IN CONTEMPT

IN CONTEMPT

Nineteenth-Century Women, Law, and Literature

Kristin Kalsem

The Ohio State University Press • Columbus

Copyright © 2012 by The Ohio State University.
All rights reserved.

Library of Congress Cataloging-in-Publication Data

Kalsem, Kristin, 1962–
  In contempt : nineteenth-century women, law, and literature / Kristin Kalsem.
      p. cm.
  Includes bibliographical references and index.
  ISBN 978-0-8142-1178-6 (cloth : alk. paper)—ISBN 978-0-8142-9274-7 (cd)
  1. Women in literature. 2. Law in literature. 3. Women—Legal status, laws, etc.—
History—19th century. 4. Literature, Modern—19th century—History and criticism. 5.
Feminist jurisprudence. 6. Women's rights in literature. I. Title.
  PN56.5.W64K25 2012
  809'.933522—dc23

                              201104364

Cover design by James A. Baumann
Text design by Jennifer Shoffey Forsythe
Type set in ITC Century
Printed by Thomson-Shore, Inc.

♾ The paper used in this publication meets the minimum requirements of the American
National Standard for Information Sciences—Permanence of Paper for Printed Library
Materials. ANSI Z39.48–1992.

9 8 7 6 5 4 3 2 1

For Cole and Andrew
Mom and Dad

CONTENTS

ILLUSTRATIONS

ACKNOWLEDGMENTS

My own history explains my fascination with the stories of the nineteenth-century women writer advocates whose texts and experiences are the keynotes of this book. After studying literature as an undergraduate, I went to law school and practiced law for several years before returning to graduate school in English, only to find myself studying law again but from a different perspective. I first had the idea for this book when I was a doctoral student in the Department of English at the University of Iowa. At its completion, I am a law professor at the University of Cincinnati College of Law. I also co-direct a joint degree program in Law and Women's, Gender, and Sexuality Studies. My scholarly life is at the intersection of law, literature, and feminism, and it is my hope that this book finds readership across disciplines. As I remind my joint degree students as they struggle to satisfy all of the members of their Master of Arts committees, truly interdisciplinary work is hard to do.

Fortunately, I have had help and encouragement from literary scholars, law scholars, and a few, like me, who are both—all of whom have embraced the promise of interdisciplinary study. This book reflects much early input from my amazing dissertation director, Garrett Stewart. I am deeply grateful to him for encouraging me at every turn and inspiring me with his eloquence. Two other Victorianists at the University of Iowa, Teresa Mangum and Florence Boos, were extremely influential in my studies. Teresa is an outstanding teacher and remains a special mentor and friend. Florence's vast knowledge of noncanonical texts and lesser-known women writers greatly enriched this study.

I came to the University of Cincinnati College of Law ten years ago with a different scholarly agenda than most law faculty. I wanted to write about law, but also about Frances Trollope, George Eliot, and many women whom my colleagues had never heard anything about. Always, they have been supportive, and I am so appreciative of their genuine enthusiasm for my work. I especially would like to thank the two deans whom I have worked with since coming to the College of Law, Joe Tomain and Louis Bilionis, and my colleagues Emily Houh, Betsy Malloy, Michael Solimine, and Verna Williams for their always-stimulating intellectual engagement, but mostly for their friendship.

This project has been supported by research grants from the Woodrow Wilson National Fellowship Foundation, the American Association of University Women Educational Foundation, the University of Iowa Graduate College, the University of Cincinnati's Friends of Women's Studies, and the Schott Foundation. This book was completed during release time generously funded by the University of Cincinnati College of Law. The staffs of the National Archives (United Kingdom) and many libraries have provided invaluable assistance, including those of the British Library, the British Library Newspaper Reading Room, the Bodleian Library, the Women's Library, the University of Iowa, and the University of Cincinnati. Special thanks to Shannon Kemen at the University of Cincinnati College of Law for her persistence in helping me locate many obscure sources, always quickly and with all good cheer. The readers for The Ohio State University Press offered thorough and thoughtful comments that sharpened and clarified the analysis. This book also benefited from careful readings of two research assistants, Maria Schneider and Kim McManus, as well as the talented editorial staff at The Ohio State University Press.

On a personal note, I wish to thank my two boys, Cole and Andrew, for all the joy that they bring to my life. They also have been especially supportive and cooperative in connection with the completion of this book, and for that I owe a debt of gratitude to my own first-grade teacher, and now dear friend, Anne Driscoll. A few months before the sabbatical year during which I planned to finish this manuscript began, she offered me two wonderful pieces of advice. First, create a writing space of my own in my home, one filled with lovely and meaningful things. Inspired by this idea, I purchased a beautiful cherry-wood Victorian writing table, set it in front of a picture window overlooking my small garden, and sat down every day to write on a comfortable chair, upholstered in a finely detailed William Morris fabric. Her second suggestion was to involve my boys in the writing process—and I did. I talked to them about the writing; they asked me about the writing; one of them even started to write a book of his own. "Make them proud to have a mom who is a woman writer advocate herself," Anne had encouraged—and that, I hope, I also did.

Other important people in my life contributed to this book's completion by helping me with other of life's responsibilities, particularly Shirley Anderson and Vona Ann and Wendell Burbank. Lastly, I want to take this opportunity to thank my parents, Ken and June Kalsem, for simply being who they are. Dad is a quiet, caring man who loves anything I do because I'm doing it. Mom, a retired librarian, gifted me with her love of books. Her favorite sweatshirt quotes Jorge Luis Borges, "I have always imagined that Paradise will be a kind of library." It is my great pleasure to present her with one more book to catalogue.

Parts of this book originally appeared in the following publications: "Looking for Law in All the 'Wrong' Places: Outlaw Texts and Early Women's Advocacy," *Southern California Review of Law and Women's Studies* 13 (2004): 273–325; "Law, Literature, and Libel: Victorian Censorship of 'Dirty Filthy' Books on Birth Control," *William and Mary Journal of Women and the Law* 10 (2004): 533–68; "Alice in Legal Wonderland: A Cross-Examination of Gender, Race, and Empire in Victorian Law and Literature," *Harvard Women's Law Journal* 24 (2001): 221–54; and "In Defense of 'Murderous Mothers': Feminist Jurisprudence in Frances Trollope's *Jessie Phillips*," *Journal of Victorian Culture* 5 (2000): 179–209. I wish to thank the *Southern California Review of Law and Social Justice* (formerly the *Southern California Review of Law and Women's Studies*), the *William and Mary Journal of Women and the Law*, the *Harvard Journal on Law and Gender* (formerly the *Harvard Women's Law Journal*), and the *Journal of Victorian Culture* (http://www.informaworld.com) for permission to reprint these materials.

Narrative Advocacy, Outlaw Texts, and Nineteenth-Century Portias

contempt

1. The action of contemning or despising; the holding or treating as of little account, or as vile and worthless; the mental attitude in which a thing is so considered. . . . 4. *Law.* Disobedience or open disrespect to the authority or lawful commands of the sovereign, the privileges of the Houses of Parliament or other legislative body; and, *esp.* action of any kind that interferes with the proper administration of justice by the various courts of law. . . .

—*Oxford English Dictionary*

Alice, in her final adventure in Wonderland, becomes increasingly bold during the trial to determine who stole the tarts of the Queen of Hearts. She knows she is growing back to her true size; she has experienced that "curious sensation" telling her that she is gaining her full personhood (94). Despite the Dormouse's warning that she has "no right to grow *here*," in this court of law, Alice decides to stay (94). And what a spectacle she makes of herself. She is loud; she literally upsets the jury; she interrupts and talks back to the judge. In fact, she shows no respect for the "stuff and nonsense" of the law itself or for any of its representatives: "'Who cares for *you*?' said Alice (she had grown to her full size by this time.) 'You're nothing but a pack of cards!' At this the whole pack rose up into the air, and came flying down upon her" (101). As Alice comes into herself, chaos becomes the order of the day, and one senses that Wonderland's system of justice will never be quite the same.

1

The Performance of Feminist Jurisprudence
in a Century of Legal Reform

In this closing episode of *Alice's Adventures in Wonderland*, Lewis Carroll dramatizes what, by 1865, was to become an increasingly popular Victorian scene: a woman questioning and critiquing the law and claiming a place for herself within its institutions. The first half of the reign of Queen Victoria witnessed Caroline Norton agitating for a mother's right to custody of her children and making minor inroads into a father's absolute rights with passage of The Infant Custody Act of 1839 (2 & 3 Vict., c. 54).[1] In 1854, Norton put the harsh realities of coverture—the legal fiction that, upon marriage, the wife's legal identity was subsumed into that of her husband—on public display in her pamphlet *English Laws for Women in the Nineteenth Century*, arguing that the law did not sufficiently protect women.[2] Barbara Leigh Smith went much further in her 1854 publication, *A Brief Summary in Plain English of the Most Important Laws of England Concerning Women*, making clear that coverture must be completely abolished for there to be any possibility of equality between men and women. Norton, Smith, Bessie Parkes, and Mary Howitt were among a group of women active in the mid-1850s debates concerning the reform of married women's property and divorce laws.[3] All were greatly distressed by the Divorce and Matrimonial Causes Act of 1857 (20 & 21 Vict., c. 85). Although the Act made it possible to obtain a divorce in England without a special Act of Parliament, it also legislated a double standard by allowing a man to obtain a divorce upon proof of his wife's infidelity, whereas a woman had to prove her husband's infidelity plus incest, bigamy, gross physical cruelty, or desertion. Rape, sodomy, and bestiality, on the part of the husband, also were included as grounds for divorce.[4]

In the 1870s and 1880s, despite numerous setbacks, feminists such as Elizabeth Wolstenholme, Elizabeth Gloyne, Lydia Becker, Jessie Boucherett, Frances Power Cobbe, and Josephine Butler worked tirelessly to reform the laws affecting married women's property. They achieved limited success with the Married Women's Property Act of 1870 (33 & 34 Vict., c. 93), followed more than a decade later by the much more comprehensive Married Women's Property Act of 1882 (45 & 46 Vict., c. 75).[5] Cobbe was also very instrumental in the passage of the Matrimonial Causes Act of 1878 (41 & 42 Vict., c. 19), which offered much-needed protection for women from domestic abuse.[6] From 1869 to 1886, Butler devoted most of her seemingly unlimited energy to the campaign to repeal the Contagious Diseases Acts (legislation to control the spread of venereal disease that allowed any woman suspected of being a prostitute to be apprehended and subject to a genital examination).[7]

Victorian women were exerting much political influence, and they were fortunate in being helped by male members of Parliament such as John Stuart Mill, Richard Monkton Milnes, and Jacob Bright.[8] As the century progressed, however, efforts were made to eliminate the need for exclusive reliance on these "middlemen" as women strove to impact the law more directly—by voting, by being elected to public offices, and by becoming members of the legal profession itself.[9]

In 1892, Charles M. Beaumont wrote a paper encouraging women to attend legal proceedings in the law courts "to see that their interests are properly cared for by Government" (1). In this paper, later published as a pamphlet entitled *Women and the Law Courts*, he explained:

> Not many years ago such conduct as I advise would have resulted in certain defeat. Then woman was generally regarded as a sort of domestic animal, on whose part any claim to political rights or to an opinion on questions of morality would be held as ridiculous as similar claims advanced by a tabby cat, though by a curious anomaly they were made to bear all responsibility for immorality. Then their intrusion into the courts would have been resented with merciless severity by the judges, who would have been supported by the public, including the majority of the female sex, whose ideas of female advocates of women's rights were fairly represented by the caricatures of Artemus Ward. Now all these things have changed. Women have become an acknowledged political force, welcomed by some, dreaded by others, but despised only by the ignorant, and a political force, in our growing democracy, is always treated with respect. The more general education of women has made the sex more restless under bondage, and the example of many of their heroine champions has roused them to some sense of the value of political and social rights. Lady advocates, lady politicians, lady lecturers, have taught the world that it is neither safe nor reasonable to treat women as a class with contempt. (4)

In Contempt: Nineteenth-Century Women, Law, and Literature focuses on women who facilitated and participated in this "intrusion" into the legal realm. In England, the nineteenth century was a period of unprecedented reform in laws affecting the everyday lives of women. Significant improvements were made, not only in the areas of child custody and support, divorce, and married women's property, but also with respect to reproductive rights, lunacy law reform, women's admission into law and politics, and domestic abuse. Women's contributions to these changes in the law, however, have been largely ignored because their work, stories, and perspectives are not recorded in law books or other authoritative sources of legal history, but rather in texts of a different kind. This book explores the legal advocacy of nineteenth-century women writers in essays, autobiographies, and other nonfiction publications, as well as in courts of law. As is more fully developed in chapter 1, this book also emphasizes the important legal forum to women that was provided by the novel form.

Specifically, this study of women, law, and literature analyzes the work of women writers who performed what today we would characterize as "feminist jurisprudence." While feminist jurisprudence encompasses multiple approaches and methodologies, broadly speaking it includes "an analysis and critique of law as a patriarchal institution" (Smith, Introduction 3).[10] Moreover, it insists on the importance to law of taking into account the voices and experiences of women and other legal "outgroups."[11]

Resistance through Narrative in Outlaw Texts

While women remained in a subordinate legal position throughout the nineteenth century, the nature and extent of that position *under* the law changed significantly over that period. Austin Sarat and Jonathan Simon, in exploring how the mutually constitutive relationship between law and culture affects the *process* of legal change, explain:

> Legal meanings are not . . . invented and communicated in a unidirectional process. Litigants, clients, consumers of culture, and others bring their own understandings to bear: they deploy and use meanings strategically to advance interests and goals. They press their understandings in and on law, and, in doing so, invite adaptation and change in legal practices. (19–20)

Legal scholars such as Richard Delgado and Kathryn Abrams have made compelling arguments that narratives offer particularly rich insights into the meanings of law from the perspectives of those who resist having the law *passed down* in a unidirectional fashion. In "Storytelling For Oppositionists and Others: A Plea For Narrative," Delgado describes the historical practice of resistance through narrative:

> Subordinated groups have always told stories. Black slaves told, in song, letters, verse, about their own pain and oppression. They described the terrible wrongs they had experienced at the hands of whites. . . . Mexican-

Americans in the Southwest composed *corridos* (ballads) and stories, passed on from generation to generation, of abuse at the hands of gringo justice. . . . Feminist consciousness-raising consists, in part, of the sharing of stories, of tales from personal experience, on the basis of which the group constructs a shared reality about women's status vis-à-vis men. (2435–36)

Specifically with respect to the value of women's narratives to an understanding of law, Abrams writes, "Experiential narratives are significant not only for the substantive message they convey but for the way they claim to know what they know. Feminist narratives present experience as a way of knowing that which should occupy a respected, or in some cases a privileged position, in analysis and argumentation" (975–76).

This book examines nineteenth-century women's stories and experiences recorded in what I will characterize as "outlaw" texts. I use the word "outlaw" to emphasize that, while these texts are not considered official legal texts and thus "out" of the purview of much legal inquiry, they are texts with respect to which "law" is an integral signifying system. Moreover, this study aims to raise awareness of nineteenth-century women's critique of unjust laws, including narrative resistance in texts that would not necessarily be characterized as legal in nature. There are no courtroom scenes in Emily Brontë's 1847 *Wuthering Heights*, for example, but, as described more fully in chapter 1, coverture and the laws relating to married women's property both underlie Heathcliff's statements and actions with respect to marriage and illuminate how he ultimately ends up owning *everything*. Similarly, an understanding of a father's absolute right to custody of his children (even if he loathes and abuses them) underscores the gravity of Heathcliff's ravings, "I'll have it [his child Linton] . . . when I want it" (178), and makes the situation of Isabella (the child's mother) all the more tragic.

In analyzing the importance of looking beyond traditional legal sources to gain understandings of law, Rosemary Coombe argues, "Rather than stress isolated decisions, statutes, or treatises, we need to attend to the social life of law's textuality and the legal life of cultural forms as it is expressed in the specific practices of socially situated subjects" (478). Outlaw texts narrate these practices, exploring the effects of law on everyday life, illustrating a primary form of nineteenth-century women's engagement with the law by examining, for example, how "[l]egal rules and practices daily influence how people act by affecting the expectations they hold and the risks they take" (Minow, "Forming Underneath" 822).

One of the primary goals of this study is to provide legal, historical, and cultural material on a selection of topics such as infanticide, birth con-

trol, and domestic violence such that readers have the context to identify moments of feminist jurisprudence in nineteenth-century writings for
what they are. This approach to women's narrative advocacy facilitates
the critical examination of what those moments might signify inside the
text (with respect to novels, for example, in relation to narrative elements
such as plot, character, and point of view) as well as outside the text—as
they "press their understandings in and on law, and, in so doing, invite
adaptation and change in legal practices" (Sarat and Simon 20).[12] In this
way, my study also responds to Christine Krueger's call in her 1999 article,
"Victorian Narrative Jurisprudence," for the need to historicize narrative
jurisprudence and attend to its complexities.[13]

I feel fortunate that my own book was early enough in the publication
process that I had the opportunity to read Krueger's recent book on this
subject, *Reading for the Law: British Literary History and Gender Advocacy*, and to incorporate discussion of the ways in which our historicized
law and literature studies complement each other. In her book, Krueger
argues for the importance of literary history to an understanding of the connections between law and literature. Concerned that some law and literature scholarship presents narratives as always critiquing legal discourse,
creating an "ahistorical opposition," her book illustrates that literary history "demonstrates the historically contingent political impact of legal and
literary texts for outsider advocacy" (2). While arguing that "literary history
presents serious challenges to the celebration of narrative—even autobiography—as intrinsically suited to outsider advocacy," she shows that "historical scholarship can also provide viable accounts of literary advocacy
that, under specific circumstances, moved forward legal recognition for
excluded groups" (3).[14] It is this type of literary advocacy, performed in
narratives that are "outlaw texts," that is central to *In Contempt*, a study
grounded in literary, as well as legal, history.

In this book, because I wish to emphasize women's important, but much
overlooked, role in legal history, I have focused primarily on outlaw texts
written by women.[15] But just as Krueger cautions against too facile an association of narrative with progressive movements, I also want to clarify that
not all legal writings by women critiqued the patriarchal nature of the law
and that many texts written by men, such as George Moore's 1894 novel
Esther Waters, did. Moore's story of Esther, an unmarried mother who is
forced to support herself and her much-loved infant by going into service
as a wet nurse, poignantly illustrates the desperate situations of young
women with infants to support and no way to pay for their food and care.
Esther has no choice but to put her own child in the keeping of an elderly
woman, but she is not at all interested in the babyminder's suggestion that

she might prefer to pay five pounds to have the child "adopted" (the idea being that the infant would die under the woman's "care"). When Esther's boy becomes ill at the babyminder's and her employer will not let her leave to see him, Esther ponders:

> By what right, by what law, was she separated from her child? . . . It was then a life for a life. It was more. For the children of two poor girls had been sacrificed so that this rich woman's child might be saved. Even that was not enough: the life of her beautiful boy was called for. And then other memories swept by. She remembered vague hints, allusions that Mrs. Spires [the babyminder] had thrown out; and, as in a dream darkly, it seemed to this ignorant girl that she was the victim of a far-reaching conspiracy. . . . (146)

The famous baby farmer case of Mrs. Waters in the 1870s (Waters was convicted of murdering one child and suspected of being responsible for the deaths of some forty others) fueled beliefs that illegitimate children were dying because their mothers were uncaring or irresponsible.[16] Narratives such as Moore's—outlaw texts that provided a different context, that insisted on the relevance of factual information such as poverty and women's sole responsibility for "immorality"—shifted the blame from individual women to a set of cultural values that conspired against unmarried women who had breached the laws of society.

Finally, certain of the texts presented in this book also are "outlaw" in that they imagine new possibilities for law and justice. Judith Resnik, in discussing the value of the interdisciplinary study of law and literature, explains, "I bring literature to law students to show them what lawyers cannot yet imagine: stories that law has yet to invent, rights yet to be seen, and how to cope with problems seen but that stymie us by their pain" (350). In the nineteenth century, writers such as Jane Hume Clapperton in *Margaret Dunmore; or, A Socialist Home* invented families that were not organized as patriarchies; novels such as Florence Dixie's *Gloriana* included women with rights to vote and sit in Parliament; *A Writer of Books* by George Paston confronts the unspeakable pain of a mother's forced (and perfectly legal) separation from her child. Literature also imagined legal advocates of a different kind. For example, Shakespeare's sixteenth-century archetypal legal woman, Portia, in the nineteenth century was given several stories all her own. Engaging in what Julie Hankey terms the "novelizing of Shakespeare's plays," women writers embellished on the positive representation of Portia from *The Merchant of Venice*, narrating her childhood, family history, education, beliefs, and desires (436). They worked to make this imagined character—the woman advocate—real.

Nineteenth-Century Portias

Making the Character Real

In *The Merchant of Venice*, Portia argues as a lawyer and presides as a judge over one of the most famous trials of all time, the proceeding to determine whether Shylock will be allowed to enforce a contractual remedy of a pound of flesh. It is Portia who tries to persuade Shylock to be merciful, and when he refuses, who articulates the fatal flaw in his desired remedy:

> This bond doth give thee here no jot of blood;
> The words expressly are "a pound of flesh."
> Take then thy bond, take thou thy pound of flesh;
> But in the cutting of it, if thou dost shed
> One drop of Christian blood, thy lands and goods
> Are by the laws of Venice confiscate
> Unto the state of Venice. (4.1.305–11)

While there was disagreement as to whether Portia or Bellario, the learned doctor of laws she had consulted, had identified this legal loophole, there was overwhelming nineteenth-century consensus about the strength of character of this "[m]ost learned judge" (4.1.303).[17]

Anna Jameson, in her 1832 *Characteristics of Women, Moral, Poetical, and Historical*, was the first to analyze Shakespeare's female characters as individuals worthy of critical attention. Prior to Jameson, critics such as William Richardson and Samuel Coleridge had dismissed the women in Shakespeare's plays as almost without character (Hankey 426–28). Richardson argued that this reflected the social inferiority of real women, explaining that "uniformity of conduct [is] frequently occasioned by uniformity of condition" (qtd. in Hankey 426).[18] Jameson disputes the uniformity of these characters, seeing them as much more realistic than the unidimensional historical representations of real women. She argues that Shakespeare's women "are complete individuals, whose hearts and souls are laid open before us—all may behold and all judge for themselves" (xvi–xvii).

Giving pre-eminence to the "characters of intellect," Jameson's first character portrait is of Portia, "a perfect model of an intellectual woman, in whom wit is tempered by sensibility, and fancy regulated by strong reflection" (xxix). However, the kind of woman Portia represents, Jameson concludes, would not thrive in the nineteenth century: "A woman constituted like Portia, and placed in this age, and in the actual state of society, would find society armed against her. . . . With her, the world without would be at war with the world within" (76). In a culture in which the legal fiction of coverture determined the plot of women's lives, Jameson lamented that either Portia's vivacious nature would be subdued or her resistance would make her proud and rigid.[19]

The nineteenth-century critic Charles Cowden Clarke noted that Portia's association with the law was particularly troubling: "There is a class of my own sex who never fail to manifest an uneasiness, if not a jealousy, when they perceive a woman verging towards the manly prerogative; and with such, the part that Shakespeare has assigned to Portia in the trial-scene would induce this prejudice against her."[20] His wife Mary Cowden Clarke, however, suggests in her collection of stories, *The Girlhood of Shakespeare's Heroines*, that *her* own sex found Portia's successful foray into legal territory particularly appealing. Like Jameson, Clarke begins her series of tales with Portia. In this very popular collection, Clarke traces "the probable antecedents in the history of some of Shakespeare's women" and tries "to imagine the possible circumstances and influences of scene, event, and associate, surrounding the infant life of his heroines, which might have conduced to originate and foster those germs of character recognized in their maturity . . ." (iii). For Portia, Clarke imagines that Bellario, the learned doctor of laws whom she consults prior to the trial, is the uncle who raised her after her mother's death in childbirth and her father's disappearance.[21] As a child, Portia sits with Bellario as he studies his law books and reviews his cases. He educates her himself, and "he would often laughingly tell her, that though she had no regular schooling, no masters, no accomplishments, no womanly teaching,—no set education in short, yet that he should in no time make her an excellent scholar, and a most capital lawyer" (48–49).

As Bellario's laughter suggests, he does not offer this as a serious course of action; he believes women "would make but poor lawyers," as Clarke has him say:

> In the exercise of their [women's] discernment, they will frequently triumph too early in the discovery of an advantage; and it is the part of a clever lawyer not to betray his own strength and his adversary's weakness too soon. To skillfully treasure up each point successively gained, and by a tardy unmasking of your own plan of action, to lead your opponent on to other and more sure committals of himself, is more consonant with the operation of a man's mind, than suited to the eager, impulsive nature of woman. (52)

Of course, the strategy Bellario accuses women of being unable to execute is precisely the one Portia adopts in the play. When Portia smilingly retorts that "one day or other you may be brought to acknowledge that I could make a profound lawyer," the readers (who are familiar with the play) know she is right (52).

Nineteenth-century women found much to admire in Portia. The actress Fanny Kemble designated Portia as her "favouritest of all Shakespeare's women" (Kemble 106); the novelist Geraldine Jewsbury named Portia as "one of [her] great heroines."[22] Also, when the *Girls' Own Paper* sponsored a contest for the best essay on "My favourite Heroine from Shakespeare," Portia was the most popular character, being the subject of more than a third of the essays submitted (Marshall 41). Manifesting some of the uneasiness noted by Charles Cowden Clarke, the *Girls' Own Paper* specifically published an admonishment of the girls whose essays suggested that Portia would be a proponent of women's rights: "Could anything be more inapropos than this? . . . How foolish girls are to become so exercised about one idea that they must fain 'drag it in,' when it has nothing to do with the subject they are writing about."[23] Clearly, some women were insisting on the contemporary relevance of "Lady Lawyer, Portia."[24]

In sharp contrast to the literary criticism that had emphasized the limited roles embodied by Shakespeare's female characters, M. L. Elliott's sketch on Portia in her 1885 collection *Shakespeare's Garden of Girls* presents the fullness of this character:

> Portia is a judge upon the bench, an advocate at the bar, a preacher at the pulpit, a wit in company, a student when alone, a philosopher in thought, a poet in expression, and, above all, a tender and romantic girl growing up into the truest of women and the sweetest of wives. (128)

While the "above all" characteristics seem to reify the ideal of Victorian womanhood, Elliott is making the case that Portia is not "strong-minded" in the derogatory nineteenth-century sense that would make her a "hard-featured, loud talking, forbidding-looking being in semi-masculine or dowdy attire"; she instead substantiates that "the possession of the highest intellectual endowments is compatible with the age and susceptibilities for tender and romantic love" (117). For Elliott, Portia is much more than a representation of women's limitless possibilities; she *is* a judge and an advocate. The references to her as a girl, woman, and wife at the end of Elliott's compiled résumé are cumulative roles, not replacement roles, and indeed, these latter "womanly" descriptions emphasize that the roles first and foremost associated with Portia are *not* manly prerogatives.[25]

Portia is an intellectual woman who can more than hold her own in the public sphere, in the male worlds of law and commerce. As Elliott notes, she can "stand side by side with learned doctors and shrewd practical men of business" (117). And while she has to dress as a man in order to gain admittance and have a voice in the courtroom, her audience knows who she is at all times. She is under the cover of a male disguise, but she is speaking her own mind.

It took until 1919, when Helena Florence Normanton and Gwyneth Marjory Thompson were admitted as law students to the English bar, for fact to catch up with fiction and for newspapers to announce, "Portia Arrives" ("Portia Arrives" 2).[26] Reporting the admission of Normanton as a student to Middle Temple and of Thompson to Lincoln's Inn, the *Evening News* stated, "Portia is to have leave to plead, in her proper person, without disguise or simulation or dissimulation of any kind" ("Sister Buzfuz" 4). Alice, at long last, had gained the right to be, speak, and even argue in a court of law.

※

In the following chapters, I present the feminist jurisprudence of numerous nineteenth-century women writers whose literal and figurative representations of women forever changed the British legal landscape. Working in real-life courtrooms, nonfiction publications, and a variety of types of novel (including Gothic, social-problem, utopian, and New Woman novels), these feminist thinkers addressed a wide array of legal issues that were central to women's lives. In the broad study of nineteenth-century women, law, and literature, choices must necessarily be made with respect to which texts to include and which aspects of law to cover. In making my selections, I have been guided by certain tenets of feminist jurisprudence. First, feminist legal scholars have developed theoretical approaches and methodologies for analyzing law that take as a central point of departure women's experiences of exclusion from the law.[27] This study takes as its primary focus works of nonfiction and fiction that, for the most part, have not been considered in legal histories or in studies of law and literature.[28] Second, women's experiences have been moved from the margins to the center of the analysis. Thus, substantive areas of the law are examined that were of particular importance to women in the nineteenth century, and specific consideration is given to "how the law fails to take into account the experiences and values that seem more typical of women than of men, for whatever reason, or how existing legal standards and concepts might disadvantage women" (Bartlett, "Feminist Legal Methods" 837).

The chapters are organized to broadly follow a legal progression in an effort to explore the myriad ways in which law—as it is drafted, enacted, adjudicated, interpreted, executed, and reformed—intersects with women's lives. Thus, after chapter 1 more specifically develops the analysis of novels as outlaw texts and more fully sets forth the state of the law with respect to women at the beginning of the nineteenth century, chapter 2 emphasizes the law as legislated, chapter 3 focuses on the trial stage, chapter 4 considers judgments, and chapter 5 addresses legal appeals. In this way, *In Contempt: Nineteenth-Century Women, Law, and Literature* takes a broad view, not only of legal texts, but also of legal actors, voices, participants, and experiences. As Judith Resnik explains, feminism can bring to law an emphasis on the importance of not limiting the study of law to texts "authored by a very few actors: Supreme Court justices in particular, appellate judges in general, and sometimes members of Congress or their staff" (351). Because such a "choice of text assumes, reiterates, and affirms the primacy of those who are currently hierarchically superior and further assumes that the hierarchy is itself fixed—and appropriate," she encourages looking beyond "a singular set of actors, positioned by class, race, ethnicity, and gender" to the work of a wider range of legal participants (351–52). Throughout the book, this study weaves larger thematic strands, such as the gradual erosion of coverture, women's ongoing struggle for legal and literary identities of their own, and the increasingly contested control of women's bodies.

More specifically, chapter 1 focuses on Mary Wollstonecraft's late-eighteenth-century unfinished novel, *The Wrongs of Woman; or Maria: A Fragment* (1897), to introduce the legal fiction of coverture, the basis for "the partial laws and customs of society" (Wollstonecraft, *Maria* 73). Also, while the concept of outlaw texts generally is described in this Introduction, chapter 1 turns more specifically to "outlaw novels," using *Maria* to illustrate the ways in which novelistic discourse and feminist jurisprudence are ideologically allied. Analyzing the imagery of "protection" in the passages on coverture in William Blackstone's *Commentaries on the Laws of England* (1765), for example, I explore the ways in which Wollstonecraft's novel revises this legal text, exposing and metaphorically reconstituting the law's cover as capture. Moreover, focusing on *Maria* as a Gothic novel, I examine how Wollstonecraft's text employs Gothic conventions such as subterranean spaces, live burial, doubles, unintelligible writings, and the unspeakable to literalize and symbolically reconfigure the buried (but very much alive) tropes of legal discourse that kept women defined, confined, and silenced within a Gothic reality. This chapter concludes with a re-examination of critical conclusions about the policing role of the novel in light of the feminist jurisprudence performed in novels that are "outlaw texts." Responding to influential studies of nineteenth-century law and literature, I also consider how other law–novel connections may be differently understood when "how gender matters" is seriously considered.[29]

The legal focus of chapter 2 is the law of infanticide and the bastardy clauses of the Poor Law Amendment Act of 1834 (the New Poor Law). The outlaw texts examined in this chapter, ones that provide *her*stories of infanticide, include *The Broad Arrow* (1859) by Caroline Leakey (Oliné Keese), *The Last Sentence* (1891) by Gray Maxwell (Mary Tuttiet) and, most specifically, Frances Trollope's 1843 novel *Jessie Phillips: A Tale of the Present Day*. *Jessie Phillips* is a novel about an unmarried working-class woman who is wrongly accused of murdering her child. I contrast the novels of Trollope, Leakey, and Tuttiet to literary and legal narratives that reinforced the law's "truth" that infanticide was a problem of deviant women. Specifically, I consider the ways in which George Eliot's novel *Adam Bede* indicted the character of Hetty Sorrel. Then I turn to an examination of the legal narrative of infanticide that begins with a 1623 English statute that applied only to "lewd women that have been delivered of bastard children" (21 James 1, c. 27). After briefly tracing the character of the "lewd woman" through two centuries of legal plotting, I provide a close analysis of the intertextual relationship between *Jessie Phillips* and narratives that emerged during the legislative debates over the bastardy clauses of the New Poor Law. An exploration of these narrative connections illuminates how Trollope's novel exposes the law's "cover" to be surveillance, its "protection" to be for the "fondly protected man," and women's "madness" to be genuine anger, particularly about their subordinate position under the law.

Chapter 3 examines the topic of birth control in the nineteenth-century contexts of law, literature, and libel. In 1877, Annie Besant and her partner Charles Bradlaugh published a tract on birth control and sold it for sixpence so that it would be available to the poor. They were arrested and charged with obscene libel for publishing an "indecent, lewd, filthy, bawdy, and obscene book" (Freethought 322). At the trial, the defendants served as their own attorneys, with Besant arguing her own case in open court. Taking the 1877 trial transcript as my primary legal text, I examine Besant's strategy of playing upon the cultural meanings of "woman." An analysis of Besant's narrative strategy shows how she used the very ideal of Victorian womanhood to subvert it. In what proved to be a stunning obfuscation of societal norms, Besant revised traditional narratives of female sexuality and good mothering to momentarily open up the possibility of a sexualized domestic ideal of womanhood. I then turn to an examination of the literary legacies of this pathbreaking trial, focusing on the first British novel to advocate openly for the use of artificial birth control, Jane Clapperton's utopian novel *Margaret Dunmore; or A Socialist Home* (1888).

I argue that *Margaret Dunmore* was a site for the reconstruction of the cultural meanings of family and the duties of women; this novel displaced representations in works such as Jane Austen's *Mansfield Park* (1814) and Charles Dickens's *David Copperfield* (1850) that ignored women's debilitating confinements or treated them as comic. I also discuss more subtle literary treatments of birth control in novels such as Thomas Hardy's 1895 *Jude the Obscure.* In the last part of the chapter, I briefly present the feminist jurisprudence of Marie Stopes, who carried the dialogue on this taboo subject into the twentieth century with her runaway bestsellers *Married Love* (1918) and *Wise Parenthood* (1918) and who sued a vocal opponent of birth control for libeling her. Stopes made the hitherto utopian idea of widespread access to contraception a reality when she opened the first birth-control clinic in Britain in 1921.

In the fourth chapter, I shift from a focus on the performance of feminist jurisprudence in legal and literary narratives to an analysis of the representations of two women who embodied the power of the law in their roles as judges: the fictional character Ayesha, from H. Rider Haggard's imperialist 1887 novel *She*, and the real-life Mary Slessor, who was the first woman appointed as a magistrate in the British Empire. In this chapter, because I am not looking at direct testimony of women's legal advocacy, but rather representations of women in the legal arena, I employ a theoretical approach that I term "cross-examination." The texts in which these representations appear, the sources of direct testimony, include fictional descriptions and iconographic images of Ayesha in her capacity as judge and written accounts of Slessor's courtroom persona. Reading these texts against the backdrop of legal proceedings in England in which women sought (and continued to be "lawfully" denied) entry into law and politics (the legal issue in these "pronoun" cases being whether a "she" was entitled to the statutory rights granted to a "person"), I discuss the negotiations at the level of narrative to keep these "Portias" within the confines of their "proper" womanly roles. Through cross-examination, one can see the chaotic attempts in these narratives of white women exercising legal power in Africa to control the disruptions to traditional roles and stereotypes that resulted from the complex negotiations of gender, racial, and national hierarchies that were endemic to the British Empire in the late nineteenth century.

Chapter 5 examines the legal and literary "appeals" of women writer advocates in the context of several late-century legal reform movements, including reform of the lunacy laws and repeal of the Contagious Diseases Acts. The first part of the chapter focuses on Georgina Weldon and Emily

Jackson. Weldon was a leader in the campaign for lunacy-law reform who wrote *How I Escaped the Mad Doctors* in 1879 and represented herself in court as a plaintiff-in-person in the 1880s in more than a hundred legal proceedings. Jackson was a quiet 42-year-old woman from a small village who found herself at the center of a national controversy when, in 1891, she was seized by a masked man (who turned out to be her estranged husband) as she was coming out of church and kept locked away in his house. She successfully appealed for a writ of *habeas corpus* to set her free and, in response to public retaliation against her by those who believed her case had dealt an irreparable blow to the institution of marriage, she wrote a four-part "Vindication," published in the *London Times*. In the second part of this chapter, I read the self-authored stories of Weldon and Jackson in the context of popular New Woman novels of the 1890s that took the intersections of law, literature, and activism as central themes. Sarah Grand's *The Beth Book* (1898), for example, explores the related roles of women writers and political activists in the context of the campaign to repeal the Contagious Diseases Acts. In *A Writer of Books* (1899) by George Paston, the woman writer heroine confronts myriad legal issues, including domestic violence and sexual harassment. Finally, Florence Dixie's *Gloriana* (1890) celebrates the possibilities of feminist jurisprudence with its representation of a woman writer elected to Parliament and, ultimately (after a revolution), to the office of Prime Minister.

In Contempt: Nineteenth-Century Women, Law, and Literature is a study of the interrelationships between legal and literary narratives in the contexts of specific chapters in nineteenth-century British women's legal history. Exploring the practice of feminist jurisprudence in certain nineteenth-century women's writing, as well as in the lives and politics of Victorian women who fought for legal reform, this book testifies to the important but much overlooked role that women have played in legal history.

CHAPTER 1

A Novel Approach to Feminist Jurisprudence

Narrating the Gothic Reality of Coverture

precedent
2. a. A previous instance or case which is or may be taken as an example or rule for subsequent cases, or by which some similar act or circumstance may be supported or justified. . . . b. *Law.* A previous judicial decision, method of proceeding, or draft of document which serves as an authoritative rule or patterns in similar or analogous cases. . . .

 —*Oxford English Dictionary*

In the advertisement to her landmark work *A Vindication of the Rights of Woman* (1792), Mary Wollstonecraft stated her intention to publish a second volume, one that would specifically address "the laws relative to women" (7). While she did not write this second political treatise, she did follow through with her proposal: she critiqued the oppression of women under the law in *The Wrongs of Woman: or, Maria* (1797)—a novel.

Wollstonecraft's purpose in writing *Maria* is unambiguously set forth in her author's preface: "the desire of exhibiting the misery and oppression, peculiar to women, that arise out of the partial laws and customs of society" (73). Her husband William Godwin, in his editor's preface to *Maria*, emphasizes her conscientious choice of the novel form in which to deliver her message: "The purpose and *structure* of the following work, had long formed a favourite subject of meditation with its author, and she judged them capable of producing an important effect" (71; emphasis added).[1] This chapter will illustrate how Wollstonecraft, with her outlaw novel *Maria*, performed feminist jurisprudence. Revolutionary thinker that she was, it is not surprising that Wollstonecraft recognized early on that the novel form was particularly suited to a feminist critique of the law.

On a practical level, the novel's accessibility to and its popularity with women made it an ideal forum for the exploration of women's lived experiences (on the part of both writers and readers). Gary Kelly argues that *Maria* was a fictionalization of the arguments in *A Vindication of the Rights of Woman* (xv–xvii), and Mary Poovey has noted that Wollstonecraft recognized that, in writing a political treatise like the *Vindication*, she had limited the number of women who would be reading her ideas ("Mary Wollstonecraft" 111).[2] Women's stories were able to call into question the law's version of reality, or its "truth," and to create new knowledge "by exploring common experiences and patterns that emerge from shared tellings of life events" (Bender 9). In *Maria*, for example, the "telling" of Maria's story, which is interwoven with the experiences of diverse and multiple other women in the novel, presents women's complex realities in resistance to the law's limiting definitions and categorizations.

But the novel also, on a formal basis, was fitting for Wollstonecraft's purpose. Specifically, the polyphonic structure of the novel form made it a fruitful site to explore the oppression inherent in legal language. In her essay "Word, Dialogue and Novel," Julia Kristeva identifies the novel's potential to "disapprove of the very structures of official thought founded on formal logic" (55) by its participation in a Bakhtinian dialogism that "situates philosophical problems *within* language; more precisely, within language as a correlation of texts" (58–59). One might say that the novel is able to engage the law in a dialogue. Kristeva clarifies that this "intertextuality" is not to be understood "in the banal sense of 'study of sources,'" but rather as the "transposition of one (or several) sign-system(s) into another" (*Revolution* 111). Words, for example, *mean* in different ways in different contexts. Explaining Mikhail Bakhtin's conception of the "literary word" as "an *intersection of textual surfaces* rather than a *point* (a fixed meaning), as a dialogue among several writings: that of the writer, the addressee (or the character) and the contemporary or earlier cultural context," Kristeva proposes the following "translinguistic" procedure for describing the word's specific operation within different texts:

> First, we must think of literary genres as imperfect semiological systems "signifying beneath the surface of language but never without it": and secondly, discover relations among larger narrative units such as sentences, questions-and-answers, dialogues, etc., not necessarily on the basis of linguistic models—justified by the principle of semantic expansion. . . . The

novel in particular exteriorizes linguistic dialogue. ("Word, Dialogue and Novel" 36–37)

An exploration of one of the law's key words for women—"protected" for example—within the larger narrative units of the novel *Maria* and the legal texts with which that novel is in dialogue illustrates how legal discourse would be markedly different if women were allowed to participate in a meaningful way.

Finally, whereas the law is an epic discourse in many respects, feminist jurisprudence is ideologically allied with the novel form. Bakhtin's distinctions between the epic and the novel provide a useful paradigm for exploring these legal and literary connections. Bakhtin characterizes the literary epic as one in which "'beginning,' 'first,' 'founder,' 'ancestor,' 'that which occurred earlier' and so forth are not merely temporal categories but *valorized* temporal categories, and valorized to an extreme degree" ("Epic and Novel" 15); the language of the epic is "unitary, completely finished-off and indisputable" ("Prehistory of Novelistic Discourse" 49). The law shares many of these epic qualities. Its authority is bolstered by its celebrated reliance on precedent, that is, that which has been decided in the past, and the requirements of legal language mean that to be heard in the legal world, one must "speak with the voice of dispassionate reason; be simple, direct, and certain; avoid the complexity of varying, interacting perspectives and overlapping multi-textured explanations" (Finley 905). Epic discourses are more about preservation than change.

In contrast to the epic, Bakhtin describes the novel as "structured not in the distanced image of the absolute past but in the zone of direct contact with inconclusive present-day reality" ("Epic and Novel" 39); the language of the novel is "a living mix of varied and opposing voices . . . developing and renewing itself" ("Prehistory of Novelistic Discourse" 49). Similarly, feminist jurisprudence is all about questioning absolutes, "especially the norms and assumptions implicit in received doctrine [precedent]"; it is about accepting and encouraging "diversity, complexity, and contradiction" (Finley 905). Like novelistic discourse, feminist jurisprudence embraces heteroglossia, which "insures the primacy of context over text" and acknowledges that "[a]t any given time, in any given place, there will be a set of conditions—social, historical, meteorological, physiological—that will insure that a word uttered in that place and at that time will have a meaning different than it would have under any other conditions" (Holquist 428). In thus exposing the oppression in the law's epic and monologic claims to be "unitary, completely finished-off and indisputable" or, more traditionally, "universal and objective," feminist jurisprudence represents a "novel" reconception of the law.

Several critics have argued that *Maria*, as a novel, does not accomplish its intended political purpose. Claire Tomalin comments that "it is probably a pity she [Wollstonecraft] allowed herself to be sidetracked from writing a second volume of polemics and chose instead to embody her ideas in fiction" (202). Harriet Jump concludes that *Maria* "cannot be called anything but a failure as it stands" because it is too didactic and lacks "any imaginative vision" (145). Mary Poovey, who characterizes *Maria* as a sentimental novel, sees this genre as "dangerously at odds" with Wollstonecraft's political insights ("Mary Wollstonecraft" 112). Poovey argues that the problem with the novel is "the difficulty Wollstonecraft had in reconciling her intended 'purpose' with the genre, which shapes the 'structure,' of the work" (112). For Poovey, "It is Wollstonecraft's recognition of this incompatibility and—equally to the point—her resistance to this recognition that account for both the hesitations of composition and the contradictions that mark the text" (112). From Godwin's preface we know that Wollstonecraft had been working on the novel for twelve months, and that she had "recommenced and revised the manuscript several different times" (71). Considering how quickly she wrote her other works (the *Vindication* was written in three months), Poovey contends that Wollstonecraft was suffering from writer's block and that "[a]lmost any passage from the text of this much belabored first part reveals that the hesitation which afflicted *Maria*'s composition haunts its prose as well. Syntax is frequently disjunctive, narratives are broken off literally in mid-sentence, and, most troubling of all, the relationship between the narrative consciousness and that of the heroine Maria is inconsistent" (111). Because I agree with critics who have characterized *Maria* as a Gothic novel, I see these hesitations and contradictions, not as flaws, but as purposeful and integral aspects of Wollstonecraft's project.[3]

Hesitations and contradictions are salient features of the Gothic, whose characteristic narrative form is "designed to create a sense of formlessness and refuses to obey our assumptions about narrative as a meaningful sequence of action" (Day 49). One expects the narratives to break off in mid-sentence because, in the Gothic, "narrators tell stories that are somehow incomplete, that lose their coherence in a jumble of other narrators telling other stories or in the muffled voices of speakers trying to tell stories we cannot hear" (Day 49).[4] The formlessness and incoherence of the narrative complement one of the Gothic's primary themes: the loss of the self. As William Patrick Day explains, the "Gothic fantasy is a fable of identity fragmented and destroyed beyond repair, a fable of the impossibility of identity" (6). It is my contention that the Gothic's preoccupation with fractured and lost identities made this genre of the novel an especially appropriate forum for Wollstonecraft to display the dissonant effects that the laws governing marriage had on women's everyday lives.

Buried Alive under Coverture

Wollstonecraft critiques various laws affecting women in *Maria;* however, she primarily attacks the "matrimonial despotism" that results from the law of coverture (Wollstonecraft, Preface 74). Coverture is a legal fiction that takes as its basic premise the idea that, by marriage, the husband and wife become one person.[5] As William Blackstone's definition in the *Commentaries on the Laws of England* makes clear, the "one" that remains is the husband:

> By marriage, the husband and wife are one person in law: that is, the very being or legal existence of the woman is suspended during the marriage, or at least is incorporated and consolidated into that of the husband, under whose wing, protection, and *cover,* she performs every thing . . . and her condition during her marriage is called her *coverture.* (430)

Thus, for a woman, coverture imposed a very Gothic reality. Upon marriage, her identity was fragmented and destroyed beyond repair as her self was subsumed into the identity of another.

In her book *The Coherence of Gothic Conventions*, Eve Kosofsky Sedgwick identifies a specific set of Gothic conventions—literal, thematic, and structural associations—that continually recur in Gothic novels. Three of Sedgwick's categories are particularly helpful in examining the Gothic aspects of coverture: (i) subterranean spaces and live burial; (ii) doubles; and (iii) unnatural echoes or silences, unintelligible writings, and the unspeakable.[6]

In Gothic novels, characters (usually heroines) often find themselves blocked off from something to which they ought to have access. They may be held captive in subterranean spaces, for example, or possibly even be buried alive (literally or metaphorically). As Sedgwick explains, "The self and whatever it is that is outside have a proper, natural, necessary connection to each other, but one that the self is suddenly incapable of making. The inside life and the outside life have to continue separately, becoming counterparts rather than partners . . ." (13). Such was the experience of a nineteenth-century woman upon marriage, when she suddenly was denied access to rights that society had determined to be proper, natural, and necessary to all but married women.[7]

A wife's *condition* (with the word itself implying an unnatural or diseased state) of coverture came with specific disabilities. Specifically, she had no right to enter into a contract, to make a will, or to sue on her own behalf in court. She also had no right to control her own property, and no right to her own wages.[8] The patriarchal ideology that informed coverture, the belief that women were inferior to and had to be controlled by men, however, was masked by language suggesting that the law protected and benefited women. In fact, Blackstone explicitly states that "[e]ven the disabilities, which the wife lies under, are for the most part intended for her protection and benefit. So great a favourite is the female sex of the laws of England" (433).

The benefits that women "enjoyed" under coverture included the right to maintenance. Also, the husband was deemed responsible for the wife's debts, as well as for any civil wrongs that she committed. The realities of these protections, however, were more imaginary than real. If her husband failed to maintain her, the wife, because she had no legal identity, had no remedy at law; her protection was unenforceable. Also, because the husband was deemed responsible for his wife's behavior, the law provided him with the power to restrain her by domestic chastisement (Holcombe 29–30).[9] Under coverture, a woman exchanged her freedom for a life of protective cover. Individual circumstances and personalities determined whether that cover was more akin to live burial.

Coverture also resulted in a Gothic doubleness. A woman's own thoughts, feelings, and beliefs (especially as they differed from her husband's) were part of her inside life, separate from the outside life in which it was deemed that she thought, felt, and believed the same as her husband. The law imposed a separation between her inner life and the outside life that, under coverture, she *performed*. Such a separation is "a fundamental reorganization, creating a doubleness where singleness should be" (Sedgwick 13). In a Gothic novel, much of the plot is devoted to attempts at reunification, to escape from this doubleness. That original oneness, however, proves impossible to retrieve. Such was the case with the condition of coverture. For many women, marriage represented a fundamental reorganization, a separation of their performing from their true selves, and in all but extraordinary circumstances, it was irrevocable. Divorce was available only by an Act of Parliament, which was prohibitively expensive for all but a select few. At the time when Wollstonecraft wrote *Maria*, no woman had successfully sued for a petition of divorce.[10]

Legal separations were available in extreme circumstances, but as an

1811 court iterated, "nothing short of actual terror and violence" would justify a wife's separation from her husband (Perkin, *Women and Marriage* 24). And if a wife left her husband without obtaining a divorce or legal separation, he could capture her, force her to return, and keep her confined so that she would be unable to leave. Her body, her very being, belonged to her husband.[11] Therefore, a Gothic novel was ideal for a textual rehearsal of the fears and terrors of a loss of identity and the anguish of an inescapable life of doubleness that also were conditions of coverture.

Finally, coverture is about unnatural echoes or silences, unintelligible writings, and the unspeakable. The unnatural echoes and silences are those of the women who had no voice to speak out against coverture.[12] Coverture was maintained by a political system that excluded women from all aspects of the legal process. In 1797, when *Maria* was written, women were not permitted to be legislators, lawyers, jurors, or judges. They were expected to accept laws and legal language that made no sense because they spoke of control and abuse in the language of protection; it was women's condition to live with the horror of the loss of self under coverture.

It is on the level of the unutterable that I see a direct link between Wollstonecraft's theme (Gothic laws) and her structure (the Gothic novel). Sedgwick explains, "Of all the Gothic conventions dealing with the sudden, mysterious, seemingly arbitrary, but massive inaccessibility of those things that should normally be most accessible, the difficulty the story has in getting itself told is of the most obvious structural significance" (13). She clarifies that this does not mean that the story doesn't get told, but rather that it gets through "in a muffled form, with a distorted sense, and accompanied by a kind of despair about any direct use of language" (14). In *Maria*, a Gothic novel, Wollstonecraft searches for a way to speak effectively *to women* about a topic that, on many levels, was unspeakable.

Wollstonecraft's Prosecution of Gothic Laws

The Wrongs of Woman: or, Maria is subtitled "a fragment." Wollstonecraft died before the novel was completed, leaving only the first volume, three chapters of a second volume, and some brief sketches of possible continuations of the story. While she could not have intended her work to be presented in this particular form, it is ironically in keeping with the fragmentary nature of the portion of the text she had completed. Typical of the Gothic form, *Maria* is a series of stories within stories. Some narratives are provided piecemeal throughout the novel; others are abruptly cut short. Day suggests that Gothic narratives resemble dreams in their lack of meaningful sequence and that such orderlessness is a way of subverting not only the narrative conventions of sentimental novels, but also the realities and values that such novels affirmed (43–45).

Maria begins *in medias res* with its heroine in a madhouse. Maria has been confined there, in her terms "buried alive," by her husband (185). The connection between the Gothic realm and the real world is made explicit in the first paragraph of the novel as the narrator draws on the reader's knowledge of "[a]bodes of horror . . . conjured up by the magic spell of genius to harrow the soul, and absorb the wondering mind" to explain the "mansion of despair" in which Maria finds herself (75).

Maria befriends the woman assigned to guard her, Jemima, and a fellow inmate Darnford, and much of the completed portion of the novel is composed of their three life stories. Darnford and Jemima narrate their stories aloud; Maria presents her two friends and the reader with her written memoirs. These memoirs describe Maria's life from her childhood to the time of her imprisonment in the madhouse, with the focus being on her disastrous marriage to George Venables. Venables gambles and drinks away all of the money that Maria receives from a benevolent uncle, has mistresses, and, ultimately, tries to prostitute Maria to a friend from whom he wishes to borrow money. When Maria finally walks out, he hunts her down like an animal, drugs her, takes her infant daughter (who, she later learns, dies shortly thereafter), and sends her to the asylum. Maria's memoirs of her past break off abruptly, and returning to her present life in the "mansion of despair," the readers learn that Maria and Darnford have become lovers; she receives him "as her husband" (188).

With the help of Jemima, Maria escapes from the madhouse and returns to London, where Darnford soon joins her. When Darnford is sued by Venables for seduction and adultery, he leaves for France, and Maria stays to take charge of his defense.[13] Wollstonecraft's narrative culminates in a trial scene, in which the future course of Maria's life will be determined. As a conclusion, Godwin appended several of Wollstonecraft's outlines for completion of the novel, all but one of which portend tragedy.

This novel, however, is much more than its Gothic plot summary suggests. It is not the story of a sentimental woman who tries to escape a bad marriage for true love and suffers as a result of her passion. Maria is not on trial here, but rather a system that, under the guise of protecting women, keeps them totally dependent on men. Rhetoric of "protection" abounds in *Maria* just as it does in the legal discourse on coverture. In the novel, the word "protection" is what Kristeva would characterize as an "ambivalent" word, one that "introduces a signification opposed to that of the other's [the Law's] word" ("Word, Dialogue and Novel" 44).[14] Working with Bakhtin's concept of "ambivalence," Kristeva explains that the term "implies the insertion of history (society) into a text and of this text into history" ("Word, Dialogue and Novel" 39). *Maria* explores (from a woman's point of view) how this abstract legal language translates in society into something very different from protection—real-life misery and oppression.

To illustrate, in an early letter to Maria in the madhouse, before they have met in person, Darnford writes, "'Whoever you are, who partake my fate, accept my commiseration—I would have said protection; but the privilege of man is denied me'" (91). With this passage, the novel clarifies that "protection" is not a benefit to women, but rather a privilege of men. The plot reinforces this assessment as Maria's situation worsens every time she turns to a man for protection. As a young woman, she seeks the protection of her genuinely caring uncle against the absolute authority of a tyrannical father and elder brother. Her uncle sees marriage as her only means of escape and encourages her to marry Venables. She soon learns the folly of her actions, commenting, "Marriage has bastilled me for life. I discovered in myself a capacity for the enjoyment of the various pleasures *existence* affords; yet, fettered by the partial laws of society, this fair globe was to me an universal blank" (154–55; emphasis added) and "I could not sometimes help regretting my early marriage; and that, in my haste to escape from a temporary dependence, and expand my newly fledged wings, in an unknown sky, I had been caught in a trap, and caged for life" (144). In these passages, Wollstonecraft linguistically signals the intertextuality between her novel and Blackstone's definition of coverture as Maria longs for "existence" and looks back on a time when "wings" signified freedom, not cover. Revising the legal text, Wollstonecraft articulates the "universal blank" that more accurately describes a woman's condition under coverture, and exposes and metaphorically reconstitutes the law's "cover" as capture. In this way, situating the wrongs of women within the very language of the law, Wollstonecraft presses new "understandings in and on law, and, in doing so, invite[s] adaptation and change" (Sarat and Simon 20). As the novel makes clear, Maria needs protection from her protector, but as she bitterly reflects, "the laws of her country—if women have a country—afford her *no protection* or redress from the oppressor" (159; emphasis added).

Finally, she turns to Darnford for protection, and while "he solemnly pledged himself as her protector—and eternal friend" (188), she soon discovers that "there was a volatility in his manner which often distressed her," and she does not taste the "uninterrupted felicity" for which she had hoped (192). The hints provided in the sketched endings of the novel suggest that Darnford is unfaithful and possibly abandons her.[15] While Poovey reads the Darnford episode as indicative of Wollstonecraft's inability to escape from romantic sentiments, I think the fact that the novel doesn't anticipate ending with Maria and Darnford living happily ever after is very much in keeping with its Gothic nature. The Darnford story line illustrates that a woman's institutionalized dependence on *any* man is problematic. Maria's husband may be a tyrant, but even the more attractive choice leaves her trapped in a Gothic reality.

Unambiguously clear in the novel is that women need to help themselves. Maria's memoirs are written with the express purpose of educating and exposing her daughter to the subtleties and harms of patriarchy. She hopes her life story "might perhaps instruct her daughter, and shield her from the misery, the tyranny, her mother knew not how to avoid" (82). While Maria is writing to her daughter, Wollstonecraft is writing to her female readers, who can become that daughter as they read the memoirs over Darnford's shoulder (Maurer 50). Wollstonecraft is thus able to encourage her readers "to form your grand principle of action. . . . Gain experience—ah! gain it—while experience is worth having, and acquire sufficient fortitude to pursue your *own* happiness" (125; emphasis added). At the same time that Maria encourages her daughter and the reader to be "mistress of your own actions" (149), however, the novel acknowledges that the laws that kept women buried alive, and in complete economic dependence on men, presented almost insurmountable barriers to the freedoms to which women should have had access. Maria's story illustrates the ramifications of a husband's absolute control over all family finances (and the lawful methods of coercion he could employ to gain control over any sources of funds available to his wife).[16] The working-class Jemima, whose story relates how she has been treated as "a slave, a bastard, a common property," tells of her harrowing efforts to feed and shelter herself through prostitution and physically debilitating labor (109). These narratives show how limited employment opportunities made it next to impossible for a woman to support—and thus protect—herself.

The novel also presents examples of women both increasing and alleviating each other's suffering. Maria's mother makes her childhood miserable by so preferentially treating her older brother. Jemima's stepmother is physically and emotionally abusive, and Jemima laments her own heartlessness in having a pregnant young servant girl turned out into the streets (the girl consequently commits suicide). The novel doesn't excuse these cruelties practiced by women against women; however, it does identify society as the root of the problem. As Maria explains in her memoirs, "By allowing women but one way of rising in the world, the fostering the libertinism of men, society makes monsters of them" (137).

Set against these monstrous behaviors, however, are examples of women protecting each other, most notably in the relationship between Maria and Jemima, a friendship that transcends class boundaries. Jemima is Maria's protector in the madhouse, keeping her company and saving her from an idleness that threatens to drive her mad. She also ensures Maria's escape, literally protecting her as she is running from the asylum from the "being, with a visage that would have suited one possessed by a devil" who seizes Maria (190). Jemima is the only person in Maria's life to respond effectively to her desperate plea of "Save me" (190).

Early in the novel, when Maria offers Jemima compensation for helping her to escape, the worldly-wise and prudent Jemima ponders what would happen if Venables successfully substantiated Maria's "madness" and gained control of her estate. In such circumstances, Jemima wonders "from whence would come the promised annuity, or more desired protection?" (83). This more desired protection seems to allude to respectability, a place in society. Later, in London, Jemima accepts Maria's protection, which then also encompasses human affection and companionship. Moreover, in the only hopeful proposed ending (and also the one that is most developed), Jemima finds Maria's daughter, who is not really dead, and arrives in time to save Maria from an attempted suicide. This ending suggests an alternative to the existing system under coverture—a society in which women do not have to be dependent on men and in which they are free to work together to cope with, and possibly transform, their own Gothic realities.

The trial at the end of *Maria* displays the irrelevance of women's stories to the patriarchal legal system that Wollstonecraft was indicting. Maria has no voice at the trial; rather, a paper she has written is presented for her. With statements such as "I wish my country to approve my conduct; but, if laws exist, made by the strong to oppress the weak, I appeal to my own sense of justice, and declare that I will not live with the individual, who has violated every moral obligation which binds man to man" (197), Maria willfully contravenes the authority of the court, claiming she will follow her own sense of right as opposed to prejudicial laws. Inviting charges of contempt, she declares that she will refuse to comply if the court orders her to return to her husband. She then appeals to the jury's humanity and sense of justice, urging them to modify the law as appropriate to her circumstances. After her heartfelt plea, the judge summarily dismisses her arguments and contemns the practice of allowing women to "plead their feelings," emphasizing that emotion has no place in legal discourse (198). In the courtroom, the judge treats rather than charges Maria with contempt.

While there may be little hope that "the jury—a body of men" (198) will override the deeply entrenched ideology of the law on marriage as summarized by the judge—"It was her duty to love and obey the man chosen by her parents and relations, who were qualified by their experience to judge better for her, than she could for herself . . ." (199)—the chapter ends without this jury pronouncing its verdict. In this way, Wollstonecraft's narrative opens up a space for the deliberations of a differently constituted body—her readers. For those who have been presented with the Gothic tale of Maria's life experiences, it is unambivalent that a truly just decision would free her from the fetters imposed by the impartial laws of society.

A *mise en abyme*, this final trial scene is an internal duplication of the feminist jurisprudence Wollstonecraft performs in and with her novel. The substance of Maria's contemptuous speech (which she writes because she has no authority to speak in the courtroom) is a summary of the law's oppression of women that she has been illustrating throughout *Maria*. Wollstonecraft's novel, like the courtroom she presents within it, is a public forum in which she interrogates the law through her writing. Also, the way the novel progresses, with the reader moving from the private pages of Maria's memoirs to the public reading of her words, enacts a method of progress that feminists increasingly embraced over the course of the nineteenth century: making generally known or *publishing* the wrongs of woman.

In *Maria*, Wollstonecraft put coverture on trial, exposing the Gothic realities of women's lives. The various women who were imprisoned, raped, beaten, and abandoned in the novel were innocent victims of a society that failed to offer them any real protection and that frustrated all efforts they made to protect themselves. Godwin writes in his *Memoirs of Mary Wollstonecraft* that all her previous works "were produced with a rapidity, that did not give her powers time fully to expand. But [*Maria*] was written slowly and with mature consideration" (111). It appears that in Wollstonecraft's considered opinion, a Gothic novel was the most appropriate form, structurally and thematically, to effect her political purpose.

Outlaw Texts

Novels That Don't Police

Since Ian Watt first noted connections between strategies of representation in courtrooms and novels and the expectations of juries and novel readers, scholars have explored a wide array of fascinating interplays between the novel and the law.[17] For example, specifically with respect to the nineteenth century, Alexander Welsh has examined changes in the construction of the novel in the context of eighteenth- and nineteenth-century developments in the laws of evidence, particularly an increased reliance on circumstantial evidence;[18] Jan-Melissa Schramm has traced the effects on literary narratives of changes in legal trial procedures such as those brought about by the Prisoners' Counsel Act of 1836 that allowed professional lawyers to represent defendants in court;[19] and Jonathan Grossman has explored how "the law courts crucially shaped the formal structures and political aims of the novel" (5).[20]

Analyzing the cultural role of the novel, D. A. Miller has argued that the novel often participated in the general economy of policing power that it purported to critique. In his Foucauldian analysis of *Bleak House*, for example, Miller reads Dickens's promotion and representation of the family as "an undeclared defense of the status quo" because, Miller explains, Dickens's advice to society to "police for the family" and his advice to the family to police itself, in effect, cancel each other out:

> For if society reformed itself so that state institutions [such as Chancery] would, if not wither away, become minimal and humane, then there would no longer exist an outside threat to consolidate the family in the face of its internal dangers; and to the extent that the family could successfully repress these dangers itself, it would only reproduce such institutions in their worst aspects. (104)

Concluding that the novel's overt disavowal of "police practices" only rendered it a more discreet form of social discipline, Miller recharacterizes the so-called lawlessness of the novel as an effective cover for its power to police everyday life (16).

Similarly, Edward Said has identified the nineteenth-century novel as "a cultural form consolidating but also refining and articulating the authority of the *status quo*" (77). With respect to law, Said also cites Dickens as an example of an author who "stirs up his readers against the legal system" but whose novels such as *Bleak House* ultimately achieve resolution, most frequently figured in "the reunification of the family, which in Dickens' case always serves as a microcosm of society" (77). It is Said's contention that the novel, "whose central continuous presence is not comparably to be found elsewhere," reinscribed rather than questioned existing institutions such as the legal system (73).

The claims of both Miller and Said are supported by thoughtful and discerning analyses of canonical or well-known nineteenth-century novels.[21] However, I believe that taking into account novels that truly are "outlaw" alters landmark literary decisions about the Victorian novel's role as aider and abettor of a patriarchal legal institution.[22]

Novels that are most obviously outlaw texts are those like *Maria* that criticize the legal institution explicitly and that include direct statements by the author of an intention to do so. Another example of this type of outlaw novel is Florence Dixie's New Woman utopian novel *Gloriana* (1890), discussed in detail in chapter 5. In her preface, Dixie states:

> "Gloriana" pleads woman's cause, pleads for her freedom, for the just acknowledgment of her rights. It pleads that her equal humanity with man shall be recognized, and therefore that her claim to share with what he has arrogated to himself shall be considered. "Gloriana" pleads that in women's degradation man shall no longer be debased, that in her elevation he shall be upraised and ennobled. (xi)

This preface concludes with an explicit statement of the novel's purpose: "If, therefore, the following story should help men to be generous and just, should awaken the sluggards amongst women to a sense of their position, and should thus lead to a rapid revolution, it will not have been written in vain" (xii).

Closely related to these outlaw novels are those that include equally sharp and specific critiques of the law or some aspect of it, but that are not introduced with a specific statement of authorial intention. In these novels, the law is indicted within and by the fiction itself. Frances Trollope's *Jessie Phillips: A Tale of the Present Day* (1843), discussed in chapter 2, is an example of this type of outlaw novel. In this novel, an unmarried woman is falsely accused of infanticide. The reader (who knows who really murdered the child) witnesses the power of legal discourse to shape the understanding of Jessie's character and to (mis)interpret her situation. By presenting the life experiences of a "fallen woman" (her seduction, her betrayal, her loss of employment upon the discovery of her pregnancy, her unsuccessful attempts to seek help from the child's father and a lawyer, and her time in the workhouse), the novel also offers a scathing critique of the bastardy clauses of the 1834 New Poor Law which made an unmarried mother solely responsible for the maintenance of her "bastard" child.

Finally, there are those novels that are less obviously in contempt of the law because they are not overtly about the law. *Wuthering Heights* is such an outlaw novel. This novel has no explicitly legal scenes; however, it would be difficult to imagine a novel in which the law of coverture and its implications with respect to married women's property, child custody, and the power relationships within marriage were more integral to the plot. In *Wuthering Heights*, in a scene that takes place a few weeks after Heathcliff marries Isabella, Heathcliff boasts to Ellen Dean ("Nelly," who at that time was a servant to Isabella's brother Edgar Linton) of his cruelties to his wife:

> Tell your master, Nelly, that I never, in all my life, met with such an abject thing as she is. She even disgraces the name of Linton; and I've sometimes relented, from pure lack of invention, in my experiments on what she could endure, and still creep shamefully cringing back. But tell him, also, to set his fraternal and magisterial heart at ease: that I keep strictly within the limits of the law. (187)

Fearing that knowledge of Heathcliff's words and actions might provoke her brother in such a way as to give Heathcliff even greater control over the Linton family, Isabella fires back:

> He's a lying fiend! a monster, and not a human being! I've been told I might leave him before; and I've made the attempt, but I dare not repeat it! Only, Ellen, promise you'll not mention a syllable of his infamous conversation to my brother or Catherine. Whatever he may pretend, he wishes to provoke Edgar to desperation: he says he has married me on purpose to obtain power over him, and he shan't obtain it—I'll die first! I just hope, I pray, that he may forget his diabolical prudence and kill me! The single pleasure I can imagine is to die or to see him dead! (188)

Heathcliff silences Isabella, "There—that will do for the present!" (188) and then impresses on her that the law would interpret her madness (rage) as madness—an all-too-typical diagnosis for nineteenth-century women:[23]

> If you are called upon in a court of law you'll remember her language, Nelly! And take a good look at that countenance: she's near the point which would suit me. No; you're not fit to be your own guardian, Isabella, now; and I, being your legal protector, must retain you in my custody, however distasteful the obligation may be. (188–89)

The law is fully on Heathcliff's side and he knows it. He is careful to act within "the limits of the law" (187), which, as this scene dramatically exposes, are really no limits at all. The emotional abuse is explicit, and the intensity of Isabella's hatred of Heathcliff suggests that his "experiments" have very likely included the completely legal act of marital rape, as well as any force that was necessary to keep her from leaving. Her rage works only to make her appear more in need of his "protection." In its presentation of speakable and unspeakable acts of this husband's cruelty, this outlaw novel shows the "protection" of coverture to be far from anything anyone could *ever* desire.[24]

Feminist legal theory and methods provide a different lens than has been used in previous law and literature scholarship through which to view interrelationships between the novel and the law. For example, such a perspective brings to the center questions such as these: When studying the impact on novelistic discourse of changing rules of evidence or trial procedures in the nineteenth century, how might it matter that women were not allowed to study or practice law? Are connections between juries and novel readers at all affected by the fact that, at the time, many women read novels but no women sat on juries? What does it say about the interplays between legal proceedings and the novel that women often were not welcome in law courts and that popular and influential women writers, such as Frances Trollope, were chided in literary reviews for daring to write about such an unfit topic as the law?[25] In her recent book, *Riding the Black Ram: Law, Literature, and Gender*, Susan Sage Heinzelman brings gender to the center of the analysis and examines the impact that this change of focus has on the traditional telling of the rise of the English novel in the eighteenth century.[26] For the nineteenth century, a particularly relevant inquiry that *In Contempt* addresses is how taking into account "outlaw" novels by women might call into question long-standing judgments that have been made about the cultural role of the Victorian novel, especially as these conclusions have been based primarily on studies of texts that have been deemed acceptable as literary precedents.[27] Among the outlaw texts analyzed in the following chapters, many are outlaw novels that were "in contempt" of the law. The performances of feminist jurisprudence in these novels cast more than reasonable doubt on conclusions about the normalizing and policing effects of novels on nineteenth-century readers.

CHAPTER 2

Legislative Histories
and Literary Herstories

Infanticide, Bastardy, and the "Lewd Woman"

law

1.a. The body of rules, whether proceeding from formal enactment
or from custom, which a particular state or community recognizes
as binding on its members or subjects. . . . b. Often viewed, with
more or less of personification, as an agent uttering or enforcing
the rules of which it consists. . . .

—*Oxford English Dictionary*

In George Eliot's novel *Adam Bede* (1859), Hetty Sorrel sits in the prisoner's
dock, dwarfed in the huge, intimidating hall in which her trial for infanticide
takes place. One of the characters describes her as "white as a sheet" and
"seeming neither to hear nor see anything" (473). For the readers, who have
no idea what has happened to Hetty since the narrative left her pregnant
and alone on the road to Stoniton, the tension and suspense are palpable.

In 1800, the year in which Eliot sets this trial, Hetty would have been
tried pursuant to the following English statute, dating from 1623, which
applied only to "lewd women that have been delivered of bastard children":

[I]f any woman . . . be delivered of any issue of her body, male or female,
which being born alive, should by the laws of this realm be a bastard, and
that she endeavor privately, either by drowning or secret burying thereof, or
any other way, either by herself or the procuring of others, so to conceal the
death thereof, as that it may not come to light, whether it were born alive or
not, but be concealed: in every such case the said mother so offending shall
suffer death as in case of murther, except such mother make proof by one

witness at the least, that the child (whose death was by her so intended to be concealed) was born dead.[1]

This first English statute to specifically address infanticide shifted the burden of proof such that the accused mother was presumed guilty unless she could produce a witness to swear that her child had been born dead. Thus, while any man (including the father) or any woman (*except* the mother) accused of killing a child would be tried for murder and presumed innocent unless proven guilty, the "lewd mother" of a "bastard," if she attempted to conceal its birth and death, was guilty under the statute *regardless* of how the child died. If a woman delivered a stillborn child alone, for example, she would be *prima facie* guilty of murder under the statute because she would be unable to produce any witnesses.[2]

Hetty did attempt to conceal the birth and death of her infant, as the schoolmaster Bartle Massey reports, "denying she's had a child from first to last" (474). At the trial, Sarah Stone's testimony that she helped deliver Hetty's baby is offered as proof that Hetty did indeed bear a child.[3] No doubt Hetty's attorney, who "puts a spoke in the wheel whenever he can, and makes a deal to do with cross-examining the witnesses, and quarrelling with the other lawyers" (473), makes the argument that this same evidence should exclude Hetty from the draconian provisions of the 1623 statute because, if Stone's testimony is accepted as proof that Hetty has borne a child, at the same time it demonstrates that there was no *actual* concealment of birth—somebody besides Hetty knew about it. If this argument is successful, the burden shifts to the prosecution to prove that Hetty intentionally murdered her child.

The testimony of the prosecution's witness John Olding seems intended to do just that. Olding testifies that he had seen Hetty the previous Monday sitting by a haystack in one of the nearby fields. Upon seeing him, Hetty got up and walked away. He describes her as having looked white and scared. He also had heard a strange cry but had found nothing when he went to investigate. Returning about an hour later, however, he found the body of a child: "And just as I was stooping and laying down the stakes, I saw something odd and round and whitish lying on the ground under a nut-bush by the side of me. And I stooped down on hands and knees to pick it up. And I saw it was a little baby's hand" (480).

At these words, "a thrill ran through the court" (480) and Hetty begins to tremble visibly. The man goes on to explain that the body had not been entirely covered, but the baby was dead. The next day he had gone back to the same spot with the constable and they had found Hetty sitting by the nut-bush.[4] Olding's testimony works to establish that the baby was alive when Hetty placed it under the nut-bush, and that she knew it was alive. It is offered as proof that the child did not die naturally, but rather as a result of Hetty's purposeful burial of it under the nut-bush.

Things move quickly after Olding testifies. Adam is now certain that Hetty is guilty of infanticide. We are told that Mr. Irwine gives evidence of Hetty's virtuous upbringing as part of a plea for mercy. The jury retires; the lawyers talk among themselves; a mere fifteen minutes later, the jury returns. There is a sublime silence: "Deeper and deeper the silence seemed to become, like deepening night, while the jurymen's names were called over, and the prisoner was made to hold up her hand, and the jury were asked for their verdict. 'Guilty'" (481–82). The judge, after ceremonially putting on his black cap, calls out the name "Hester Sorrel." Hetty, wide-eyed, stares at the judge "as if fascinated by fear" (482). When he pronounces that she is "to be hanged by the neck till you be dead" (482), Hetty's piercing shriek echoes through the hall.

This courtroom scene has the potential to be the site for a powerful performance of feminist jurisprudence. So many questions go unasked and unanswered at this trial: Were there other reasons Hetty might have left the child under the nut-bush? Why did she come back? Does she understand the nature of the strange proceedings going on around her? How many of the gaps in the prosecutor's narrative are filled in by the "knowledge" that the law has helped to constitute that "lewd women" are inclined to dispose of their "bastard" children?

While the novel sets up the possibility for this type of gender and class critique of the law's condemnation of Hetty, other aspects of the narrative are at odds with this reading. Specifically, readers bring to Hetty's trial prior knowledge of "deviant" aspects of her character. So while it is true that Hetty's circumstances have made her vulnerable and that she is presented as childlike in many respects,[5] the narrator also has emphasized since the early pages of the novel that she is vain, selfish, cold-hearted, and—most disturbing in connection with the accusation of infanticide—not maternal.[6] As I will discuss more fully below, this prior characterization of Hetty as deviant, supplemented by a prosecuting narrative voice, results in a trial scene that does not call into question and critique the law's association between "lewd women" and infanticide. Rather, as Rosemary Gould concludes, "though the tragic outcome of Hetty's story exists to create sympathy for her, the concept that she is the kind of woman who would commit infanticide remains" (266).

Feminist legal scholars have explored the impacts of "causal attribution," a cognitive mechanism by which people assign causes to outcomes, in a wide array of legal contexts. Research on causal attribution has shown ways in which group stereotypes affect decision makers, specifically suggesting that

> when behavior appears to confirm a stereotype about the group, we tend to attribute that behavior to a dispositional factor, that is, one within the control of the actor. Only if the behavior is inconsistent with our stereotype about the group are we apt to seek out an external explanation and then attribute the behavior to situational factors. (Chamallas 185)[7]

Thus, in many respects, when women come to law, character carries more weight than circumstances in explaining outcomes. In this chapter, I contrast legal and literary texts that helped to constitute the causal attribution in law between the character of the "lewd woman" and the outcome of infanticide with alternative *her*stories that unequivocally problematize and discredit stereotypes and dominant narratives about "fallen women."

The Law's "Truth" about Infanticide and the Literary Judgment of Hetty Sorrel

> Under no possible system of police, however elaborate, could all working mothers in England be watched in order to make certain that they should not murder their own children. We could, perhaps, prevent their eating them, or burying them secretly for children can be counted; but their killing them is not preventable. . . . There is, in fact, no defence for young children, and can be none except the mother's feeling for them; and when that is absent, or has been changed into abhorrence, they must, as far as society can help it, just die at their mothers' discretion. The only cure worth anything is a change in the women's hearts.
>
> —"*The Judges' Opinion Upon Child-Murder*," Spectator *1890*

Studies of real nineteenth-century women who were accused of criminal acts confirm that the law tended to judge the woman rather than the crime. In *Women, Crime, and Custody in Victorian England*, Lucia Zedner reports that "[d]escriptions of women's crime frequently referred to past conduct, marital status, protestations of regret, or shamelessness, and even to the woman's physical appearance" (30). Virginia Morris's research shows that women's crimes often were explained in terms of natural feminine traits gone awry: "[T]he perception that violent women acted from individual rather than environmentally produced motives and that there was something wrong with them as women if they chose aggression rather than acquiescence run as constant themes through the journal articles, charges to juries, and crime histories of the century" (27). Specifically with respect to infanticide prosecutions, Ann Higginbotham's examination of actual child-murder cases tried in the Central Criminal Court in London reveals a "surprising leniency" on the part of judges and juries, with few women being convicted and those found guilty being pardoned (323).[8] However, her research also shows that the "more unconventional the woman's behavior and background, the more likely she was to lose the sympathy of the court" (333). Regardless of actual conviction rates, Higginbotham reports that many Victorians were all too ready to suspect unmarried women of murdering their infants, to make the connection between "lewd women" and infanticide. These assumptions about unmarried mothers "may have sent women to the dock even when their infants died naturally or accidentally" (329). It is my contention that the narrator of *Adam Bede* presents Hetty Sorrel in ways that worked to reinforce cultural ideas about sexuality, deviance, and crime.

The reader is first introduced to Hetty as she is trying to catch a glimpse of "the pleasing reflection of herself" (117) in the polished surface of an oak table. The narrator makes clear that he has access to what other characters cannot see, reporting that Hetty looks at her reflection in the table, the round pewter dishes, and the hobs of the grate only "when her aunt's back was turned" (117). Moreover, as Lisa Rodensky explores in her study, *The Crime in Mind: Criminal Responsibility and the Victorian Novel*, third-person narrators "can hold themselves out as representing thoughts directly" (6), which is the case with the narrator in *Adam Bede*. So when Hetty's seducer Arthur Donnithorne visits her in the dairy and she is described as tossing and patting her butter with a "self-possessed, coquettish air," we also are told that she is "slyly conscious that no turn of her head was lost" (127). Such information works to undermine the characterization of Hetty as an "innocent" victim of seduction. Indeed, at times, the narrator implies that Hetty's innocence is feigned, that her nature is cunning:

> Hetty's was a springtide beauty; it was the beauty of young frisking things, round-limbed, gambolling, circumventing you by a false air of innocence—the innocence of a young star-browed calf, for example, that, being inclined for a promenade out of bounds, leads you a severe steeplechase over hedge and ditch, and only comes to a stand in the middle of a bog. (128–29)

While the novel clearly places much censure and responsibility on Donnithorne, Hetty's "false air of innocence" also is blamed for Hetty's and

Arthur's "promenade out of bounds."[9] As this passage suggests, Hetty has played a significant role in leading them into the quagmire that their story becomes.

Moreover, it is difficult to feel compassion for Hetty when she is presented as seemingly incapable of feeling for anyone else. Portrayed by the narrator as callous and completely self-absorbed, Hetty is indifferent to Adam's pain when his father drowns, and she cares little about her uncle, who has welcomed her into his family. In fact, we are told that "Hetty did not understand how anybody could be very fond of middle-aged people" (199–200). Moreover, the narrator records that, while she has no intention of marrying "a poor man," Hetty exercised a "coquettish tyranny" over Adam, enjoying the "cold triumph of knowing that he loved her" (144).

Most damning, however, may be Hetty's attitude toward children. Far from nurturing, she is presented as actively hostile toward them:

> Hetty would have been glad to hear that she should never see a child again; they were worse than the nasty little lambs that the shepherd was always bringing in to be taken special care of in lambing time; for the lambs *were* got rid of sooner or later. As for the young chickens and turkeys, Hetty would have hated the very word "hatching," if her aunt had not bribed her to attend to the young poultry by promising her the proceeds of one of every brood. (200)

In a novel in which the "good women" are loved by and loving toward children, this passage portrays Hetty as far outside that norm. To her, children are a burden; young things needing care and attention are hateful. In light of how her story will unfold, Hetty's line that the lambs at least "were got rid of sooner or later" is particularly chilling.

Even when Hetty is on the road to Stoniton, the narrative voice is constantly interrupting the reader's burgeoning feelings of sympathy. Thus, as we commiserate with Hetty on her desperate wanderings, as she makes her "toilsome way in loneliness, her peaceful home left behind for ever, and nothing but a tremulous hope of distant refuge before her," the narrator reminds us that Hetty "thought of all she had left behind with yearning regret for her own sake: her own misery filled her heart: there was no room in it for other people's sorrow" (417).

The same is true during Hetty's trial. From the description of the courtroom scene with which I opened this chapter, I purposely omitted the comments of the narrator—and thus there was the potential for sympathy for this young, terrified girl. The same scene, however, viewed in light of the information that the narrator already has imparted about Hetty's character, and including his courtroom commentary, shows the condemning effect of this narrator/prosecutor.[10]

Rather than characterizing Hetty as frightened and silent at the trial, the narrator tells us that she is in a state of "blank hard indifference" (481). The following description of Adam's response when he first sees Hetty in the courtroom emphasizes her deviance from any feminine norm:

> Others thought she looked as if some demon had cast a blighting glance upon her, withered up the woman's soul in her, and left only a hard despairing obstinacy. But the mother's yearning, that completest type of the life in another life which is the essence of real human love, feels the presence of the cherished child even in the debased, degraded man; and to Adam, this pale hard-looking culprit was the Hetty who had smiled at him in the garden under the apple-tree boughs—she was that Hetty's corpse, which he had trembled to look at the first time, and then was unwilling to turn away his eyes from. (477)

While "objective" others see that Hetty is monstrous, demonized, with a withered soul, Adam, in his blind devotion, views her differently. With the maternal metaphor, the narrator accentuates Hetty's crime. Hetty, given the opportunity to feel that mother's yearning, the essence of real human love, felt nothing. In this passage, Adam is the loving, nurturing mother, while Hetty is a pale, hard-looking culprit; unwomaned, she is the equivalent of a "debased, degraded man." The language itself suggests guilt by association because if Hetty is capable of "killing" her previously innocent self (she is now *that* Hetty's corpse), she also could have murdered another innocent. In this passage, Hetty is so far removed from the ideal of Victorian womanhood that she becomes a "realistic" representation of a woman capable of killing her child.

After the trial, through the intervention of Eliot's strong woman preacher Dinah Morris, Hetty is able to voice her story.[11] Krueger, who sees Hetty as "too terrified to defend herself" when "she is accused in man's court of law" (*Reader's Repentence* 253), argues that "Dinah empowers the fallen woman's voice, which in turn obliquely indicts patriarchal sins" (253). I agree that Hetty's own narrative does soften her portrayal somewhat by suggesting that she had hoped the baby would be found, as well as by emphasizing the ways in which her crime was motivated by her (well-founded) fear of severe judgment by her family and community. However, at the same time, her story also reflects "a startling rejection of the role of motherhood which was so sanctified during the Victorian era" (Hancock 305). Moreover, her descriptions of the baby as "like a heavy weight hanging round my neck" (499) and her confession that "I seemed to hate it" (499) echo her earlier troubling sentiments toward children, never letting Hetty "escape from her culture's underlying main assumption about the 'infanticidal woman': that she is not made of the same stuff as you and I" (M. Jones 323).

With its characterization of Hetty, the novel does little to disrupt legal discourse about "lewd women" and infanticide. Several critics have argued that Eliot actually was more harsh with Hetty than was the law, with Miriam Jones suggesting that the strength of the argument that the novel is a critique of a legal system that silences women like Hetty is lessened by the fact that Hetty is "shut out from the narrative as surely as she is from testifying at the trial" (312). Indeed, the law, by sending Hetty away, is instrumental in bringing about reunification of the community.[12]

Unlike the outlaw novels discussed below, *Adam Bede* concludes with more of a sense of resolution than of grave injustice. Arthur is allowed to return after being appropriately diminished in health and esteem. Adam finds true happiness with Dinah and benefits from the "fuller life which had come to him from his acquaintance with deep sorrow" (574). Dinah, overindulgent of her children and no longer preaching, represents an appropriate feminine ideal. The memory of Hetty is present and there is a "tinge of sadness" (Creeger 238), but Creeger argues that this "hint of sorrow" is most appropriate to the resolution of this novel because "in the world which George Eliot reveals to us, life not only contains sorrow, it needs sorrow in order that there may be love" (238).[13] Gould describes, at the end of the novel, "a perfected Hayslope/England, perfected not because the unmarried mother and child are accepted and cared for, but because they no longer exist" (275).

Thus, in its portrayal of Hetty, the novel serves as a reinscription of what feminist legal scholar Carol Smart describes as law's claim to "Truth," its authoritative claim to ultimate correctness ("Law's Truth/women's experience" 2). As Schramm notes, Hetty's confession is "a tentative confirmation of the court's finding that her intent to harm her child could be inferred from her actions" (138). The novel, in fact, makes the explicit connection between law and truth in an early passage in which the narrator "pauses a little" to inform the readers that he will be giving a "faithful account of men and things as they have mirrored themselves in my mind" (221). Offering something akin to a narrative oath, bolstering his credibility, the narrator avers, "I feel as much bound to tell you, as precisely as I can, what that reflection is, as if I were in the witness-box narrating my experiences on oath" (221). This passage is exemplary of the shift in novels that Alexander Welsh has identified toward a preference for "making strong representations," which "can be reduced to the idea of telling stories, but only stories of a particular kind: the representation purports to be true, for one thing, and therefore in literature the expression is generally appropriate to realism" (8).[14] While representations "should appear to be dispassionately devoted to the facts" (9), Welsh explains that they are, by definition, of a particular view:

> To make a representation in practice means to subordinate the facts to a conclusion that makes a difference one way or another. In other words, the representation is conclusive: if it purports to review all the facts that is because, in the opinion of the person making the representation, the facts when considered rightly all point in one direction. . . . People need not go about telling their stories and hoping for the best; instead, the stories should be managed with a careful view of the consequences. This management obviously takes ability and experience and, above all, hard work and therefore can best be left to professionals—and professional representation is thought to be an impressive performance in its own right. (9)

Eliot's narrator in *Adam Bede* gives just that kind of impressive professional performance, and with his crafted presentation of the narrative facts, he makes strong representations in support of the law's "truth" about deviant women and infanticide.[15] A review of *Adam Bede* in the *Athenaeum* testifies to the effectiveness of his performance: "the story is not a story, but a true account of a place and people who have really lived . . . but that everything happened as here set down we have no doubt in the world" (284). In this way, the representation of Hetty Sorrel helped to constitute lasting ideas about infanticide as a problem of deviant women, and the enduring critical acclaim of *Adam Bede* has ensured that literature's "truth" about infanticide in the nineteenth century is strongly represented by Hetty Sorrel.[16]

Evidence to the Contrary

Infanticide in Outlaw Texts

Other literary texts such as Frances Trollope's *Jessie Phillips: A Tale of the Present Day* (1843), Caroline Leakey's *The Broad Arrow* (1859), and Mary Tuttiet's *The Last Sentence* (1891), however, are resolutely "outlaw" in their resistance to the law's causal attribution between unmarried mothers and infanticide.[17] In *The Broad Arrow*, for example, the heroine Maida

Gwynnham is discovered burying her illegitimate child, who the reader knows has died of natural causes, most likely malnourishment. Gwynnham subsequently is convicted of child-murder and transported to Australia. Published the same year as *Adam Bede*, Maida's story begins where Hetty's leaves off. After Hetty's dramatic reprieve from the scaffold, we hear no more of her story. Narrative concern shifts to those people who will continue to be a part of the community, away from the one who has disrupted it. In contrast, *The Broad Arrow*, which was the first major novel to address convict life in Australia and the only convict novel to concern itself with female transportees, takes up the story of the "fallen woman," exploring the realities of her "pardon."[18]

The literary criticism of *The Broad Arrow*, not surprisingly, has focused on its account of life in Van Dieman's Land (Tasmania), Australia, the place where Leakey lived and observed the convict system from 1848 to 1853.[19] At the same time, however, this criticism dismisses the seduction and infanticide narratives in the novel as nothing more than "an irrelevant frame around the main narrative" (Hergenhan 142). I disagree with the consensus that Maida's early trials are unimportant, instead seeing them as integral to an understanding of Maida's "guilt."

While Maida is innocent of infanticide, she was tricked by her seducer, Captain Norwell, into committing forgery. Sacrificing herself to protect Norwell (although unable to repress completely her own anger), she tells him, "your *hand* did not commit the forgery, your fame must not be touched, it stands too high: but Maida Gwynnham, that outcast! it matters not how low her fall" (Leakey 16). Thus, she offers no protest when wrongly accused of infanticide because she knows this more serious charge likely will forestall any inquiry into the forgery.

Having for many months suffered society's judgment of her as an unmarried mother, Maida knows how the law will read her story. She is not at all surprised when proofs such as the sudden start she made when the constables examined her baby's body for signs of violence and the bottle of poison found in her cupboard (she had contemplated suicide when first abandoned by Norwell) are produced in such a way as to make her guilt "unquestionable"—"The dreadful crime could, without doubt, be traced" (21). Whereas in *Adam Bede* the readers wonder whether a crime has been committed, there is no such suspense during Maida's trial. It has been made clear to the reader that Maida did not commit infanticide. Thus, the trial only goes to prove that, try as it might, the law does not get it right. While Maida is escorted to her cell, where a "doubly-locked door swings itself solemnly back, and there is silence, darkness, despair" (4), we are told that the truly guilty party, Norwell, left the courtroom and "gladly crept out of the loophole opened by circumstance (Providence, he said), and still wider opened by the fair law of England; he crept but into—The ball-room! No harm either—it was the assize ball" (21). In this scene, the law's claim to "truth" (and fairness) is severely undermined.

As Maida is not guilty of infanticide and only technically (not morally, since Norwell had deceived her) guilty of forgery, what she is punished for, in effect, is her sexual fall. Through transportation, she literally becomes the outcast she has been made to feel in England. While Leakey's descriptions of the degradations of convict life—particularly female convict life—provide important historical information, they also serve metaphorically to show the overly severe societal and legal judgment and punishment of "fallen women."[20]

Another woman wrongly accused of infanticide appears in the late-century novel *The Last Sentence* by Mary Tuttiet (who wrote under the pseudonym Maxwell Gray). In this novel, the judge who erroneously sentences Cicely Rennie to death is her own father Cecil Marlowe. Marlowe had refused to acknowledge Cicely's peasant mother Renée as his wife and, when Renée died outside his window frozen in the snow, Marlowe left the infant Cicely with a stranger and later lost track of her completely. How to judge his own abandonment of the child and the misjudgment of his and her characters are among the many questions posed in this novel's feminist interrogation of the rules of law and society.

In this chapter, however, in order to elaborate on *how* novels perform feminist jurisprudence, I will be focusing on Frances Trollope's *Jessie Phillips*. Whereas Eliot, Leakey, and Tuttiet portray legal trials and sentences, Trollope reproves the law as legislated. In her literary narrative, she critiques and exposes the presumptions and biases involved in the *production* of legal texts.

Frances Trollope's *Jessie Phillips*

What about Her Story?

The particular clause of the Act which [Mrs. Trollope] has selected for reprobation is the *bastardy clause*—not perhaps the very best subject for a female pen. And then, in order to give dramatic effect to this subject, we have the seduction of Jessie Phillips, her pregnancy, the birth of the child, and its supposed murder by the guilty mother, discussed by two young ladies (Ellen Dalton and Martha Maxwell), of which discussion, the discovery of the body, the probabilities of Jessie being in a condition, just after parturition, to be able to

destroy the child, and the enormity of the crime, are the prominent
points. We admit that Mrs. Trollope manages these details with as
much delicacy and reserve as their nature would admit of, but they
are essentially unfit materials. They are, of necessity, suggestive of
circumstances which are always repulsive in their character, and
peculiarly so when made the subject of lengthened conversation
between two young, artless, and inexperienced girls.

—*Review of* Jessie Phillips, *in* John Bull *1843*

Frances Trollope, one of the most prolific and popular British authors of
the 1830s and 40s, unacceptably breached legal, literary, and gender boundaries when she entered the dialogue on infanticide with her serial novel
Jessie Phillips: A Tale of the Present Day (1843). Contemporary reviews
of this social-problem novel, while couched in terms of literary impropriety
and writerly disabilities, betray anxieties about Trollope's choice of subject
matter.[21] The review of the novel in *John Bull* announced that "for the sake
of thus having a Poor Law story with which to blend heavy accusations
against the Poor Law itself, Mrs. Trollope has sinned grievously against
good taste and decorum" (732), and *The Athenaeum* cites as one of the
novel's flagrant faults that in "illustrating the iniquity of 'the law,' Mrs. Trollope could not turn away from so tempting a subject as its dealings with
Woman and her Seducer; and 'Jessie Phillips' is accordingly the old tale of
the Lamb and the Wolf" (956).

I would argue, however, that *Jessie Phillips* was pronounced such a
"bad book" because it unapologetically is *not* that same old tale, but rather
a "novel" forum in which Trollope puts into practice feminist jurisprudence. Published serially from December 1842 to November 1843, *Jessie
Phillips* is peopled with needlewomen, clergymen, dukes and duchesses,
fashionable young ladies, squires, and lawyers, all participating in a variety
of subplots. Unlike her literary competitor Dickens, however, who delights
in making a mystery of the relationships among his characters, Trollope
emphasizes her characters' interconnectedness.[22] Her narrative strategy of
weaving together the story of Ellen Dalton, the eldest daughter of the parish
squire; the tale of Jessie who is seduced by Frederic (Ellen's brother); and
the narrative of Martha Maxwell, a friend to both Jessie and Ellen and
"engaged" to Frederic, accentuates how the law's regulation of a "deviant"
woman such as Jessie is premised upon and authorized by its institutional
control of the behavior of all women.

When Jessie Phillips, a beautiful and talented seamstress, is seduced by
the charming (but diabolical) Frederic Dalton, he convinces her that they
must keep their relationship a secret and wait a few years before marrying

(allegedly so he will not lose an inheritance). The two of them exchange vows, and Jessie believes that, while the public ceremony has to be delayed, "she was in spirit and in truth his wedded wife" (2: 20).[23] True to the conventional Lamb and Wolf plot, Frederic abandons a pregnant Jessie, who after losing her reputation, and hence her livelihood, disappears behind the walls of one of the Union workhouses established pursuant to the New Poor Law. While not literally dead, she is presumed literarily so. With Jessie seduced and abandoned, the Lamb's story is supposed to be over. In Trollope's "bad" novel, however, Jessie's tale is just beginning.

Breaking out of the traditional story, transgressing barriers separating fact from fiction, politics from aesthetics, and law from literature, Trollope's narrator follows Jessie into the workhouse and reports on the conditions inside. The descriptions emphasize the isolation and dehumanizing aspects of the workhouse where families are separated, no visitors are allowed, and the "inmates," who must wear prescribed uniforms and their hair cut short, are not permitted to exercise or engage in any type of productive activity. Whereas Dickens's 1837 novel *Oliver Twist*, which also critiqued the conditions within the workhouses, considered those "regulations having reference to ladies . . . not necessary to repeat" (55), Trollope's text focuses on women and their concerns within this space. In her novel, the workhouse stands as a physical manifestation of the law's otherwise tacit regulation of women's bodies.

Not wanting her child to suffer the miseries of the workhouse, Jessie escapes to seek support from Frederic, who not only refuses to help her, but also solicits Mr. Lewis, the village lawyer, to impress upon her that she has no legal remedy. Desperately wandering after her confrontations with Frederic and the lawyer, she gives birth to a baby girl alone in a shed. While Jessie is unconscious after the birth, Sally, "one of those harmless, imbecile unfortunates of which almost every parish can show a specimen" (1: 228), finds the mother and child and goes in search of milk, taking the crying baby with her. When Jessie is discovered without the baby, she is arrested for infanticide. Meanwhile, through a series of crossed paths, Frederic chances upon the child where Sally has temporarily placed her and forever silences the infant's piercing cries with his booted foot. When the body is found near the shed, Jessie's fate seems sealed. She, of course, has no idea what happened while she was unconscious, and grieves the horrible possibility that she may have killed her child unknowingly.

Ellen and Martha, however, suspect Frederic of the murder. So strong is Ellen's belief in her brother's treachery that she calls off her marriage to Lord Pemberton (their romance being one of the primary subplots) to avoid involving him and his family in the scandal. She then slips in and out of delirium for much of the last part of the novel. Martha, appearing more than a decade before the allegedly "first" fictional female detective and almost a century before women practiced law, has been investigating the Phillips/Dalton case since her suspicions had been aroused by Frederic's unexpected marriage proposal to her.[24] Throughout Jessie's trials, Martha serves as her counselor and advocate, although, as a woman, she is unable to represent Jessie in any official capacity. Trollope, like Martha, had no access to the authoritative language of law. Having much to say about legal issues, however, she entered the dialogue through literary language.

If, as studies such as Said's and Miller's suggest, nineteenth-century novels typically achieve resolution through reunification of the family, and if the family plays a vital role in social discipline, then what is the cultural meaning of a novel such as *Jessie Phillips* that stirs its readers up against the legal system and sustains the challenge by presenting a familial "microcosm of society" as a murderous father, a dead infant, and an angry mother? Such an outlaw novel demonstrates that what Miller describes as the "fully panoptic view" of the omniscient narrator may indeed *not* support the status quo and its institutions but instead be lawless in the way that it shifts the perspective to show the innocence of a "fallen woman" and to make a spectacle of the law.

A HAUNTING PRESENCE: THE "LEWD WOMAN" AND THE LAW

> WHEREAS many lewd women that have been delivered of bastard children, to avoid their shame, and to escape punishment, do secretly bury or conceal the death of their children . . . whereas it falleth out sometimes (although hardly it is to be proved) that the said child or children were murthered by the said women, their lewd mothers. . . .
>
> —*21 James 1, c. 27, 1623*

In *Jessie Phillips*, when Frederic visits Lawyer Lewis to explain that "a young hussy" is threatening to swear a child to him in order to extort money, Lewis confirms that all such efforts have been rendered "utterly harmless and abortive" by "the admirable clause" in the new act. In a protective, fatherly manner, Lewis makes his assurances palpable by producing the act itself: "'[H]ere we have it, safe and sound' (laying his hand upon the act, which made part of the furniture of his table), 'and as completely the law of the land as that which awards hanging for murder'" (3: 61). In this passage, Trollope signals the intertextuality between *Jessie Phillips* and the legal text that furnishes her novel's pages and dialogue. While Lewis's further comment, "We have nothing to do with facts now in cases of this sort; the law is comprehensive enough without them" (3: 61), suggests that the law may be *mere* text—completely removed from lived experiences— the allusion to capital punishment reminds of the killing authority of legal language.

The "act" referred to is the Poor Law Amendment Act of 1834 (the New Poor Law), which includes the "admirable" bastardy clause(s) that made an unmarried mother solely responsible for the maintenance of her child.[25] The debate over these clauses is the particular legal moment in which Trollope's "tale of the present day" is situated, and the connections between the bastardy clauses and the law of infanticide are implicit in Lewis's seemingly random allusion to "hanging for murder," the legal sentence for infanticide. In *Jessie Phillips*, Trollope actualizes the law's potential infanticide—"the lewd woman"—who historically and thematically informs and haunts the legislative text of the 1834 bastardy clauses.[26]

While the crime of infanticide itself is no part of these bastardy clauses, that same woman who needed to be prevented from murdering her children is also the subject of this legal narrative. This time she is preying on innocent men. According to a report prepared by a nine-man Royal Commission to Investigate the Poor Laws (a source of the legislative history of the New Poor Law), the old system's attempts to regulate morality by forcing a woman to publicly declare her infamy and to name the father of her child were instead empowering women to force men into marriage: "a woman of dissolute character may pitch upon any unfortunate young man whom she has inveigled into her net, and swear that child to him; and the effect of the law, as it now stands, will be to oblige the man to marry her" (Commissioners' Report 176, evidence of Mr. Simeon).[27] Still trying to capture and punish these "deviant" women, the new strategy was to silence them and make them solely responsible for the maintenance of their illegitimate children. All laws enabling a woman to charge a man with being the father of her child and collecting maintenance from him were repealed to ensure that "a bastard will be, what Providence appears to have ordained that it should be, a burthen on its mother . . ." (Commissioners' Report 350).

The Commissioners' Report makes passing reference to concerns about the seduction of young girls and infanticide only to write them off as irrelevant. The Commissioners' final word on seduction is that "[c]ases will no doubt occur of much hardship and cruelty, and it will often be regretted that these are not punishable, at least by fine upon the offender. But the object of law is not to punish, but to prevent" (351). The suggestion that the incidence of infanticide might increase is dismissed with moral indignation: "We believe that in no civilized country, and scarcely in any barbarous country, has such a thing ever been heard of as a mother's killing her child in order to save the expense of feeding it" (351). The actual welfare of a "bastard child"—how it is to be fed—is of no concern in this text.

In *Jessie Phillips*, Lawyer Lewis "had carefully read, and commented upon at length, every page of every report from the select committee on the Poor Law Amendment Act, with the whole body of the evidence produced before them" (1: 218).[28] His notes and comments on the Commissioners' Report had furnished him with "a very neat sort of bird's eye view of the *leanings* of the honourable committee themselves" (1: 218–19). Lewis, as close reader and interpreter of the legal text, sees it in a way that exposes the leanings or subjectivity of the lawmakers. Sycophant that he is, Lewis hopes to use this "secret fund of authority" to ingratiate himself with the assistant commissioner who has come to Deepbrook to oversee the enforcement of these leanings (1: 219). The novel itself makes different use of this "secret fund of authority" identified within it, this recognition and understanding of the Commissioners' Report as a crafted narrative that presented the body of evidence in a particular way. In the legal text, the "evidence" (the voice) is exclusively male and "the body" is female. Trollope's revisionary novel gives "the body" a story of its own and a voice to change the tenor of the legal dialogue.

In the discussion of the bastardy clauses in the Commissioners' Report, the evidence of twenty-two men is presented as if they were engaged in a casual conversation. One anecdotal story follows another. Mr. Tweedy tells of an "instance in Carleton of a woman who is now receiving 4s. for two children, and is about to have a third; and she said, if she had a third, she could live as well as anybody," which seems to remind Mr. Cowell of a woman "in receipt of 18s. per week, the produce of successful bastardy adventures" (171). Colonel A'Court's comment, "Middle-aged women will sometimes unblushingly swear mere lads to be the fathers of their bastard children; lads whom they have perhaps enticed to the commission of the offense" (168), apparently rings true to Mr. Power, who concurs, "the female in very many cases becomes the corrupter; and boys, much under the age of twenty, are continually converted by this process into husbands" (173). Only the footnotes to the Commissioners' Report reveal that these pieces of conversation have been selected from reports from different parishes and that it is highly unlikely, for example, that Mr. Tweedy and Mr. Cowell have ever met each other, let alone participated in a dialogue on bastardy. This presentation of the evidence has the effect of neutralizing the role of the Commissioners, who appear merely to be summarizing the "facts" and making the only recommendations that make sense in light of the evidence.

The following story from the Commissioners' Report, told by a "Captain

Chapman," is a typical example of the "proof" offered of the "oppression" under the Old Poor Law:

> At Exeter, an apprentice under eighteen years of age, was recently committed to the house of correction for want of security [to indemnify the parish for providing for an unborn child]. It was admitted that there was no chance of his absconding, but the overseers said he had been brought for punishment. The woman stated that she was only three months gone with child; and thus the boy is taken from his work, is confined five or six months among persons of all classes, and probably ruined for ever, on the oath of a person with whom he was not confronted, and with whom he denied having had any intercourse. (167)

What lies at the heart of this and all of the other testimony in the Commissioners' Report is the threat to men posed by women's bodies. In the above passage, not only is there the suggestion that the woman may be swearing her child to the wrong man; there is also the concern that she may not be pregnant at all (she "states" that she is three months gone with child). Her unruly and, more importantly, unknowable body puts her in an unacceptable position of power, which is emphasized by the stress laid on the "boy's" youth. That women's bodies were the focus of the bastardy clauses is tellingly revealed by the interesting piece of "evidence" offered by a solicitor at Nuneaton parish, who reports "that his house looked into the churchyard; that he was in the habit purposely of watching persons resorting to the church for marriage, and that he could confidently say, that seventeen out of every twenty of the female poor who went there to be married were far advanced in pregnancy" (173).

In *Jessie Phillips*, it is the young woman who is under eighteen, unable to work, confined for months among persons of all classes and more than probably ruined forever, all because of a false oath of marriage sworn to her by a person who denies having had any intercourse with her. In Trollope's novel, the watched bodies of women talk back.

"THE MISCHIEF THAT AN OLD WOMAN MAY DO": TROLLOPE OPENS A DIALOGUE

While *Jessie Phillips* is situated within this broad legal context, Trollope chooses, as a literary setting, the small, rural village of Deepbrook. She creates a sense of interconnectedness by introducing her characters as neighbors, moving from the tranquil, gentleman-like dwelling of Reverend

Rimmington, to the attractive house and grounds of Lady Mary Weyland, to the large, though not picturesque, mansion of the squire, Mr. Dalton. What is most striking about this initial scene, however, is the abundance of lawyers and the paucity of wives. The lawyer who lives next to Mr. Dalton, Ferdinand Lewis, is a widower and the father of two daughters. Henry Mortimer, the lawyer whose house stands next to Lewis Lodge, is also a widower and lives with his sister, his daughter, and his son, who is studying to be a lawyer. Reverend Rimmington is a bachelor, Lady Weyland is not the wife but the widow of a baronet, and Mr. Dalton (although his wife is alive and well) is described as having a family consisting of ten daughters and one son.

The absence of wives from the narrator's descriptions of the traditional and patriarchal "leading families" who reside in Trollope's "legal landscape" introduces one of her central themes—the "non-existence" of wives under the law. Literalizing how Mrs. Dalton, for example, lives in Deepbrook— under the legal condition of coverture—Trollope describes her (by not describing her at all) as covered (by the description of the large mansion she inhabits) and as having her identity subsumed into that of her husband.

Mrs. Dalton soon appears on the scene, however, as Trollope abandons her legal world view for a more intimate look. The second chapter of *Jessie Phillips* opens in the middle of a dialogue between Mr. and Mrs. Dalton about the new poor law commissioner. Mrs. Dalton is "perseveringly pursuing her occupation of putting sugar into ten breakfast-cups" (1: 12), and while her "occupation" at the tea table may seem trivial, the enormity of her labor in producing eleven children is accentuated by her need to rest before pouring cream into each of their cups. Described as immoderately fat and suffering from *vis inertiae* of mind as well as matter, Mrs. Dalton answers most of her husband's inquiries about a dinner party for the commissioner with her signature line, "I am sure I don't care a single straw about it" (1: 24). Her general apathy may be symptomatic of her wifely condition of coverture, a condition that encourages silence and discourages any thoughts of her own. The law worked to ensure the domestication of a wife and then relied on her husband to "keep her covered." One might say that, having delegated its surveillance responsibilities, the law reciprocated Mrs. Dalton's sentiments—it didn't care a straw about her either. In light of Mrs. Dalton's condition, the lack of respect displayed by Mr. Dalton's "hastening out of the room in time to escape 'the straw' that sometimes almost overwhelmed him" (1: 26) appears more sad than comic, and we can read Mrs. Dalton's preferred pastime of "doing nothing" as a tragic but real consequence of the law's fiction. With Mrs. Dalton, Trollope's narrator begins tellings of the life experiences of several women whose "varied and opposing voices" problematize legal constructions of women, specifically those of "wife" and "mother."

Of course, to be a wife and "protected" in both legal and social discourse, a woman had to be legally constituted as such. Since the passage of Lord Hardwicke's Marriage Act in 1753, to be a lawfully wedded wife, a woman had to be married in a church, have her marriage entered in the parish register and signed by both "contracting" parties, and have the consent of her parents or guardians if she was under the age of 21. The Act, although requiring the ceremony to be performed in a church, in fact secularized marriage by providing that a religious ceremony was not valid unless it also complied with the legal requirements. The Act also provided that verbal spousals, that is, oral contracts of marriage, were no longer binding.

The primary purpose of this Act was to protect wealthy families from the consequences of "unfortunate" marriages, and it was enacted despite objections that it facilitated the seduction of young girls by making promises of marriage unenforceable, and that it would result in a rise in concubinage, bastardy, and infanticide by making legal marriage too expensive for the poor.[29] To the upper- and middle-class men who were debating this issue in Parliament, the Marriage Act was really about the wealthy. The seduced young women and "the poor" who would suffer because of this Act were irrelevant; their legally sanctioned absence and silence made them as abstract as the terms "bastardy" and "infanticide" when removed from lived experience.

In the novel, Jessie believes she has entered into a valid marriage contract with Frederic. Prior to the passage of the Marriage Act, their agreement would have been a contract *per verba de futuro*, an oral promise to marry in the future which, if witnessed and if followed by consummation, would have been legally binding for life. Jessie's thoughts and actions upon discovering that she is pregnant, however, reveal that she not only is ignorant of her vulnerable position under the law but also has little sexual knowledge. She had thought it "impossible" that her connection with Frederic should be known, suggesting that pregnancy had never crossed her mind.[30] The narrative voice is quick to defend Jessie's ignorance, implicating instead "our theories of popular education" that erroneously equate innocence with virtue (2: 24). While Jessie may not have realized how she came to be with child, she is not unaware of the social judgment of a pregnant woman whose union has not been proclaimed to the world. She hastens to tell Frederic her news, with "such perfect and entire confidence in him, that the idea of his refusing to *ratify* the promise so repeatedly and so solemnly given, when she should *demand its performance*, never entered her head for a single moment" (2: 25; emphasis added). Jessie has taken Frederic at his word; to her, his solemn avowal of marriage was fully performative of the act. Describing the thought she *doesn't* have in terms of legal language, however, the narrative voice emphasizes that the law matters, that words spoken outside its purview, in effect, are meaningless.

To the surprise of no one but Jessie, Frederic refuses to acknowledge what she has considered to be a valid marriage contract. If the story had taken place before the passage of the Marriage Act, it would have been lamentable that Jessie could produce no witnesses to his promises, and that in agreeing to protect his interests through concealment, she had left herself unprotected. In Trollope's novel, this was of no matter, however, because after passage of the Marriage Act, it was easy for the Frederics of the world to escape on any number of technicalities. To Jessie's desperate entreaties that he acknowledge her position in front of his sister Ellen, "Tell her at once, Frederic Dalton—tell her, without subterfuge or delay, what and who I am," he replies with a loud laugh (2: 56). From Jessie's point of view, she is Frederic's wife and the mother of "an unborn treasure" (2: 22). When Frederic laughs off his responsibilities, she becomes a fallen woman, and, in legal terms, the lewd mother of a bastard.

A "wife," by definition, is secured within the confines of the law's construction; a "mother" is a more "unruly body." In the context of nineteenth-century legal discourse, which Carol Smart argues constructs Woman as "a problematic and unruly body; whose sexual and reproductive capacities need constant surveillance and regulation because of the threat that this supposedly 'natural' woman would otherwise pose to the moral and social order," the unmarried mother is the most dangerous body of all ("Disruptive Bodies" 8, 24). Outside the protective cover of any man, the law distinguished the "lewd" mother from the "wife" mother, and constructed her as someone to be protected against.

Martha Fineman, in her analysis of twentieth-century discourses of poverty, remarks that the label "mother" is still modified by the woman's legal relationship (or lack thereof) to a man, with single motherhood being constructed as a deviant family form (285). Citing legal rhetoric, Fineman demonstrates how single motherhood has been constructed as a primary *cause* of poverty, as well as implicated in the degeneration and destruction of society as a whole. She explains that the representation of single mothers as "bad mothers," with corresponding "good mothers" being those situated within traditional, patriarchal families, is possible because motherhood is "a colonized concept—an event physically practiced and experienced by women, but occupied and defined, given content and value, by the core concepts of patriarchal ideology" (287–88).

In *Jessie Phillips*, Trollope explores the usurped concept of motherhood by doing what is notably rare in literature: presenting the subjective experiences of mothers.[31] While focusing on a "murderous mother," she presents Jessie's narrative in dialogue with the experiences and voices of multiple mothers in a way that disrupts attempts to label them, as well as exposes the class bias inherent in the law's categorizations. I will focus this part of my discussion around the two women in the novel who "go to law" as mothers in the novel, Widow Greenhill and Jessie Phillips, both of whom as "uncovered" women have a legal identity. The tellings of their stories uncomfortably challenge notions of what constitutes good and bad mothering.

Early in the novel, Mrs. Greenhill, a well-respected former servant of the Duke of Rochdale, is forced to appear before the Board of Guardians for the local Union workhouse to seek financial relief for her son's family.[32] More successful in sport than in business, her son Tom had accumulated such a vast amount of debt that even the pledge of his mother's generous annuity from the Duke was insufficient to keep him from prison. While Tom was in jail, his wife worked in the fields to feed the family while Mrs. Greenhill minded her five grandchildren. As the birth of their sixth child approached, however, Tom's wife was no longer able to work, and Mrs. Greenhill had no choice but to apply to the parish for relief. Greenhill and her daughter-in-law are "good mothers," both from a legal perspective—all of their children are "legitimate"—and from the perspective that they are loving caretakers. When they are no longer able to support themselves, however, they are stripped of "good mother" status.

Appalled by the daughter-in-law's "profligate maternity," one of the louder members of the Board berates a stunned Mrs. Greenhill:

> Are you not ashamed—a woman of decent appearance as you are, to come and ask the active, honest, intelligent, thrifty part of the population to rob themselves and their own children (honestly brought into the world, with the consciousness that there was power to maintain them)—are you not ashamed, old woman, to come here to take their money out of their pockets, in order to feed this litter of brats, that you know in your own heart and conscience ought never to have been born at all? (1: 66)

As his reiteration of the word "woman" accentuates, Mrs. Greenhill (not her son) is implicated in the "profligate maternity" of her daughter-in-law; it appears that "brats," like "bastards," are a female problem. Of course, other related "female problems" are irrelevant to this representative of the law. Another interpretation of young Mrs. Greenhill's "annual *accouche-ment*," for example, is that she is fulfilling her legal obligations as a wife;

she always is sexually available to the sporting young Tom. Moreover, this Board member doesn't take into consideration how higher wages for women, different childcare arrangements, or the accessibility of information about birth control might alter the Greenhills' situation. From his perspective, considerations such as these would unnecessarily involve and implicate "the active, honest, intelligent, thrifty part of the population" in problems that really were about "bad mothers."

Mrs. Dalton further disrupts the good mother/bad mother dichotomy. As the mother of eleven children, almost twice the number as the young Mrs. Greenhill, is she guilty of profligate maternity? If not, is that because her husband is the acting head of the household, because of her family's status as gentry, or because she needs no funds from the parish? Would she still be a "good mother" if the family lost all of their money (which happened to the Trollope family *twice*)? What about the fact that she is described as incapable of performing domestic duties (Ellen supervises the servants and writes letters for Mr. Dalton), and that the children's favorite on an affectionate level is none other than Jessie Phillips? The narrative itself suggests these questions in the way it moves back and forth between the stories of the Dalton and Greenhill families, putting these two tellings in dialogue across class boundaries. It is only after calling into question the norms and assumptions implicit in the cultural meanings of a "good mother" that Trollope presents Jessie, a "bad mother," in confrontation with the law.

Jessie appeals to the Board to seek admittance into the workhouse when she is no longer able to support herself by sewing because the young women in the parish refuse to associate with someone in her condition. The male Board members, however, despite much looking, fail to notice Jessie's pregnancy:

> Every eye (and in consequence of the previous business [a proposal to dismiss the workhouse medical attendant whose drunken behavior had resulted in the death of one child and the near fatality of another] there were many persons present)—every eye was fixed upon her; but, contrary to what was usually the case among the many busy individuals there assembled, none seemed anxious to undertake the customary task of examining her, relative to the business which brought her there. (2: 183)

The text emphasizes Jessie's body as the focal point of these eyes, describing how she was "without visible tremor in any limb or fibre," although her "fluttering pulse throbbed, stopped, and throbbed again" (2: 183). At length, Jessie "brought this *silent examination* to a close by raising *her eyes* to those of the reverend chairman, with *a look* that seemed to beseech his attention for her case" (2: 183–84; emphasis added). The examination relative to the business that brought her there—her life experiences—begins only when Jessie is able to meet the gaze of the Board.

As she stands before this group of men, with every eye fixed upon the "sedate stillness of her look and manner, joined to the pale beauty of her marble features" (2: 183), the fawn-like Jessie Phillips bears no resemblance to the seductress of the Commissioners' Report, out to inveigle innocent men in her net. She "was more likely to suggest the idea of a being rising supernaturally from the tomb" (2: 183). In fact, Jessie is the embodiment of the seduced young woman whose haunting presence is only barely visible in the legal texts of the Marriage Act and the Commissioners' Report. This scene in the novel is also haunted by the "idea" of infanticide that was "the previous business" that textually interrupts the Board's consideration of Jessie.

While she struggles to explain, "my health is gone; I have not a shilling in the world, and I must perish if I am refused shelter here," Jessie becomes unable to control her "unruly" body and faints (2: 185).[33] The accompanying illustration shows her collapsed on the floor before the Board. Jessie is uncovered (her bonnet lies beside her on the floor) and in need of protection (from starvation, from the elements), and these men—all unmoving, some unmoved—can only stare as she literally becomes a fallen woman before their collective eyes. This portrait of ten administrators of the law, looking on with a mixture of shock, perplexity, and indifference, not only depicts women's subjected position under the law, but also shows that the law is unable, if not unwilling, to "see" in a way that takes women's experiences into account. (See figure 1.)

Once Jessie is visibly pregnant, however, the law does know how to view her. As she "goes to law" for a second time, with the law this time represented by Lawyer Lewis, she is described as a "strange-looking figure, half-ghostly, half-grotesque, slowly but decisively approaching the lawyer's door" (3: 62). To Lewis, she is ghostly in a ghastly way, figuring that dangerous conniving seductress, preying on innocent men such as his friend Frederic. She is grotesque in that she has dragged her pregnant body out into the open to have her say. In his article "Patriarchal Territories: The Body Enclosed," Peter Stallybrass discusses legal and cultural assumptions that a woman's body is "naturally" grotesque, necessitating constant scrutiny: "The surveillance of women concentrated upon three specific areas: the mouth, chastity, and the threshold of the house. These three areas frequently were collapsed into each other. The connection between speaking and wantonness was common to legal discourse and conduct books" (126).[34]

Figure 1 "Jessie before the Board." Illustration by Leech taken from the first one-volume edition of *Jessie Phillips* (1844). This illustration also appeared in the first three-volume series (1843).

Faced in this passage with a breach of all these boundaries, Lewis is outraged that Jessie has appeared at the threshold of his house, in an obviously unchaste condition, and is particularly interested in silencing her. Interrupting her story, he assures her that "you may stand all day swearing that one man or another is the father of your child, and no more notice will be taken of it than if you whistled" (3: 65) and "Let the father be a king or a cobbler, it will not make the slightest difference, so you need not trouble yourself to say any thing about that" (3: 66). This time Jessie has approached the law seeking protection for her unborn child, only to discover that the purpose of the new legislation was "to spare the pocket of the fondly *protected* man" (3: 67; emphasis added). When she dares to utter the name of Frederic Dalton, the embodiment of that "fondly protected man," Lewis flies into a rage, seething as he verbally assaults her, "How dare you come to me, of all men living, in the hope of having your impudent way in the very teeth of the statute?" (3: 68). As Jessie races from his house, she is filled "with a feeling of terror, such as she might have experienced if an angry bulldog had been let loose upon her" (3: 68). In this scene, the law is presented as what Jessie and her child need to be protected against.

It is through the character of Martha that Trollope envisions a law of a different kind. Described as having "a shrewdness of observation and character," Martha knows Jessie and rejects the conflation of sexuality and monstrosity implicit in the legal and social judgment of her character. A self-described "lawyer," Martha shares a business-like way of doing things with Lawyer Lewis. They go about their business, however, in a most dissimilar way. When Martha learns of Jessie's pregnancy, rather than judging and condemning her, undeterred by boundaries of class and propriety, she seeks her out to offer counsel. Instead of looking first to the law (which she, in fact, knows very well), Martha begins with Jessie's experiences: "Jessie Phillips, I wish I could persuade you to open your heart to me fully and completely. . . . Without knowing exactly how matters stand between you and Mr. Frederic Dalton, it is impossible I can be of any real service to you; but if you would trust me entirely, it is possible I might be" (2: 141–42). In Jessie's "telling" to Martha, "the part of her story which she dwelt longest upon was that which related to the solemn promises of marriage she had received" (2: 144). Martha is well aware, however, that what seems most important to Jessie, the law has "objectively" deemed irrelevant.

While some of Martha's legal work for Jessie (who is referred to as Martha's "client") is presented almost playfully, the vilification of Martha in nineteenth-century literary reviews of the novel illuminates the real threat she posed. One review was particularly worried about a promise of marriage that Martha drafted and persuaded Frederic to sign. Purposefully leaving the woman's name blank, Martha hoped that the document would in some way prove useful to Jessie. It was most important to this reviewer to recast Martha's "male" acts of lawyering as "female" scheming (*Athenaeum* 956–57). As the review accuses, Martha does enjoy keeping "the villain on the rack" (957), but that is because she is angry about his attempts to dupe her into marriage, as well as outraged by his behavior toward Jessie. Once Jessie is accused of infanticide, however, there is nothing at all playful about Martha's advocacy.

For Lewis, it was the most natural of things that a socially deviant woman, monstrous in her sexuality as evidenced by her pregnant body, would act monstrously toward her child. After Jessie is arrested for infanticide, Lewis brags, "I won't deny that I do feel a little proud of my own sagacity . . . I saw at once that there was something desperately bad about that hussy" (3: 159). The similar reactions of other characters prove the power of legal discourse to shape how things are seen. The farmer who discovers an unconscious Jessie in his shed "felt not the shadow of a doubt that she had given birth to a child, destroyed and concealed it" (3: 87), and he is afraid to be at all associated with the "horrible infanticide" (3: 86). The same verdict is reached by the village doctor and the caretakers of the workhouse, who feed and care for Jessie simply to ensure that she doesn't cheat the hangman, "horrid monster as she is" (3: 93). Even the clergyman who is sent to Jessie believes that she is guilty, "for who but yourself could find benefit or profit of any kind from the deed?" (3: 123). When Jessie claims to have no knowledge of what happened, she is told that no jury will believe "any such worn-out story," for all women in her condition say the same thing (3: 274). The law has constructed its own knowledge about fallen women and infanticide, and Jessie's experiences must be made to fit that epic narrative.

Refusing to accept the law's "truth," Martha cannot believe that Jessie murdered her child and visits Jessie in prison to see for herself. During their meeting, Martha learns that Jessie has no recollection of what happened after the baby's birth. She asks Jessie why she has led everyone to believe she is guilty:

> Then why is it that you have suffered more than one friend, who was disposed to believe you innocent, why have you suffered such to leave you, Jessie, with the persuasion that you had murdered your child? Surely they could not have left you with such an idea if you had spoken to them as you have now spoken to me! (3: 270)

Jessie's response illustrates how the law's claim to knowledge authorizes itself and disqualifies alternative accounts:

> "There was no difference," returned Jessie, calmly, "in what I said to them and what I have said to you, Miss Maxwell, except what came from the difference of their questions. You asked me what I remembered, and I could safely tell you that I remembered nothing; but, when they told me that my child was murdered, and that nobody could have done the deed but myself, how could I help believing that I had done it?" (3: 270)

Jessie is the victim of legal discourse that "tells us how we should understand a problem and which explanations are acceptable and which are not" (Finley 905). Free to unravel outside the purview of the legal narrative, Jessie's own story reveals the machinations of the law's "truth."

While the readers know Jessie is innocent, suspense builds as Trollope whittles away at the possible infanticide defenses that are acceptable in legal terms. Much is made of the fact that Jessie admits to having heard the baby cry, making any defense based on the child being stillborn impossible. A skilled needlewoman, Jessie also cannot claim the popular and successful benefit-of-linen defense. A woman who could show that she had done sewing for the baby before its birth usually was acquitted. Having spent the last few months of her pregnancy confined in the workhouse, however, where no labor of any kind was allowed, Jessie had neither the opportunity nor the materials to prepare linen. Sally, in fact, had procured clothes for the infant, but Frederic is careful to strip the baby of these garments prior to his concealment of its body. The extreme violence of Frederic's murderous act also forecloses the broadly interpreted want-of-help defense, which was based on arguments that the infant had died from causes such as failure to tie off the umbilical cord or a fall into a basin of water because the mother lacked skill or self-possession or was medically incapacitated.[35]

The most popular defense, temporary insanity, is the one pled for Jessie at her trial. (Martha, who has been convinced by Lewis and Reverend Rimmington that her suspicions about Frederic are unfounded, in fact, comes to believe that Jessie did kill her child when she was out of her senses.) While not specified in the text, the "causes" of her insanity most likely would have been explained in terms of her morality and her biology. James Pritchard in 1833 had introduced the term "moral insanity" to describe deviant behavior, and this could account not only for her murderous act, but also for the excessive sexuality that led to Jessie's fall in the first place. Correspondingly, her female body, especially after childbirth, also made her susceptible to madness and moral perversion.[36] While a defense of temporary insanity may have saved certain women from being held accountable for their actions, it is a problematic defense because it reinforces ideas of madness as essentially female. *Jessie Phillips* is subversive in that, while Jessie is determined to be "not guilty by virtue of temporary insanity," the readers know she is simply "not guilty." I would argue, however, that Trollope goes much further than this by reconfiguring the discourse of madness to show her female characters, particularly Jessie and Ellen, to be "not mad (insane) but mad (angry)" in a justifiable and politically powerful way.[37]

Madness is introduced in the novel in the figure of Sally. Sally lives in the workhouse; however, she is granted the singular privilege of being allowed to come and go as she pleases, making her position as the local madwoman the envy of the other inmates. She is known for two qualities, her tenderness toward infants and her truthfulness. She always spoke the truth and "there was nobody in the parish who, if they wanted to ascertain a fact about which she knew any thing, but would have taken her testimony in preference to all others" (1: 229). For Sally, truth was not an abstract principle. She simply told things as she saw them—hers was a truth grounded in lived experience. In a pictorial representation of Sally, she looms large as the central figure in a group of women—her associations with madness, the maternal, and truth situate her as an important character in Trollope's revised narrative of infanticide. (See figure 2.)

Jessie is first described as mad when she goes to demand that Frederic acknowledge her as his wife. Refusing to accept a docile and silent role, Jessie boldly asserts her rights. Frederic can fathom her unexpected pluck only as a form of madness: "By your mad conduct you have, of course, banished yourself from the house," the whole and horrible truth of which she is just beginning to grasp (2: 63). For her, the mad conduct has been to believe his false promises of marriage; for him, it is to suggest he suffer the consequences. Playing the role of the innocent and betrayed man of the Commissioners' Report, Frederic asks Jessie, "Is it your purpose mad woman, as you are, to drive me mad too?" (2: 61). Repositioning women to have agency and a voice, *Jessie Phillips* is threatening because it suggests an affirmative answer to this rhetorical question.

Once she realizes the extent of Frederic's perfidy, Jessie truly is mad (angry), declaring, "I would not be the wife of Mr. Frederic Dalton if doing so would make me a crowned queen!" (2: 168). Jessie (and the reader) know that she and the child would be better off without this particular father, whom the narrative has shown to be hateful and violent. Single motherhood is the preferable choice; however, societal attitudes toward "uncovered" mothers have made it impossible for Jessie to find work. Given her limited economic choices, her decision to seek maintenance from Frederic makes practical sense. Because the bastardy clauses were legislated with the "reasonable" view being that of the "fondly protected man," however, Jessie's sound determination "much more resembled the dominating idea of a maniac" than "the steady resolution of a rational being" (3: 42). In this passage, the text exteriorizes the oppression in the law's appropriation of words such as "reasonable" and "rational" to describe itself. Legal language, by its very terms, protects itself from criticism. Any perspective other than the law's may be dismissed as *un*reasonable or *ir*rational or, when that perspective is female, as "emotional" or "mad." Frederic is quick to point out that the law is on his side, taunting her with "Where did you get

Figure 2 "The Idiot." Illustration by Leech taken from the first one-volume edition of *Jessie Phillips* (1844). This illustration also appeared in the first three-volume series (1843).

your law from, Jessie Phillips?" (3: 48). His thoughts, however, reveal what his cruel words try to mask—he is beginning to crack under pressure.

Unable to conceive that Jessie could be so bold, he becomes paranoid that she is "*acting upon orders*" (3: 49), specifically those of that villainous Martha Maxwell. Frederic is so self-absorbed that Jessie's story is nothing more to him than a devious plot by Martha to destroy him. Confronted with Jessie's pregnant body, he visualizes his own fall:

> All his greatness, all his fashion, all his pre-eminence, were seen crumbling into ashes before the blasting eyes of the miserable object before him; while a phantom of Martha Maxwell appeared peeping over her shoulder, showing its white teeth from ear to ear in delighted laughter, while its head nodded and its finger pointed to himself. (3: 52)

Frederic's terror in the face of female power (Jessie's blasting eyes create a genuine castration anxiety) mirrors the tacit fear of women's bodies evidenced in the testimony in the Commissioners' Report. At the same time, this passage displays the threatening possibility of a shift in perspective. Seeing (eyes), hearing (ears), voicing (laughter), and thinking (head) in a different way, this "strange-looking figure, half-ghostly, half-grotesque" (3:52) (an apt description of the law's construction of Woman—non-existent or Other) is empowered by an accusatory phallic finger.

In this confrontational scene, Jessie symbolically manipulates legal terminology by going under cover and performing madness in order to speak the truth as she sees it and to stop protecting Frederic from the consequences of his false promises. In order to escape detection (from the workhouse officials), Jessie has covered herself with the well-known oversize bonnet belonging to Sally. As she is speaking with Frederic, the unfastened bonnet falls to the ground and an "uncovered" Jessie angrily declares:

> Well may you tremble now. . . . At a day not long ago, I think I would have crept into a hole that a dog would have turned from, so I might have hid my shame and its wretched fruit. . . . But that is all gone together now: I care not for my shame—I care only for my child, though it has such a wretch as you are for its father, and I will not die without telling the whole world what you are. (3: 52)

While the law may place all shame and blame on Jessie, her voice of resistance is empowered by the context of her narrative. She no longer seeks the law's degrading and silencing cover (the "hole" that represents the workhouse and marriage to Frederic); she will take cover only as necessary to protect herself and her child. Moreover, the fallen bonnet serves to remind that her anger is *not* madness. Linguistically reconfiguring the law's way of seeing, Jessie's anger exposes, or one might say un*cover*s, the "madness" that Frederic, wretch that he is, is the "fondly protected" favourite of the law. Having taken him under its protective wing, the law becomes implicated in *his* infanticide.

It is Ellen's suspicions of her brother's murderous act that drive her "crazy." Reading fear and guilt in Frederic's face when he learns that the child's body has been found, she collapses, suffering from a paroxysm of fever that "threatened her life as well as her reason" (3: 262). When her fever abates, Ellen informs Frederic of her decision that he is to go abroad, leaving behind a declaration of his guilt. Justifiably furious, she then orders him out of her sick room. Frederic, shaken but sufficiently recovering himself to leave the room, announces that Ellen is worse than people think, "for every word she has uttered to me was as mad as Bedlam" (3: 295). The doctor, after examining her, however, responds, "take my word for it, Mr. Frederic, she is more in her right senses than you are" (3: 299), which is more insightful than the doctor realizes. While the law would go far to cover Frederic, to make sure he was the subject of no undue suspicion of infanticide, considering he actually committed the crime, he no longer is privy to the law's protection. Occupying the position of Other, he feels constantly under surveillance; he is described as increasingly irrational, and indeed as feminized.

When he hears that the child's body has been found, for example, he turns "ghastly pale" and rushes from the room calling for "Water! Water!" He darts through the parlor to where he "was presently sheltered from every eye by the thick plantations of shrubbery" (3: 177). The announcement had "unmanned" him (177–78). Later, misinterpreting the doctor's innocent comment about Ellen being in her right mind to mean that he was about "to be seized upon and conveyed to prison," Frederic, "too thoroughly bewildered by terror to have any judgment left," rehearses the earlier scene and rushes out of the room to escape "the spot where he then stood and the eyes that were then gazing on him" (3: 300). Seeking shelter among the copses, Lear-like in his ravings, Frederic passionately curses the women who have "wronged" him:

> "They have not hunted me to death yet," he murmured, with a ghastly laugh; "the game is not yet up with me, most beauteous Martha! . . . Hideous, spiteful fiend, and fury as thou art! thou shall not conquer me! There is much more to do, my lovely duchess sister, and my most peerless promised wife, before you succeed in your amiable schemes against me." (3: 302)

It is at this juncture that madness approaches in the figure of Sally, and Frederic's misbelief that she has witnessed his crime causes him to rush "*madly* forward to the steep bank" and plunge headlong into the stream to his death (3: 305). It is what Sally represents—the power of women, when angry (mad) to find a voice to speak the truth as they see it, not as it has been constructed for and about them—that ultimately brings about "justice."

Weakened from physical hardships and mental suffering, Jessie dies in the courtroom when she learns of "the death of her destroyer" (3: 313). Frederic has "destroyed" both Jessie and her baby girl, so we can read this comment to mean that Jessie realizes her own innocence and Frederic's guilt before her death. Still, it is disappointing that Jessie has lived through her trial only to die at the end of it. This conclusion, however, is in keeping with the legal and social critique that the novel performs. Not only does Trollope's plot expose the injustice of nineteenth-century legal "truths" about women accused of infanticide, but it also dramatizes that, while technically acquitted, Jessie has no place to go.

Having read the story of Jessie's experiences—her education, her seduction, her betrayal, her loss of employment, her suffering upon the death of her child, and her futile attempt to make the legal system work for her—the readers know she is neither deviant nor insane. She also is not "lewd" in that she sincerely believed in the validity of the marriage vows she had exchanged with Frederic. Unlike the prosecuting narrator in *Adam Bede*, the narrator of *Jessie Phillips* has made strong representations in support of Jessie, judged a fallen woman because of a class-based legal technicality. Thus, the law itself is indicted when it pays no heed to Jessie's experiences and when it insists on its own version of her story. The irony in the narrative's closing statement on Jessie barely masks a bitter indictment of "the law," which has *mis*judged Jessie in every respect:

> Jessie Phillips—too weak, too erring, to be remembered with respect, yet not so bad but that some may feel it a thing to wonder at that she, and the terribly tempted class of which she is the type, should seem so very decidedly to be selected by the Solons of our day as a sacrifice for all the sins of all their sex. . . . I will not venture any protest against this seemingly one-sided justice, beyond the expression of a wish that the unhappy class thus selected for victims were not so very decidedly and so very inevitably the weakest, and in all ways the least protected portion of society. There is no chivalry in the selection, and to the eyes of ignorance, like mine, there is no justice. (3: 316–17)

After the novel had engaged the British reading public in a dialogue on this issue for more than a year through serial publication, this belittlement of the narrative's protest is comic, and its "ignorance" is belied by the knowledge of the law demonstrated in the novel itself. Trollope may have been nodding to the policers of the circulating libraries with these duplicitous comments, as well as with the "humble" statement of the wise widow Buckhurst (who most likely sits in and speaks for Trollope in *Jessie Phillips*), "I would recommend no man to judge of the danger of rash legislation, by estimating the mischief that an old woman may do" (1: 306). More likely, however, these were clever responses to reviews of early installments of *Jessie Phillips* such as the following:

> It is [her] extreme view of principles, and her hard, exaggerated painting, which render Mrs. Trollope so utterly powerless upon public opinion, *not-*

withstanding her shrewdness, cleverness, and constant activity. Whilst the notice of an abuse by Boz [Dickens] will excite general attention, and probably induce some movement towards a reform, Mrs. Trollope's exertions have no effect; for she has no influence except upon folly and ignorance, which have no influence upon affairs till a case is ripe for counting polls, *and not much even then.* ("New Fictions" 18; emphasis added)

In its efforts to distinguish Dickens from Trollope (implying that characters such as Mr. Bumble and Mrs. Corney are *not* caricatured), this review acknowledges the power of fiction to effect social change. This makes its anxious qualifications about Trollope's potential political influence particularly telling, and, indeed, *Jessie Phillips* may have played a role in changing the bastardy clauses. While much of the New Poor Law remained intact into the twentieth century, in 1844, one year after the publication of *Jessie Phillips*, the "Little Poor Law" was enacted, reinstating the right of unwed mothers to sue putative fathers for maintenance in Petty Sessions. Heineman suggests that it can be surmised that Trollope, "as the only novelist who dramatized the disastrous implications of this law for women," in some way contributed to this statutory amendment ("Sexual Politics" 102).

Regardless of whether there is any direct connection between this novel and the change in the law, it is important to acknowledge this lost voice that spoke in resistance to the law's "truth" that infanticide was a problem of "deviant" women. By focusing on a woman's experience, *Jessie Phillips* raised questions about infanticide that were not being discussed in other forums: Was the woman really the guilty party? How was a woman to support a child if she couldn't find work? What role should education play in addressing this issue? Later in the Victorian period, the dialogue Trollope opened with *Jessie Phillips* was continued by The Committee for Amending the Law in Points Wherein It Is Injurious to Women (CALPIW). This Committee, formed in 1871 by Elizabeth Wolstenholme, Josephine Butler, and Lydia Becker, questioned the law's one-sided narrative about infanticide and attempted to make women's views legally relevant. In a pamphlet entitled "Infant Mortality: Its Causes and Remedies," CALPIW offered a well-documented, compelling critique of proposals that had been suggested to curb the incidence of infanticide. Specifically, the Committee condemned proposals involving compulsory registration, licensing, and supervision of all infant caretakers (including daycare providers), arguing that they interfered with women's employment opportunities and involved inappropriate surveillance, "increasing officialism, police interference, and espionage" (7).[38] The Committee also expressed its conviction that "direct infanticide has little to do with the terribly high death-rate prevailing among young children" (24), and accused lawmakers of diverting attention away from the real causes of infant mortality, specifically low wages for women, seduction, lack of education, a wife's conjugal duties, male sexual and financial irresponsibility, the difficulty of unmarried mothers in finding work, and unjust laws resulting from "the natural inclination to regard every question from an exclusively masculine point of view" (24)—all problems that had been foregrounded thirty years earlier in *Jessie Phillips*.

Immediately upon the novel's publication, *The Athenaeum* assured that "'Jessie Phillips' will be no sooner 'out of sight' than it will be 'out of mind,'" reiterating warnings to its authoress about "the dangerous responsibility of such one-sided appeals to passion and prejudice" (956). Prescient and self-fulfilling, this literary review accurately portended the fate of this daring and unconventional novel. The name of Jessie Phillips has been all but erased from literary history; only a few copies of the novel are known to exist.[39] What is shocking is that Frances Trollope, who published thirty-six novels and six books of travel and of whom *The New Monthly Magazine* wrote in 1839, "No other author of the present day has been at once so much read, so much admired and so much abused," similarly has been forgotten.[40] I would suggest, however, that "Jessie Phillips" (both the character and the novel) help to illuminate why Trollope shares their obscurity—because her "subjectivities" were so troubling.

First, her own subjectivity as a wife/mother made her public activity of writing suspect. Unwilling to confine her activities to the domestic sphere, she was "called amazonian, a 'man-woman,' and the connotations of her name were used against her" (Heineman, *Frances Trollope* 10).[41] Moreover, Kissel suggests that, through critical interpretations of her son Anthony's writings, Frances is remembered as ambitious, selfish, thoughtless, and the mother who loved Anthony least of her children (20–23). In other words, Trollope has been categorized as a "bad mother," which has silenced her voice and sharply curtailed the inquiry into her own experiences.[42] Also, widowed in 1835, as an "uncovered" woman she dared to write about such controversial subjects as slavery in *Jonathan Jefferson Whitlaw* (1836), evangelical excesses in *The Vicar of Wrexhill* (1837), child-labor laws in *The Life and Adventures of Michael Armstrong, The Factory Boy* (1840), and bastardy and infanticide in *Jessie Phillips*, topics considered most inappropriate for "a female pen."[43]

It is interesting that while Anthony's literary engagement with the law accounts for much of the critical attention he receives today, Frances's feminist jurisprudence has almost ensured her oblivion.[44] Yet, any history/narrative of nineteenth-century infanticide law would be misleadingly monological if it failed to take into account the voices of resistance such as Trollope's, Leakey's, and Tuttiet's. Attempts to analyze and understand these laws by looking only to the statutes, the legislative debates and reports, and voices that support law's "truth" (such as the writer of *The Spectator* epigraph and the narrator in *Adam Bede*) would only perpetuate what Robin West describes as "masculine jurisprudence":

> Jurisprudence is "masculine" because jurisprudence is about the relationship between human beings and the laws we actually have, and the laws we have are "masculine" both in terms of their intended beneficiaries and in authorship. Women are absent from jurisprudence because women *as human beings* are absent from the law's protection: jurisprudence does not recognize us because law does not protect us. ("Jurisprudence and Gender" 60; emphasis in original)

Peter Fitzpatrick argues that it is possible to think about the law differently if more emphasis is placed on the connection between law and context. To do this, it is necessary to "evoke those otherwise suppressed, disregarded or marginalized perspectives" so as to avoid "the protective and premature closure around law which jurisprudence continually seeks to effect" (2).

Jessie Phillips evokes suppressed, disregarded, and marginalized (women's) perspectives on infanticide, as well as on the larger issue of women's subordinate position under the law. Moreover, its resistance to the protective and premature closure typically effected in nineteenth-century novels by scenes of familial bliss sheds light on women's "maddening" position within that legally constituted and socially sanctioned domestic setting. In its focus on women *as human beings* and its thematic exploration of the law's failure to protect them, *Jessie Phillips* calls into question legal and literary precedents in the true spirit of feminist jurisprudence. *That* is the kind of "mischief" Trollope's novel performs.

CHAPTER 3

Birth Control on Trial

Law, Literature, and Libel

trial

1. *Law.* The examination and determination of a cause by a judicial tribunal; determination of the guilt or innocence of an accused person by a court. . . . 2. a. The action of testing or putting to the proof the fitness, truth, strength, or other quality of anything; test. . . . 9. That which puts one to the test; *esp.* a painful test of one's endurance, patience, or faith. . . .

—*Oxford English Dictionary*

When Sue Bridehead, heroine of Thomas Hardy's 1895 novel *Jude the Obscure*, tries to explain to her stepson Little Father Time that she and Jude are expecting yet another child, their third in three years, he angrily upbraids her:

> "O you don't care, you don't care!" he cried in bitter reproach. "How *ever* could you, mother, be so wicked and cruel as this, when you needn't have done it till we was better off, and father well!—To bring us all into *more* trouble! No room for us, and father a-forced to go away, and we turned out to-morrow; and yet you be going to have another of us soon! . . . 'Tis done o'purpose!—'tis—'tis!" (407–8)

His fury is directed specifically against Sue; she, the mother, is the "you" who doesn't care, who is wicked and cruel. She is the "you" who purposefully acts against the "we" of the family, the "us" of the children, and the father who is forced away and ailing. To Little Father Time, that Sue is and will again be "mother" is entirely her fault and failing. Much affected by the accusatory "you," Sue stumbles for an appropriate response:

> "Y-you must forgive me, little Jude!" she pleaded, her bosom heaving now as much as the boy's. "I can't explain—I will when you are older. It does seem—as if I had done it on purpose, now we are in these difficulties! I can't explain, dear! But it—is not quite on purpose—I can't help it!" (408)

While Sue's hesitant and ambiguous declaration ("But it—is not quite on purpose—I can't help it!") has been discussed in terms of her sexuality, its meaning and significance in light of her probable views on family limitation have been largely unexamined. Similarly scant attention has been paid to the relevance of birth control to the chilling suicide note that Little Father Time writes the following morning before hanging himself and his half-brother and half-sister: "Done because we are too menny" (410).[1] With the subjectless verb, Little Father Time claims no agency nor admits any responsibility for this act; rather his language accuses: the murder/suicide is *done* because of what Sue has "*done* o'purpose" (408; emphasis added).

As a well-read New Woman, Sue would have been familiar with the topic of birth control, one of "the common talking points of the new womanhood" (Cunningham 2).[2] She (like Hardy) was also an admirer of John Stuart Mill, who as early as 1848 was writing about the benefits to women of family limitation:

> It is seldom the choice of the wife that families are too numerous; on her devolves (along with all the physical suffering and at least a full share of the privations) the whole of the intolerable domestic drudgery resulting from the excess. To be relieved from it would be hailed as a blessing by multitudes of women who now never venture to urge such a claim, but who would urge it, if supported by the moral feelings of the community. (*Principles of Political Economy*, qtd. in McLaren 97–98)

While birth control is never explicitly mentioned in *Jude*, Sue's concerns with closely related topics such as a husband's "right" to sexual access to his wife and the importance of sex education suggest that family limitation is one of the many "modern" ideas to which Sue has been exposed.[3]

Sue's desire to control her own body is one of the central themes of the novel. In speaking of her marriage to Phillotson, she explains, "What tortures me so much is the necessity of being responsive to this man whenever he wishes . . ." (273–74). Early in her marriage, she literally removes her body (to the closet, out the window) in dramatic attempts to evade this enforced responsiveness (sex) and its possible consequences (pregnancy). When she finally, in an exchange of notes, explicitly asks Phillotson to let her live in his house "in a separate way," she writes, "I implore you to be merciful! . . . I would not ask if I were not almost compelled by what I can't *bear!* No poor woman has ever wished more than I that Eve had not fallen, so that (as the primitive Christians believed) some harmless mode of vegetation might have peopled Paradise" (287; emphasis added). Sue's desire to abstain from sexual relations with Phillotson is motivated by more than "a physical objection" (271) to him personally; part of what she fears is the offspring that she cannot bear to bear. While arguing that a marital separation would be morally right, she adds, "especially as no new interests, in the shape of children, have arisen to be looked after" (285). Sue conceives of the potential issue of her marriage to Phillotson, born of a legal not a loving union, not as children, but as mere legal "interests."

This, then, raises the question of what Sue thinks about the children born of her loving relationship with Jude, those children she has "not quite on purpose." If one agrees with the critics who read Sue as essentially passionless, sleeping with Jude primarily to keep him, then her response to Little Father Time seems almost a personal defense, emphasizing that the children have resulted from a painful situation to her, not really of her own making—"*I* can't help it" (emphasis added).

On the other hand, this same statement could be an acknowledgment of the real passion she feels for Jude—that despite the possibility of children, she cannot help having a sexual relationship with him.[4] This reading is supported by Sue's earlier comment to Arabella that "it seems such a terribly tragic thing to bring beings into the world—so presumptuous—that I question my right to do it sometimes!" (382). Her use of the phrase "my right" suggests a voluntariness that works to negate the idea of coercion by Jude and that also suggests the idea of family limitation as a counter-obligation. In telling Little Father Time that she is having another child "not quite on purpose," Sue may be suggesting that while she and Jude did not plan to have all of these children, they were the inevitable result of their sexual desires. Bolstering this argument is Sue's later description of the years in which the children were conceived as a time when she and Jude were "indulging ourselves to utter selfishness with each other" (413), not considering the consequences of their actions.

But what about artificial forms of birth control that would have allowed Sue and Jude to act on their sexual passions while also limiting the size of their family? One possibility is that, like other feminists of her time, Sue is against artificial birth control because it might have the effect of allowing men to overindulge their passions.[5] Even if Sue is sexually attracted to

Jude, she does often accuse him of being much more passionate than she. Another possibility is that her failure to put methods of birth control into practice is yet another example of her not having "the courage of [her] opinions" (303).[6] Throughout the novel, the readers are told of Sue's independent views, only to watch her act in the most conventional of ways. Therefore, it would not be out of character for her to be a proponent of birth control and still find herself pregnant on a yearly basis. In this scenario, Sue's comment to Little Father Time would be one of her many after-the-fact expressions of remorse: "But it—is not *quite* on purpose" (emphasis added), meaning "I realize 'now we are in these difficulties' that I could and should have done something about it, but 'I can't help it!'; my 'theoretic unconventionality' (284) always seems to break down." Similarly, Sue's comment to Arabella about feeling "presumptuous" about bringing all of these children into the world also suggests some belated regret on Sue's part for not having acted more responsibly.

While we cannot be certain of Sue's specific views on family limitation, there is no denying that "too menny" children played a significant role in the tragic climax of this novel. Little Father Time, so often read as merely a symbolic figure, asks questions and expresses concerns of a real and practical nature.[7] He knows the family has very little money, that his father is sick and out of work, and that they are being turned out of their lodging. While Sue and Jude cogitate on the meanings and effects of their unconventional union (they never marry each other), Little Father Time focuses on the realities he sees and hears.[8] Typical of children, he takes things literally. So why is it that so little attention has been focused on what he literally has to say—"Done because we are too menny"?

I would argue that the neglect of this obvious issue in the novel is symptomatic of a larger problem—that history has painted nineteenth-century feminist thinkers as having little interest in the issue of birth control. The classic statement of this view is set forth in a 1964 study by J. A. and Olive Banks, *Feminism and Family Planning in Victorian England,* in which they argue that "neither feminism as such nor the emancipation of the middle-class woman from her traditional role of home-maker were important causal factors in the decline of family size" (qtd. in McLaren).[9] Fortunately, work has been done to refute this view, with Angus McLaren's study, *Birth Control in Nineteenth-Century England* (1978), presenting a powerful case against the Banks' thesis.

McLaren traces the link between feminism and family planning throughout the nineteenth century, arguing that "all the birth controllers could be called feminists to the extent that they took an unprecedented interest in the health of women and in their right to control their own bodies" (94–95). While most of the writings on birth control in the early part of the century were by men, McLaren produces evidence showing that women not only approved of these writings, but were often influential in their composition.[10] With respect to the latter part of the century, McLaren provides a thoughtful analysis of why few leading nineteenth-century feminists publicly defended birth control (including concerns about alienating supporters from their more specific goals), and others actively opposed it (particularly those social purity reformers who associated birth control with activities such as prostitution). His analysis of the writings of such women as Josephine Butler, Christabel Pankhurst, and Elizabeth Blackwell, however, leads him to conclude that the women's movement "was far from indifferent to the question of fertility control, that its interest is indeed one of the lost dimensions of Victorian and Edwardian feminism" (197).

Feminists may have disagreed on the method of family limitation (advocating methods as diverse as complete chastity, periodic abstinence, "natural" and "artificial" means of birth control); however, McLaren concludes that "the goal—to win for a woman the right to control her own body—was the same" (198). Considering the extremely controversial nature of this topic, it is not surprising that Hardy's novel does not directly address it. But in more subtle ways, *Jude* does speak to this issue. Reading late-century texts with more of an awareness of this important cultural context should help to illuminate this lost dimension of nineteenth-century feminism.

While many feminist advocates did not speak out explicitly on family limitation, a few dared to make birth control central to their work for women's rights. In this chapter, I focus on two Victorian women who broke the silence on this taboo subject: one in law and the other in literature. Their work and the resistance to it are evidence that much was at stake. Annie Besant defended birth control in a courtroom in 1877; Jane Clapperton chose a novel as her public forum, publishing *Margaret Dunmore; or, A Socialist Home* in 1888. In these unprecedented "trials," with Besant acting as her own attorney, advocating for both herself and birth control, and with Clapperton presenting a utopian or "trial" society in which artificial birth control is an integral aspect of domestic life, both women embrace the power of storytelling to challenge the silencing judgments of law and society. I conclude with a discussion of the early-twentieth-century reformer Marie Stopes, who sued a vocal opponent of birth control for libeling *her* and who helped make Clapperton's utopian vision of increased education about, and access to, birth control a reality with her books *Married Love* and *Wise Parenthood* and the opening of the first birth-control clinic in Britain.

Annie Besant Defends "A Dirty, Filthy Book"

In 1877, Annie Besant and her partner Charles Bradlaugh published a tract on birth control and sold it for sixpence so that it would be available to the poor. They were arrested and charged with obscene libel for publishing an "indecent, lewd, filthy, bawdy, and obscene book, called 'Fruits of Philosophy'" (Freethought 322).[11] The indictment accused them of inciting and encouraging "obscene, unnatural, and immoral practices," and of bringing youth and others "to a state of wickedness, lewdness, and debauchery."[12] At the trial, Besant and Bradlaugh served as their own attorneys, with Besant arguing her case in open court. At a time when women played no official roles in the enactment, administration, enforcement, or adjudication of the law, amidst all the gentlemen of the jury, the Lord Chief Justice, the three male attorneys for the prosecution, and Mr. Bradlaugh, sat Mrs. Besant.

Before focusing on Besant's climactic courtroom performance, I will briefly situate the 1877 trial within nineteenth-century Britain's narrative of birth control, which begins with the ideas set forth by the Reverend T. R. Malthus in his 1798 *Essay on Population*. In this essay, Malthus argues that the population will outstrip available food supplies if its growth is not checked by vice, misery, or self-restraint; he identifies the cause of poverty as the reckless overbreeding of the poor. This "scientific" analysis was popular with conservatives because it blamed the working class for their own misery and concluded that charity would only exacerbate the problem. Malthus identified two types of checks on the population: positive and preventive. Positive checks were influences that increased the death rate, such as wars and famines; preventive checks decreased the birth rate. His recommended "solutions" to overpopulation were postponement of marriage and moral restraint on the part of the poor.

While Malthus advocated late marriages, he specifically opposed artificial birth control: "I should always particularly reprobate any artificial and unnatural modes of checking population, both on account of their immorality and their tendency to remove a necessary stimulus to industry" (qtd. in Chandrasekhar 11).[13] John Wade, one of Malthus's followers, commented that "any artifice to frustrate conception, might be positively mischievous, since, by the disgust it would excite, like an indecent attack on established religion, it would prevent the temperate investigation of a subject of national importance" (327). It is interesting that Wade speaks of this "disgusting" and "indecent" topic in the very language of playful eroticism ("mischievous," "excite"). McLaren summarizes the basic ideology of the Malthusians as follows:

Their concern was that the preaching of birth control could completely undermine both the economic and moral foundation of their argument. They saw in it a new optimistic ideology that ran counter to their own which held that civilisation was based on self-denial and progress on competition resulting from pressure of numbers. The Malthusians did not seek to abolish population pressures. At the very heart of their doctrine lay the belief that such a force was necessary to drive man—at least working-class man—from his naturally lethargic state. (51)[14]

Others who were concerned with population control, however, did not espouse Malthus's conservative views or politics. In 1823, for example, Frances Place, a tailor and political advocate for the working class, printed and distributed handbills addressed "To the Married of Both Sexes of the Working People." Recommending as a birth control method the use of a piece of sponge placed in the vagina prior to intercourse, and afterwards withdrawn by means of an attached string or bobbin, the handbill states that no injurious consequences result from the use of the sponge; "neither does it diminish the enjoyment of either party."[15]

In 1826, Richard Carlile published *Every Woman's Book; or, What is Love?*, also advocating the use of the sponge, as well as a type of condom known as "the glove."[16] Robert Dale Owen, an American reformer and the oldest son of Robert Owen, published *Moral Physiology; or, A Brief and Plain Treatise on the Population Question* in 1831 (reprinted in England in 1833). This book recommends *coitus interruptus* as opposed to any artificial method of birth control.[17] Owen's book argues, however, that family limitation is moral, as well as economically and socially beneficial. The American physician Charles Knowlton incorporated many of Owen's arguments in his 1832 book, *Fruits of Philosophy*, the contested text in the 1877 Besant trial.

In *Fruits of Philosophy*, Knowlton emphasizes the political and social benefits of not always being fruitful and multiplying. He cites the prevention of hereditary diseases, as well as reductions in poverty, profligacy of young men, and infanticide, as benefits of contraception. Knowlton also is particularly concerned with women's health, querying, "How often is the health of the mother, giving birth every year to an infant . . . and compelled to toil on, even at those times when nature imperiously calls for some relief from daily drudgery—how often is the mother's comfort, health, nay, even her life thus sacrificed?" (101). Specifically countering Malthus's proposal of late marriages, Knowlton argues that celibacy is both ineffectual and of a demoralizing tendency. He contends that birth control is unnatural only if all efforts of civilization to control nature (to stop disease, to subdue the forest) are considered as such. The birth control method Knowlton advocates consists of douching the vagina with a solution that will act chemically on semen.[18] He expresses a clear preference for keeping contraception in the hands of women (138).

Fruits of Philosophy was originally reprinted in Britain in 1834, with approximately 1000 copies being sold each year from 1834 to the time of the Besant trial (Himes 243). The book slipped into the foreground in 1877 when a Bristol publisher, Henry Cook, published it with illustrations alleged to be obscene. Cook was arrested and sentenced to two years of hard labor. The original publisher of *Fruits of Philosophy*, Charles Watts, was also arrested and ultimately pleaded guilty to the charges of publishing an obscene book. In order to counter Watts's admission that such a book was obscene, and to establish the right to publish contraceptive information, despite warnings from friends that such actions would mean "ruin to you as a lady" (A. Taylor 109), Besant persuaded Bradlaugh to join her in setting up the Freethought Publishing Company so that they could publish *Fruits of Philosophy* themselves.[19] After publishing the book and then notifying the police where and when they would be selling it, as they had anticipated, they were arrested. Thus began one of the landmark events in British social history, the Besant–Bradlaugh trial.

The trial began on June 18, 1877, and contemporary witnesses estimated that 20,000 people gathered outside the Guildhall on each of the four days of the trial (Chandrasekhar 38). After the scathing indictment had been issued, a magistrate at an early hearing offered to dismiss Besant from the case. This strong-minded woman, who had separated from her authoritarian husband four years earlier and pressured Bradlaugh into taking on this cause in the first place, not unexpectedly refused.[20]

At the trial, the Solicitor-General's argument was in keeping with the terms of the indictment, the basic premise of which was as follows:

> I say that this is a dirty, filthy book, and the test of it is that no human being would allow that book to lie on his table; no decently educated English husband would allow even his wife to have it, and yet it is to be told to me, forsooth, that anybody may have this book in the City of London or elsewhere, who can pay sixpence for it! . . . The object of it is to enable persons to have sexual intercourse, and not to have that which in the order of Providence is the natural result of that sexual intercourse. That is the only purpose of the book, and all the instruction in the other parts of the book leads up to that proposition. (Freethought 251)

Throughout his case, the Solicitor-General was reluctant to actually read

passages from the book aloud, preferring to have the jury read to themselves to save them "the pain and trouble" of hearing it (18). Several times
he professed it "really extremely painful to me, (hesitating) very painful, to
have to read this" (19). The Lord Chief Justice, seemingly irritated by the
Solicitor-General's extreme delicacy, insisted that the "book must be read,
sooner or later, either by you, Mr. Solicitor, or the officer of the court" (18).

When Besant presented her defense in the courtroom, her feminist
method was strategic and understated. This was in sharp contrast to the
combative tone and stance she often took in her written narratives, such
as in the 1876 article in the *National Reformer* entitled "The Legislation of
Female Slavery in England."[21] At the trial, rather than directly taking on the
gender bias in this application of the law of obscene libel, highlighting the
subordination of women implicit in the law's (and the husband's) presumed
right to "allow" women access to birth-control information, Besant told
stories. Law, with its claim to universality and objectivity, its strict reliance
on established form and pleadings, and its exclusionary rules of evidence,
is a mode of analysis and argument that tries to maintain an "exclusive
hold on the truth" (Minow, "Stories in Law" 36). As Martha Minow explains,
"Stories disrupt these rationalizing, generalizing modes of analysis with a
reminder of human beings and their feelings, quirky developments, and
textured vitality" (37). With narratives of her own personal experiences
and those of other women, Besant disrupted and called into question the
law's knowledge or "truth" about birth control, female sexuality, and good
mothering.

Young wives of all classes, she argued, wanted to know about family
limitation. Explaining that birth-control information was available in more
expensive books such as Dr. Chavasse's *Advice to a Wife*, a book she had
been given by her doctor as a young wife (Freethought 139), she brought
the class implications of this lawsuit to the forefront: "I will ask you not to
allow it to go out from this court as the verdict of twelve English jurymen
that you measure indecency by the price at which it may be bought, and
that you would allow that to pass at a high price which you count worthy
of condemnation at a low" (147). After clarifying that information on family
limitation was available to those who could afford it, she proceeded to narrate the tragic lives of those living in families too large to sustain.

Citing the ramifications of overcrowding as one of the justifications for
the checks advocated in Knowlton's book, Besant offered personal anecdotes as evidence. Reminiscent of Engels's descriptions in *The Condition
of the Working Class in England*, she reported: "I have myself seen four
generations of human beings crowded together into one small room, simply
divided into two or three beds, and I will ask you if, after such an experi-

ence as that, you wonder that I risk even prison and fine if I can bring some
salvation to those poor whose misery I have seen" (Freethought 89). She
corroborated her own stories with those of other witnesses to the devastating effects of unchecked population growth. She quoted George Godwin,
from an essay he had presented to the National Association for the Promotion of Social Sciences: "It was but the other day that a child was found
dead in Brownlow Street, and, on inquiry, it was learnt that the mother, a
widow, and six children slept in one bed in a small room. The death of the
child was attributed to the bed clothes" (85).[22] Similarly, she related the
words of the Bishop of Manchester:

> Modesty must be an unknown virtue, decency an unimaginable thing, where,
> in one small chamber, with the beds lying as thickly as they can be packed,
> father, mother, young men, lads, grown and growing up girls—two and some-
> times three generations—are herded promiscuously; where every operation
> of the toilette, and of nature—dressings, undressings, births, deaths—is per-
> formed by each within the sight or hearing of all. . . . It is a hideous picture;
> and the picture is drawn from life. (89)

With these and other life stories, Besant translated the abstract concept
of "obscene libel" into the real-life contexts of unplanned, undesired, and
unsupportably large families.

She also presented evidence of the particular disadvantages to women
of keeping practical birth-control information from them. Arguing the dan-
gers to a woman's health of having too many children, she told the following tale:

> I have often myself seen a poor woman, a mother of a large family, standing
> over the wash-tub three or four days after having borne a child, and upon
> my representing to her the utter ruin to her health which was involved in
> such a proceeding I would get the reply: "What am I to do? There is another
> mouth to feed; the children are there and must be provided for, and I must
> get about." (117)

Besant brought into the courtroom the voices of women who had no opportunity to speak out against their oppression, insisting on the legal relevance
of their experiences. In discussing the positive aspects of feminist narrative scholarship, Kathryn Abrams explains, "Narratives are more likely to
reveal a neglected perspective or theme that needs to play a role in legal
decisionmaking, or to establish a new context or backdrop for legal discussions" (1031). In Besant's story, the woman's simple question—"What am I

to do?"—presented against the backdrop of the washtub, sign and site of the toil from which she has no rest, is a powerful plea for justice.

In addition to bringing neglected perspectives and stories into the courtroom, in what proved to be a stunning obfuscation of societal norms, Besant revised traditional narratives of female sexuality and good mothering. Speaking openly about sexuality, she commented matter-of-factly that "there is nothing wrong in a natural desire rightly and properly gratified" (Freethought 61). Possibly making reference to the extreme modesty exhibited by the Solicitor-General, she claimed that "it is only a false and spurious kind of modesty, which sees harm in the gratification of one of the highest instincts of human nature" (61).

Moreover, she explained that "good" mothers wanted their daughters to be educated in sexual matters and to understand how to limit the size of their families. Speaking to the jury "as mother of a daughter whom I love," she applauded what she argued was a recent effort by the government to encourage both boys and girls at a school in South Kensington to study physiology. Referring to her daughter, she commented, "I believe it will tend to her happiness in her future, as well as to her health, that she shall not have made to her that kind of mystery about sexual functions that every man and woman must know sooner or later" (128). On the matter of birth control, she reported that among the hundreds of the poor who were her "clients" (28) were "mothers who beg me to persist in the course on which I have entered—and at any hazard to myself, at any cost and any risk—they plead to me to save their daughters from the misery they have themselves passed through during the course of their married lives" (29). Besant made the most of the fact that the public was watching this trial, and that "the people" were not only on her side, but whom she was representing ("I speak as counsel for hundreds of the poor, and it is they for whom I defend this case" [28]). The crowds of many thousands gathered outside of the courtroom no doubt made this a powerful argument.

In speaking to the judge and jury, Besant became a public woman; moreover, she was publicizing the most intimate aspects of private life. Indeed, Besant herself may have been as inflammatory as her topics. No ordinary speaker, she was known for the passion she inspired in her audiences. One young man, who heard a speech she delivered for the National Secular Society in 1875, described the impact she had had on him as follows:

> She still seems incomparably young and attractive, her face alive with emotion and expression, her voice full and sonorous, but musical and not unfeminine. . . . She was, or we thought she was, a martyr; she had won freedom from domestic and clerical oppression at the cost of social proscription. She

faced a hostile world on behalf of liberty and truth. We young men, who had a passion of these things in our souls, responded readily to the passion with which she pleaded for them. We were carried away.[23]

She pleaded with this same intensity in the courtroom, and her ability to "carry men away" may have intensified her associations with other "public" women. Throughout the trial, however, she strategically presented her arguments and herself in such a way as to resist that cultural construction. Rhetorically moving the boundaries of respectable womanhood, she never appeared to cross them.

She emphasized, for example, the self-sacrifice involved in her support of this cause:

> I had nothing to gain in publishing this work—I had much to lose. It is no light thing for a woman, whose ambition is bound up in the name which she hopes to make, to have the imputation thrown upon her of publishing indecent books and of disseminating obscenity amongst the young. I risk my name, I risk my liberty; and it is not without deep and earnest thought that I have entered into this struggle. (29)

She understood that her reputation was on the line, but she underscored that, in keeping with the ideal of Victorian womanhood—for the sake of others—she had decided to put aside her own interests.

Careful to present herself as a caring and proper woman, she expressed concern at the amount of the jury's time she was taking in presenting her case. At one point, she requested that the lighting be changed so that it did not fall directly on the jury box, commenting amiably that it "is a great point to me to keep the jury in good temper" (46). In her personal anecdotes, she emphasized her own position as wife and mother. While the judge and jury may have been aware of her estrangement from her husband, inside the courtroom she went by and was always referred to as *Mrs.* Besant.

She also exhibited a mastery of more traditional legal argument. Vast amounts of preparation had familiarized her with the legal precedent, and she referenced relevant case law not only in her prepared defense, but also in response to specific questions from the judge and during the cross-examinations of witnesses. She provided statistics, studies, and references to support all of her factual assertions. The clear presentation of her argument was commended by the judge several times throughout the proceedings.

Sometimes practicing feminist jurisprudence, other times reifying more traditional ideas about wives and mothers, as in most courtroom performances, Besant acted in the way that best supported her case.[24]

In her closing remarks, in what appears to be an appeal to the chivalry and nationalism of the jury, she masterfully manipulated gender roles to her advantage, summarizing the case in such a way that what was truly at stake was her reputation. Arguing that a guilty verdict would mean that the jury believed her speech to be one mass of falsehoods, that her intent in publishing the book was to corrupt the morals of youth, and that she was the worst character of woman, she pleaded, "Unless you are prepared, gentlemen, to brand me with malicious meaning, I ask you, as an English woman, for that justice which it is not impossible to expect at the hands of Englishmen—I ask you to give me a verdict of 'Not Guilty,' and to send me home unstained" (151). In her plea for her reputation, she was completely successful; she was less so on the issue of the obscenity of the book.

At the end of the trial, the jury returned the following verdict: "We are unanimously of the opinion that the book in question is calculated to deprave public morals, but at the same time we entirely exonerate the defendants from any corrupt motives in publishing it" (267). Everyone, including the judge, seemed surprised at this verdict, which the judge stated must then stand as a verdict of guilty. The defendants were released on their own recognizances until sentencing.

Bradlaugh's daughter Hypatia, who was present in the courtroom, wrote the following about the peculiarities of this verdict:

> The jury, however, were by no means so decided at heart and so unanimous as the prompt bow of the foreman led one to believe. . . . two [jurors] returned each their guinea fee to be put down to the defence; one wrote that he did not agree with the verdict, subsequently stating that six of the jury did not intend to assent to a verdict of guilty, and that it had been arranged that if the Lord Chief Justice would not accept their special verdict they should again retire and consult. During the time they were locked in they discussed so loudly that they were heard outside, and their discussion was found to be by no means confined to the offence which they were supposed to be considering, as it included amongst other things the heretical views of the defendants.[25]

At the sentencing hearing, Besant argued that the verdict could not be interpreted as guilty, because with no corrupt motive, there could be no crime. The Lord Chief Justice, however, did not agree. Moreover, he was angry with the defendants because, in the time between the decision and the sentencing hearing, they had claimed to a full house at the Hall of Science that they were sure that a new trial would be declared and that the Lord Chief Justice had supported their cause in his summing up of the case. Copies of *Fruits of Philosophy* also were sold at this meeting. While he originally had planned to let Besant and Bradlaugh off with a warning, because they had defied the jury's verdict by the continued sale of the book, the Lord Chief Justice sentenced them to six months' imprisonment and a large fine. He did release them, however, until the time of their appeal.

In February 1878, the judgment was reversed on a technicality. Besant and Bradlaugh had "won" the case, although not on the principles that they had set out to establish. Bradlaugh recovered the seized copies of *Fruits of Philosophy*, which were then sold stamped with the words "Recovered from Police" (Chandrasekhar 41). They continued to sell the book "till all prosecution and threat of prosecution were definitely surrendered" (Besant, *Autobiography* 220). During the time between the verdict and the appeal, Besant published her own treatise, *Law of Population: Its Consequences, and Its Bearing Upon Human Conduct and Morals* (1877).

In the end, this prosecution was self-defeating, serving only to facilitate the widespread distribution of information about birth control. All of the major newspapers carried extensive coverage of the trial, moving the discussion of birth control from the publications of the radicals to the headlines of the mainstream press. Many newspapers printed lengthy speeches from the defendants, and others printed actual excerpts from "that dirty, filthy book."[26] It is estimated that 125,000 copies of *Fruits of Philosophy* were sold between March and June of 1877 (Banks and Banks 24), and more than 200,000 copies in the three and one-half years following the trial (Chandrasekhar 45). Besant's *Law of Population* sold over 175,000 copies before she withdrew it from circulation in 1891 (Himes 243–44).

In this respect, the Knowlton trial was most definitely a victory for birth control and a personal triumph for Besant. This success, however, came at a high cost. While her dazzling performance at trial momentarily opened up the possibility of a sexualized domestic ideal of womanhood, "the law" soon came to its senses and, reaffirming traditional narratives of woman as mother, found Annie Besant unfit to be one. Besant lost custody of her eight-year-old daughter Mabel in a custody battle tried before Sir George Jessel. Jessel cited Besant's conviction of publishing an obscene book as a ground for removal of the child, stating that "although the conviction was set aside on a technicality, no Judge, so far as I am aware, has doubted the propriety of that conviction," and that "[o]ne cannot expect modest women to associate with her" (qtd. in A. Taylor 131–32).[27] He was particularly outraged that she served as her own counsel in his courtroom: "Appear in person? A lady appear in person? Never heard of such a thing! Does the lady really appear in person?" (Besant, *Autobiography* 214). As *advocate* for birth control and for herself, Besant was too unsettling. The law disciplined her feminist jurisprudence by taking away her child.

A few years later, Besant became a Fabian Socialist, still adhering to her advocacy of birth control despite widespread socialist opposition to it.[28] She wrote "The Law of Population and its Relation to Socialism" to make clear that birth control was not a ploy of the upper classes. She saw socialism as offering the possibility of complete equality for women, and it was her conviction that women ultimately would be the ones to implement effectively family planning: "I believe that one of the strongest arguments in favour of the limitation of the population will come from women. . . . They will be willing to give all the care that is necessary for two or three children, but will refuse to have their health ruined, and the whole of public life shut to them, by having families of ten or twelve . . . ." [29] In 1891, Besant gave up both socialism and Neo-Malthusianism when she embraced Theosophy.[30] At this juncture in her life, she silenced herself on the issue of birth control. However, having already made arguably the nineteenth century's "strongest arguments in favour of the limitation of the population," her message had been heard. One of the women who continued Besant's line of argumentation was the author Jane Hume Clapperton. Seeking more of a "jury of her peers" than Besant had faced in the courtroom, Clapperton chose to perform her advocacy of birth control in a novel—middle-class women's literature of choice.

Margaret Dunmore; or, A Socialist Home
Jane Clapperton's Literary Trial of Family Planning

Three years prior to the publication of her utopian novel *Margaret Dunmore; or, A Socialist Home*, Jane Clapperton wrote a treatise entitled *Scientific Meliorism and the Evolution of Happiness* (1885). Many of Clapperton's arguments for family limitation in this treatise echo those of Besant, whose *Law of Population* Clapperton footnotes as having been received with gratitude by many overburdened mothers. In the 1880s, however, birth control remained subject matter against which moral and proper women needed to be protected, as the following "compliment" in a review of Clapperton's treatise illustrates:

> However repulsive her subject [birth control] may be, her treatment of it is never open to the charge of indelicacy, while at the same time it is absolutely frank and unreserved. Indeed, we may go so far as to say, that if we except

her perilous doctrine of Neo-Malthusianism, there is nothing in this book which would be unwholesome for persons of either sex who approach it sober-mindedly. (*Westminster* 251)

Such was the climate in which Clapperton chose to open a dialogue on this "perilous doctrine" in a novel.

Judging from her comments in *Scientific Meliorism*, I believe that Clapperton's use of the novel as a forum for her politics was a most conscious decision. She saw fiction as playing a vital role in education. Preferring the best light literature of her own day to the ancient classics, which she believed carried "moral ideas completely out of date" (*Meliorism* 186), Clapperton argued that people may see in contemporary fiction "the standpoint average humanity has reached, and the confusion of ideas upon the subject of right conduct, natural to a transitional epoch" (*Meliorism* 134). Recognizing what Bakhtin theorized, that the novel is "structured not in the distanced image of the absolute past but in the zone of direct contact with inconclusive present-day reality" ("Epic and Novel" 39), Clapperton saw the novel as a place to critique unequal laws and an unjust society and to promote discussion of revisions and alternatives.

Like many other late-nineteenth-century women, she specifically chose to write a utopian novel, a popular and highly marketable form of fiction.[31] Darby Lewes identifies several reasons why this genre was so attractive to women writers, including "its unique correlation to nineteenth-century women's own alienated, ambiguous situation" (10–11).[32] In their fictional utopias, women were able to "spurn the grim uniformity of woman's place in men's texts," and "the very possibility of change began to emerge" (19). Jane Baron, in discussing the value of stories today to considerations of law, writes that "stories can depict or construct a 'reality' in tension with the one portrayed in law's dominant tales" ("Resistance to Stories" 268). In the nineteenth century, Clapperton's novel performed feminist jurisprudence by presenting, through a utopian narrative, a different set of rules for women, a less alienated "reality," an alternative textual place, and an alternative social text.

Guided by the philosophy of scientific meliorism, which provided that through a process of controlled evolution, ultimately it would be possible to "create conditions under which no suffering can exist" (L. Ward 468), Clapperton believed that social activists could begin to effect an evolutionary movement toward socialism.[33] In *Scientific Meliorism*, she argued that real reform could begin with "*socially localized* . . . groups," living under conditions of voluntary socialism (427).[34] In her novel, this abstract theoretical idea is translated into the concrete "reality" of a communal home named La Maison, which is peopled with a wide range of characters including an heiress, a retired governess, two newly married couples, in-laws, widows, a fallen woman, children, widowers, socialist activists, and a doctor.

La Maison is the brainchild of Margaret Dunmore, an intellectual young woman who is discontented with her life as an heiress, and her friend Miss José, a committed socialist. These two women conceive of socialism much differently than the radical Monsieur Martin, for example, who advocates violence and large-scale revolution. Their new-era socialism emphasizes that true progress must begin with a change in home life. The novel's revolutionary ideas about domestic arrangements, specifically regarding marriage, divorce, and adultery, provoked *The Saturday Review* to accuse it of showing "contempt of the law" (236).

Within La Maison, the patriarchal structure of the traditional British home is dismantled. Emphasizing from the beginning that they are a reconstituted family, Dunmore explains, "We are deposing, man . . . from headship in our family group. Ours is not a family despotism" (91). Instead, La Maison is run by committee. The Executive Committee, composed of two men and two women, is elected by ballot every six months; it organizes work arrangements. Other committees, also with elected members, include the Finance Committee, the Amusement Committee, the Education Committee, and the Public Service Committee.

The novel covers a four-year period and the narrative progresses in what Clapperton might term a series of displacements. In speaking of real-life character development in *Scientific Meliorism*, she makes the following observation:

> Changes within ourselves occur in similar fashion to changes without. Old laws give way to new; old institutions are replaced by institutions of a better kind, but nowhere do we see a clean sweep (if we may call it) of what is old, leaving a blank and arid waste unfulfilled with what is new. And so it is with human sentiment. The changes are *displacements*. (135)

In La Maison, everything is in a state of transition, and much of the "plot" takes the form of literally and figuratively negotiating change. One of the important "changes without" is the rejection of traditional gender- and class-based work roles. Men perform many of the domestic tasks, including cooking, and, despite objections from some of the members, this middle-class family (which has no servants) does its own "dirty housework" (88). An admirer of the work of Wollstonecraft, Clapperton put the ideas on education that Wollstonecraft advocated in *A Vindication of the Rights of*

Woman into place at La Maison.[35] Boys and girls are educated together in the associated day school, which also is open to all social classes.[36]

Clapperton clearly understood, however, that reproductive control for women was key to lasting displacements. So while other types of "family planning"—decisions about who should do the dusting and who should work in the garden, and where the kitchen should be located in relationship to the nursery—merit serious discussions, birth control is acknowledged as foundational to this "homely" experiment. It is in the context of re-evaluating the institution of marriage, specifically the inequalities between husband and wife, that the subject of birth control is first broached. One of the young husbands, Joe Ferrier, who had only reluctantly agreed to live at La Maison, remains steeped in patriarchal values. While he submits to the "house rules" in most instances, he tries to maintain husbandly authority. After a few months, his wife Vera has had enough. When Joe accuses her of not behaving as a good and affectionate wife, of not considering his wishes and desires, she angrily retorts: "You command me to do this and that! Why am I to consider your wishes always, and you not consider mine?" (121–22). They storm off in different directions, with their fight continuing into the next day. That evening, Vera takes a serious fall and loses the baby that Joe was unaware was on the way.

While she is convalescing, Joe "flung his notions of sex distinctions in work to the wind" and helped to nurse her (125). He still was upset, however, that she had talked back to him: "She was bound to honour her husband; indeed, the Church says obey! He would waive the obedience—some women are touchy on that point; but Vera had clearly dishonoured him that night" (125). When he makes reference to their argument, however, he is amazed to learn that she is unhappy with him. Rebuking him for being cold and harsh to children, she explains that she is not sorry they lost the child because "it cannot be right to bring a child into the world if one of the parents does not desire it" (126). Joe, initially, is shocked and full of resentment. As time passes, however, some of his ideas about marriage and fatherhood begin to be displaced.

It is in connection with Joe and Vera that Clapperton explicitly raises the issue of artificial birth control. This discussion is set within the context of allusions throughout the novel to excessive childbirth ruining women's health and happiness. The Rector's wife, the mother of Rose, one of the young women who lives at La Maison, is one such example. Early in the novel, the narrator comments, "Within the Rectory of Westbrook a babe was born at intervals of never more, sometimes less, than eighteen months; the normal state of the gentle mother was one of feeble health, and Rose had been her prop and stay from very tender years" (14). The Rector, father of this ever-increasing family, is described as "a man who applied all his logic to the squaring and fitting of practice to old dogmas under new conditions, rather than to the examination of new doctrines in the light of simple truth" (15). In light of organized religion's opposition to birth control (McLaren 207–8), it is not surprising that Clapperton presents a Rector as a perpetrator of the population problem. Annie Besant also emphasized that wives of the clergy were supportive of her cause: "there was the passionate gratitude evidenced by letters from thousands of poor married women—many from the wives of country clergymen and curates—thanking and blessing me for showing them how to escape from the veritable hell in which they lived" (*Autobiography* 223–24).

In *Margaret Dunmore*, when Rose's mother matter-of-factly tells her husband, "Oh, marriage disappoints every woman," she responds to his surprise by clarifying that she is not complaining about him specifically; rather she explains that "the position tries a woman in every way, and when the family is large—" (164). The Rector's dogmatic response to his wife, "Lo, children are an heritage of the Lord: and, the fruit of the womb is His reward" (165), is cruel in the casual way that it dismisses her simple truth—that her large family has resulted in poor health being her "normal" state. Although her voice trails off, she does not stop short of speaking her experience. And Clapperton, the tenth of twelve children herself, who spent years tending to her ailing mother, does not stop short in her novel of holding out hope for "new doctrines" in the experience of Joe and Vera.

Joe, as the reader has seen, is much like the Rector in his desire to square and fit old dogmas to new conditions; however, he agrees to the use of artificial birth control to protect Vera's health after the miscarriage. After she is up and about, the narrator comments that "a new phase of married life began for the young couple. Both were to some extent altered, and Joe had, strange to say, submitted himself voluntarily to authoritative dictation on a matter of purely personal conduct" (126). I believe this novel to be unprecedented in nineteenth-century fiction in its explicit clarification of this conduct as the practice of birth control:

> In La Maison the power of bringing fresh human life into existence is bound to be controlled in unfavourable conditions by unhurtful scientific methods. No massacre of innocents is permitted there, and the birth of unhealthy infants is pronounced nothing else, *in an epoch of conscious evolution.*
>
> For unhealthy persons to become parents is a crime against Humanity. Vera for the present is delicate. The responsibilities, the joys of parenthood, must be guarded against, deliberately relinquished till health is fully restored. (126–27)

The syntax of the last sentence suggests that just as the responsibilities and joys of parenthood go together, so too do the ideas that parenthood sometimes of necessity ("must") literally be guarded against (as with birth control) and figuratively relinquished (given up as a right). While phrases such as "conscious evolution" and "crime against Humanity" echo the eugenic-like practices Clapperton espouses in *Scientific Meliorism*, the emphasis in the novel is on the health of mothers, the necessity of providing a loving and nurturing environment for children, and the right of women to control their own bodies.[37] Soon, Joe and Vera are studying physiology together; a class for instruction has been organized at La Maison, and outsiders are welcome. Joe and Vera thus grow into the kind of marriage that Wollstonecraft described as possible only when women are educated with men, "prepared to be their companions rather than their mistresses," and when "the affections common to both are allowed to gain their due strength by the discharge of mutual duties" (*Vindication* 165). Specifically on the issue of sex education, the novel takes up Besant's discourse that women, as well as men, should be fully aware of their bodies and sexuality.

Even more radical than Wollstonecraft's proposals or Besant's defense are the ways in which this novel disrupts traditional ideas regarding the roles of wife and mother. While there are married couples living at La Maison, close relationships among persons of all ages and sexes are encouraged. People are drawn to each other because of mutual interests, as opposed to filial or marital connections.[38] Moreover, parenting is just another one of the group's shared tasks, albeit a most important one. When a widowed mother of two sons first joins the group, for example, she has to give "a solemn pledge to resign her maternal freedom in the management of the boys. Their training and discipline must be under the authority of the Unitary Home" (65). Joe learns to love all of the children in the house, not just his own. In fact, as a reader, it is difficult to tell which child belongs to which biological parents, as the children are seen in the hands of a myriad of caregivers. The cultural constructions of mothering become those of parenting.[39]

In *Margaret Dunmore*, Clapperton not only adopted the novel form; she adapted it to her own purposes. In her communal home, a place of transition and revision, the women—spinsters, wives, fallen women, widows, and mothers—are given new stories. The reader immediately is aware that this is a novel of a different kind when Dunmore, an unmarried, attractive heiress, announces on the first page that she is done with romance and chooses instead to nurture her socialist dreams for the future. The "plots" of the couples are focused on the difficult negotiations of married life, including family planning. The fallen woman suffers no tragic fate, instead finding acceptance and happiness in her new family. And the two widows play key roles in organizing a conference for mothers, the first event sponsored by the communal family in their efforts to educate others in an enlightened way of living.

Having nurtured their domestic socialism, the participants in the Unitary Home feel ready to "assume the grave responsibilities of extended public action" (200). The conference for mothers, the dramatic climax of the novel, emphasizes that women's rights to control their own bodies and their own lives must be of primary concern in bringing about social change. As one of the widows, Mrs. Plimsol, explains:

> There are delicate matters for mothers alone. They must limit their families. They must learn what their duty is to their own health, the health of their children, and the health of the nation. We women will instruct them in self-respect, and show them how to support one another in cases where men are brutal and ought to be resisted. (203)

As they assemble in La Maison's newly constructed lecture hall, these mothers are released figuratively from an isolating domestic system that has offered a false sense of duty and protection. Late in the nineteenth century, after decades of performed feminist jurisprudence, Clapperton envisions women released from the Gothic reality of Wollstonecraft's *Maria* and able to work together toward positive change—and not just in intimate groups of one or two, but rather as a large movement of women. Moreover, addressing family planning directly, this novel serves as a displacement of earlier novelistic representations that tended to legitimate women's debilitating confinement, either by ignoring the tragic lives of women, such as the mother of Jane Austen's Fanny Price in *Mansfield Park* (1814), who gladly sends one of her daughters to a new family as she prepares for her ninth lying-in, or by presenting their situations as comic, such as Dickens's passing reference to Sophy Traddles's mother in *David Copperfield* (1850), who has ten children and has "lost the use of her limbs" (554). In Clapperton's novel, mothers are no longer defined by and confined within narrow and idealized conceptions of home and family.

With the establishment of La Maison and the important first step of the mother's conference, Margaret Dunmore accomplishes the goal she had set out for herself at the beginning of the novel. Having traced the defects of English character to the "defects in the English home," she had committed to "accomplish something, however small, in the exposure of these defects, the inauguration of a remedial system" (72). With *Margaret Dunmore*, Clapperton, too, took an important first step. Daring to show contempt for the law, risking charges of inciting and encouraging "obscene, unnatural, and immoral practices," and bringing youth and others "to a state of wickedness, lewdness, and debauchery," Clapperton advocated for artificial birth control in the public forum of the novel.[40]

In its review of this novel, *The Saturday Review* called *Margaret Dunmore* the "history of a scheme" (236), and it was right to do so. The communal home in the novel was more than a fictional representation; it was a blueprint. More than a setting, it was a site for the reconstruction of the cultural meanings of home, family, and the "duties" of women. So, too, was the novel itself. In situating her alternative domestic system within this literary forum, bringing her political ideas "in the zone of direct contact with inconclusive present-day reality" (Bakhtin, "Epic and Novel" 39), Clapperton created an imaginary space in which her political ideas could be "tried"—treated and tested, not as utopian fantasies, but as real possibilities.

From the Obscene to the Offensive

Birth-Control Advocate Marie Stopes Sues for Libel

In 1921, Marie Stopes took another first step, making Clapperton's "utopian" idea of teaching women practical knowledge about contraception a reality with the opening of the first birth-control clinic in the British Empire. Just as Margaret Dunmore used her money to finance the Unitary Home, Stopes and her husband Humphrey Roe used their own funds to set up and run this clinic in Holloway, North London. Already the author of two enormously successful books on marriage and contraception, *Married Love* (1918) and *Wise Parenthood* (1918), Stopes wanted to reach those women who might not have access to her books, just as Clapperton earlier had turned to the novel as a more accessible forum than her treatise *Scientific Meliorism*. As Stopes explained, "the very overburdened working-class mother does not read our literary reviews; she does not read these books of health, and she has not the time to read them, even if she had the money and wished to buy them" (Box 78).[41]

Hundreds of women came to the clinic to receive information and advice on birth control, as well as for the fitting of contraceptives by qualified nurses. Everything was free except for the birth-control devices themselves (small rubber cervical caps called check pessaries), which were sold to the women at cost. In light of the success of this clinic, Stopes proposed to the Prime Minister, David Lloyd George, that the government set up birth-control clinics around the country as a public service. Not opposed to the idea, but fearing adverse political consequences, Lloyd George wanted Stopes to provide evidence that public opinion on this still publicly taboo subject had changed.[42]

In the spirit of Clapperton's mothers' conference, Stopes organized a large meeting at the Queen's Hall, where birth control was openly discussed in a very public forum. Speakers included prominent politicians and doctors, with the arguments echoing many of the same ideas that Besant had presented over forty years before. The Rt. Hon. G. H. Roberts, P.C.M.P., proclaimed, "It is a deplorable fact today that while the better-to-do possess this knowledge, and are, in my opinion, ordering their lives so as to give their children greater and fairer opportunities, the class to which I belong, groveling in their ignorance, are still producing in excessive numbers" (qtd. in Box 23). Dr. Jane Hawthorne, much like Besant, presented real-life examples of the hardship resulting from the lack of availability of practical birth-control information: "I am here today . . . to represent those who have neither the opportunity nor the power to make their own appeal, and therefore I am anxious to put before you as clearly as possible the position of the very poor, hardworked wife and mother" (qtd. in Box 23). When Stopes finally began to speak, highlighting the harmful effects of lack of sexual knowledge and sexual repression, Labour leader J. R. Clynes became "conscious of a spiritual fire somehow beginning to blaze up" (qtd. in Box 24).

Within a few weeks of this most successful public debate on birth control, Dr. Halliday Sutherland attended a lecture given by a noted gynecologist, Dr. Anne McIlroy, in which she referred to the rubber check pessary as "the most harmful method of contraception she had encountered in her experience" (qtd. in Box 27). A Scottish Catholic doctor much opposed to the idea of birth control, Sutherland knew that this type of pessary was the one in use at Stopes's clinic. A year later, Sutherland published an anti–birth-control book, *Birth Control*, that included the following passage in the chapter titled "Evils of Artificial Control":

> The ordinary decent instincts of the poor are against these practices, and indeed they have used them less than any other class. But, owing to their poverty, lack of learning and helplessness, the poor are the natural victims of those who seek to make experiments on their fellows. In the midst of a London slum, a woman who is a doctor of German Philosophy (Munich) has opened a birth control clinic where working women are instructed in a method of contraception described by Professor McIlroy as "the most harmful method of which I have had experience." . . .
>
> When we remember that millions are being spent by the Ministry of Health and by local authorities—on pure milk for necessitous, expectant

and nursing mothers, on maternity clinics to guard the health of mothers before and after childbirth, for the provision of skilled midwives, and on infant welfare centres—all for the single purpose of bringing healthy children into the world, it is truly amazing that this monstrous campaign of birth control should be tolerated by the Home Secretary. Charles Bradlaugh was condemned to jail for a less serious crime. (qtd. in Hyde 248–49)

Outraged by this attack on her work and herself, Stopes challenged Sutherland to a public debate. When she received no response, she had a writ for libel issued against him and his publishers. Thus, birth control became the subject of yet another highly publicized trial—only this time it and one of its most outspoken advocates were on the offensive.

In a trial lasting nine days, from February 21 to March 1, 1923, issues were argued ranging from the Catholic church's position on contraception, the implications of specifying Stopes's degree from a German University at a time in England (post–World War I) when anti-German sentiments were rife, to whether there was sufficient medical knowledge about the rubber check pessary to consider it non-experimental. There also were passionate and explicit arguments concerning whether Stopes's books (which were part of "this monstrous campaign of birth control") were indeed more obscene than *Fruits of Philosophy* (thus making true Sutherland's comment that Bradlaugh had been condemned to jail for a less serious crime).[43]

After deliberating for four hours, the jury answered the following four questions put to it by the Lord Chief Justice as follows:

1. Were the words complained of defamatory of the plaintiff?
    Answer: Yes.
2. Were they true in substance and in fact?
    Answer: Yes.
3. Were they fair comment?
    Answer: No.
4. Damages, if any?
    Answer: £100.

(Box 390)

Seeming to ignore the answers to questions one, three, and four, the judge found for Sutherland, basing his judgment on the fact that the jury determined the alleged libel to be true in substance and in fact (even if it was not fair comment).

This surprising interpretation of the jury's verdict is less so in light of the Lord Chief Justice's far from impartial summation of the case. After explaining the law of libel and the applicable defenses, he had gone on at length about the details presented at this particular trial. Stating that there obviously were those who believed in a "sort of public duty to spread abroad, on the widest possible scale, without discrimination of sex, or age, or marriage, or absence of marriage, the truth about the check pessary" (Box 363), he asked whether it did not also occur to the gentlemen of the jury that others held stoutly to an opposite view:

> Contraception may be, as more than one of these witnesses have said, in some cases a deplorable necessity, always at the best a second best; but, for heaven's sake, do not let this information be published broadcast to all and sundry, to persons of all ages and of all circumstances as to marriage or non-marriage. And if they are to be published in that way, let us be very careful as to the language, the tone, the manner, the style, in which the publication is made. . . . Sex teaching, yes, but in cold scientific language, not mixing up physiology with emotion, not teaching such truths as need to be taught in the language of adjective and rhetoric, but with austerity, with coldness, stating the facts and no more. (Box 363)

The literary presentation of this information (the language, tone, manner, style, the use of adjective and rhetoric) seemed most perturbing to this judge. In light of his admission that birth control may be "a deplorable necessity," he most likely feared the effectiveness and persuasiveness of this type of written word.

In protecting "unfair comment" about birth control, the law itself came under attack. In a letter to the *Daily News* about the ruling, George Bernard Shaw commented as follows:

> What has just happened in a case quite as important in its way as the trial of the seven bishops makes it unnecessary to say anything more except that if jury men are not better instructed in their rights and duties than they are at present, the continuous pressure of the Bench to usurp their functions will end in nothing being left to the jury but the responsibility for the Judge's decision.[44]

The *Westminster Gazette* concluded, "Women who desire to know how to prevent unwanted children are bad women. Such is the law as it stands. The law is not functioning usefully."[45]

Stopes acknowledged the verdict as a victory: "The result of the trial is indeed remarkable, but I feel absolutely vindicated as I obtained a clear finding for damages from the British public as represented by a Jury, though this is withheld as a legal technicality. Even this has worked for good and led to many public expressions of sympathy and indignation."[46] Moral victory not being enough, however, she appealed the decision, and in July of 1923 the Court of Appeal reversed the judgment and ordered Sutherland to pay Stopes £100 damages, plus half the costs of the action. Supported and funded by Catholic newspapers and a committee to counteract the evils being perpetrated by the advocates of birth control, Sutherland appealed to the House of Lords, which overturned the decision of the Court of Appeal, ordered Stopes to repay the damages and costs, and determined that there were no grounds for a new trial.[47]

As with the Besant prosecution, the tremendous publicity these trials received did a great deal to spread the word about birth control. While ultimately losing the case, at a steep cost of approximately £10,000 (Hyde 276), Stopes herself admitted that her defeat had "roused so much more enthusiasm for me than simple success would have done that I cannot regret it" (qtd. in Hall 243). The number of women visiting the clinic in 1923 was more than double the number who had visited in 1922. One postal delivery alone in 1923 brought 350 letters to the clinic, and newspapers around the world carried coverage of the trials (Hall 246). "Stopery" had become the talk of the town.[48]

The actual practice of birth control was not illegal in England; what was dangerous was to advocate it in print. And the greater the audience of readers, the greater the "crime." Thus, the threat of being charged with obscenity and immorality, whether in a legal indictment, in a literary review, or in the court of public opinion, effectively kept many writers from openly addressing this pressing issue. It was clear from those who did speak out that the risks were high. Efforts were made in 1873 to keep John Stuart Mill from being buried at Westminster Abbey because he was sympathetic to family limitation (McLaren 93). Annie Besant was ostracized from "decent" society and unwelcome in many feminist groups because of her Neo-Malthusian views (Bland 196). Most shockingly, her outspoken views were "proof" in a court of law that she was unfit to raise her own child. Jane Clapperton's novel was dismissed as "didactic," and she has slipped into such obscurity that we do not know what ramifications she may have suffered on account of her contemptuous views (Review of *Margaret Dunmore, Athenaeum* 177).[49] In the early twentieth century, Stopes's personal trials included the receipt of many life-threatening letters, the refusals of newspapers to advertise her books (The *Times* even refused to print the announcement of the birth of her son), and arson at one of her birth-control clinics (Soloway 247; Briant 176).

Statistical evidence on the birth rate, however, suggests that these efforts at silencing were far from 100 percent effective. In 1876, one year before the Besant trial, the birth rate in Britain peaked at 36.3 births per thousand. Then it began to plummet. By 1901, fertility had dropped more than 24 percent; in the course of fifty years, the average size of British families fell by nearly two-thirds (Soloway xi). As Richard Soloway explains in his study *Birth Control and the Population Question in England, 1877–1930*, by the early twentieth century, "it was widely acknowledged that the decided shift toward smaller families was not a result of later marriage, alterations in diet, or the diminished fecundity of an evolving, or, as the more pessimistic suggested, a decaying race. On the contrary, the decline was the effect of the rapid spread of family limitation, or birth control . . ." (xii).[50]

While it may be impossible to measure the influence of any one person or event, after Annie Besant raised her voice in court, thousands of people purchased pamphlets providing practical guidance on birth control, and in the same year as the trial, a Malthusian League was formed that openly promoted the discussion and use of contraception throughout the Victorian and Edwardian periods.[51] Stopes reached out to a much greater public than the Malthusian League with her campaign for "constructive birth control," which focused on the right to sexually fulfilling marriages and desired children as opposed to the League's emphasis on the economic consequences of overpopulation.[52]

The explicit discussion of birth control in Clapperton's "lost" novel, as well as the relevance of this issue to the tragedy of Hardy's much more famous one, also suggests that this taboo subject may have been explored in literature much more than has been previously considered. There may be other novelists like Clapperton who wrote, as one reviewer of *Margaret Dunmore* commented, without "an eye to the circulating libraries" (*Academy* 147), whose controversial subject matter may have ensured that their fiction was deemed unremarkable.[53] Still others, like Hardy, may have commented more subtly in order to evade the severe and silencing judgment of "Mrs. Grundy" (the term Hardy used to refer to critics and other upholders of conventional propriety).[54]

Just because a novel does not address a topic explicitly, however, does not mean that it was not written with those ideas very much in mind.[55] Reading Victorian novels from our contemporary perspective that birth control was not really a nineteenth-century issue, we have failed to take into account, because it virtually necessitated euphemism and self-censorship, a social context that truly mattered. It is less likely that middle-class Victorian readers, who other evidence suggests had knowledge and access to birth-control information, also would have read over these important cultural references.

With the knowledge that various methods of family limitation were available, the hangings in *Jude the Obscure* may be read as all the more tragic. For Sue *could* have helped it. That is unless she was one of those working-class women whom Besant and Clapperton recognized as having little practical guidance on how to limit the size of their families. Or unless, growing up without a mother, she was as ignorant about sexual matters as many of the women who wrote gratefully to Marie Stopes for the information she provided in *Married Love*. Or maybe, as her hero Mill had suggested, she was too hesitant (as the hesitancy of her remark itself underscores) to acknowledge desires and methods that were so unsupported by the moral feelings of the community. These possibilities would have further complicated the tragedy of everyday life that Hardy was trying to portray, especially for the many Victorian readers to whom the full significance of Little Father Time's message would not have been obscure.

CHAPTER 4

Sitting in Judgment

A Cross-Examination of Women, Law, and Empire

judgement, judgment
1.b. Phr. *to sit in judgement:* (a) *lit.* to sit as judge, to preside as a
judge at a trial; (b) *fig.* to pass judgement *upon* . . . to judge, criticize
(with an assumption of superiority).
    —*Oxford English Dictionary*

As set forth in the Introduction, by the time Lewis Carroll penned the courtroom scene in his 1865 *Alice's Adventures in Wonderland,* women had
exerted significant influence in legal reforms relating to child custody and
divorce and were advocating for substantial changes in laws governing
married women's property. With women starting to claim a right to enter
and participate in the sphere of law, judges found themselves stumbling,
like the King in the following scene from *Alice,* for applicable rules to keep
them out.

> At this moment the King, who had been for some time busily writing in his
> notebook, called out "Silence!" and read out from his book, "Rule Forty-two.
> *All persons more than a mile high to leave the court.*"
>   Everybody looked at Alice.
>   "*I'm* not a mile high," said Alice.
>   "You are," said the King.
>   "Nearly two miles high," added the Queen.
>   "Well, I shan't go, at any rate," said Alice: "besides, that's not a regular
> rule: you invented it just now."
>   "It's the oldest rule in the book," said the King.

"Then it ought to be Number One," said Alice.

The King turned pale, and shut his notebook hastily. (98)

Flustered by the threateningly large presence of Alice in his courtroom, the King (who sits as judge in this proceeding) tries his best to make her leave. From his position of authority, he declares the law—which, it appears, he just made up. When Alice gets nowhere disputing the facts (she is not a mile high), she questions the law itself. At this point the King confidently invokes precedent ("It's the oldest rule in the book"). But it is not at all lost on Alice that this argument makes no sense.

In the first part of this chapter, I examine several legal cases in which women sought entry into law and politics. These cases illuminate how the common law (often referred to as judge-made law) sometimes really was law *made up* by judges. While professing their impartiality, Victorian judges greatly influenced women's legal roles (by ruling that they could not have any). I will then engage in a "cross-examination" of the representations of two surprising nineteenth-century characters—female judges, one fictional and one real: *She-Who-Must-Be-Obeyed*, or Ayesha, from Rider Haggard's 1887 novel *She*; and the real-life missionary, Mary Slessor, who was the first woman appointed as a magistrate in the British Empire (Buchan 138).

In the field of law and literature, the term "cross-examination" is most closely associated with Brook Thomas's excellent study of the American Renaissance, *Cross-Examinations of Law and Literature: Cooper, Hawthorne, Stowe, and Melville* (1987). Focusing on the period of American history in which, Thomas argues, law and literature "were severed," he cross-examines these two fields to "reconstruct the narratives that different segments of American society imagined in response to the social and economic transformations that they experienced, as well as the narratives that helped to legitimize and structure those transformations" (16). In *In Contempt*, I generally engage in the type of cross-examination espoused by Thomas, one that analyzes legal and literary narratives and their intersections in order to illuminate historically specific cultural histories and legal ideologies. However, in this chapter, I use the term cross-examination to describe two, more specific, methodological approaches. First, as in a legal proceeding, a cross-examination provides an opportunity to clarify or discredit testimony that is offered on direct examination. It is a method of probing gaps and openings in the direct testimony—places where it is possible and necessary to bring out important unstated, but related, issues (whether or not they have been omitted intentionally) in order to reveal a more complete story. Second, by cross-examination, I mean examining texts from various interrelated perspectives. Therefore, while my focus will be on representations of women, law, and power, my cross-examination will also take into account the imperial context in which they were set. In reading these texts that cross continents, I will also explore the intersections of gender and race. Both Ayesha and Slessor exercised legal power in Africa, and my analysis explores the ways in which, in the context of Empire, traditional ideas about gender were complicated and disrupted by racial politics when white women were ruling and judging indigenous people in Africa.

Judge-Made Law

Attempts to Regulate a Growing Concern

In 1866, Barbara Leigh Smith Bodichon and several fellow feminists collected 1,499 signatures on a petition for women's suffrage. John Stuart Mill presented this petition to the House of Commons in 1866, and in 1867, he introduced an amendment to the Representation of the People Act (30 & 31 Vict., c. 102). This effort to give women the right to vote in national elections was rejected, with "every conceivable argument, many of them contradictory . . . employed to defeat the amendment" (St. John-Stevas 263).[1]

In several parts of the country, however, women householders registered to vote. When the names of 5,347 women were excluded from the lists of voters in the borough of Manchester, these women took the matter to court.[2] Having to make their arguments within acceptable legal frameworks, in *Chorlton v. Lings* (1868) they contended first that women historically did have the right to vote and that no subsequent legislation had taken that right away, and second (alternatively) that the 1867 Representation of the People Act had conferred the right to vote if women did not possess it before. This latter argument was based on the applicability of Lord Brougham's Act (13 & 14 Vict., c. 21 [1850]), which provided that "in all Acts Words importing the Masculine Gender shall be deemed to include females, unless the contrary . . . is expressly provided" (s. 4). Powerful ethical and philosophical arguments (such as that the fundamental principle underlying the Representation Act was that there should be no taxation without representation) had to be "fitted" into those arguments deemed legally relevant.

As Chief Justice Bovill made clear in the opening remarks of his opinion in *Chorlton*, consideration of such nonlegal arguments would be most inappropriate: "It is quite unnecessary to consider the general question of whether it is desirable that women should possess the franchise of voting at the election of members of [P]arliament. What we have to determine is, whether by law they now possess that right" (382). The court proceeded to find that they did not, concluding that under the common law, women had been and still were legally incapacitated from voting, and that if the legislature had intended to make such an important alteration in the personal qualifications for voting in the 1867 Act, they would not have used the word "man" in the relevant provisions. This was the holding of the case despite arguments by the women's attorney that if the legislature had intended to exclude women, they would have used the words "male person" (which had been used in a provision of a related act) rather than "man," which "by the express provision of Lord Brougham's Act, includes women" (*Chorlton* 379).

While women were thus foreclosed from voting on a national level, the Municipal Franchise Act 1869 (32 & 33 Vict., c. 55) gave women the right to vote in local elections on the same terms as men. This right was gained from a late-night amendment offered by Jacob Bright; however, few seemed bothered by women's exercise of this municipal franchise, most likely because these elections primarily impacted issues closely associated with women's "appropriate" sphere (such as local schools and care of the poor and elderly) (Shanley 109).[3]

The right to vote in a local election, however, did not grant a corresponding right to run for office—that is, if you were a woman. Despite a provision in the applicable municipal corporations act that "every person shall be qualified to be elected and to be a councillor who is, at the time of the election, qualified to elect to the office of councillor," the Court in *Beresford-Hope v. Sandhurst* (1884) determined that the word "person" as used in this provision did not include women (even while agreeing that there were places in the act where "person" and even "he" had to be read to also mean "she") (qtd. in *Beresford-Hope* 82). Therefore, the election of Lady Sandhurst (who ran and won a seat as county councillor by a clear majority) was declared void, the votes for her thrown out, and the defeated candidate (who brought the suit in the first place) deemed duly elected.

Judgment was given against Sandhurst by Sir James Fitzjames Stephen (Virginia Woolf's uncle), and his decision was upheld on appeal. Expressing commonplace judicial reverence for what (and who) had gone before, one of the appellate judges, citing the *Chorlton* case, stated, "I take it that by neither the common law nor the constitution of this country from the beginning of the common law until now can a woman be entitled to exercise any public function. Willis, J., stated so in that case [*Chorlton*], and a more learned judge never lived" (*Beresford-Hope*, Esher opinion 95).

Soon thereafter, another woman was elected to the London Council. In order to take advantage of a provision in the applicable statute that an election not questioned for one year is deemed valid, she waited one year to act and vote as a member of the council. While the court in *De Souza v. Cobden* (1891) held that this validity provision was inapplicable to the election of a woman, it had no problem holding her liable under the penalty section of the same statute—even though, to do so, they had to interpret the word "he" to also mean "she."[4]

The inconsistent wordplay in these "person" cases—with "man" sometimes meaning "person," "person" sometimes meaning "he," and "he" sometimes meaning "she"—made it uncomfortable to decide a case solely on the basis of the "clear" meaning of the statute. As a result, the common law was cited to lend credibility and authority to these decisions. A hallmark of the English legal system, the common law is a theory of judicial precedent—judges are bound by the decisions of the judges who have gone before them. Citing the common law not only gave a judge the backing of the law's valorized past; it also excused him from considering present-day realities. But as Sachs and Wilson explain, much of the common law's venerated "history" is really "fiction":

> In the seventeenth century the common law had been yoked to a principle of the fundamental rights of the people of England as a weapon to challenge the divine right of the Kings of England. It drew its doctrinal strength from a claim to have existed since time immemorial, having its roots in an antiquity that predated the prerogative rights of the kings. In order to establish this ancient origin, a history was invented by the judges. This retrospectively created history was almost entirely fictional, but so strong was the need of the judges to assert the supremacy of the common law and the concomitant idea of uninterrupted custom, that contrary facts were simply ignored or treated as irrelevant. Essentially this fictionalized history represented a projection into the past of the current world-view of the judges. Coke was the leading exponent of this asserted antiquity, and it was Coke's manufactured views that were relied upon for the next three centuries as having set out immemorial custom. (43–44)

It was the fiction of the uninterrupted custom of women not holding public or political office that ultimately decided most of these "person" cases. Evidence to the contrary was ignored or deemed too scanty or insubstantial to call into question a grand common-law tradition of exclusion. Hence, in response to several fifteenth-century examples of women participating in elections provided by counsel to the women in the *Chorlton* case, the Court responded:

It is quite true that a few instances have been brought before us where in ancient times, viz. in the reigns of Henry IV., Henry V., and Edward VI., women appear to have been parties to the returns of members of parliament; and possibly other instances may be found in early times, not only of women having voted, but also of their having assisted in the deliberations of the legislature. . . . But these instances are of comparatively little weight, as opposed to uninterrupted usage to the contrary for several centuries; and what has been commonly received and acquiesced in as the law raises a strong presumption of what the law is. . . . (Bovill opinion 383)[5]

This "acquiescence" continued as judges strove to characterize interruptions as anything but, with Lord Esher in *De Souza*, for example, determining that "by the common law of England women are not in general deemed capable of exercising public functions, though there are certain exceptional cases where a well-recognized custom to the contrary had become established, as in the case of overseers of the poor" (691). The court in *Jex-Blake v. Senatus* (1873) (the case in which Sophia Jex-Blake and others sought the right to study and receive degrees in medicine from the University of Edinburgh) dismissed the notorious Victorian interruption, Queen Victoria herself, as an "illustrious and solitary exception" to the well-established common-law rule. In this way, "the anti-feminism of one generation of judges was carried by the common law to the anti-feminism of another generation" (Sachs and Wilson 44)—all under the guise of judicial neutrality. The mantra "women have always been excluded from public office" became one of the law's "truths"—one of the oldest rules in the book. But like the mile-high rule encountered by Alice, it had been made up.

While the courts would not address the issue of whether a woman was a "person" under the statutes governing admittance into the legal profession until 1913, women were actively considering legal careers as early as the 1870s. In 1876, a woman first applied to sit for the solicitors' examination but was refused (Sachs and Wilson 171–72). The aspirations of another "young lady candidate" were foiled in 1879 when the Law Society, that "ungallant body" as the *Solicitors' Journal* somewhat smugly reported, "definitely said that they do not feel themselves at liberty to accept the notice of any woman" ("Lady Lawyers" 139).[6] That same year, ninety-two women signed a petition requesting admission to the law lectures at Lincoln's Inn. They were told "that in the opinion of this Bench it is not expedient that Women should be admitted to the Lectures of the Professors appointed by the Council of Legal Education" (Roxburgh 178).[7]

In the midst of these pronoun controversies and inexpedient requests, the young lawyer Rider Haggard penned one of the most popular novels of his day—an imperial adventure story about an unprecedented ruling queen and judge who is unambiguously "She."[8]

She-who-must-be-obeyed

Queen of the Imagination

The novel *She* is the story of three Englishmen who penetrate into the depths of a feminized African landscape and discover an all-powerful queen, *She-who-must-be-obeyed*.[9] The novel consists of a first-person manuscript of one of these travelers, Ludwig Horace Holly, which is presented to the reader by an anonymous editor as a "record," or testimony concerning "one of the most wonderful and mysterious experiences ever undergone by mortal men" (1).[10] The editor counsels the reader in jury-like fashion "to form his own judgment on the facts before him" (6). Before their journey, Holly, his ward Leo, and Job, a "suitable male attendant" (19) who has taken care of Leo since childhood, live together in a university setting, an all-male family in an almost exclusively masculine world.[11]

Holly, a Cambridge scholar in his forties, identifies himself as "a bit of a misogynist" (88); Leo, described as "a statue of Apollo come to life" (1), loves women; and Job, one of a family of seventeen (this being yet another example of a humorous presentation of a tragic situation), is a comic, feminized character who displays the fears and concerns of an overbearing mother and the moral prudishness of a stereotypical "spinster aunt."

In the novel, Leo is called to the Bar "to pass the time away" until he turns twenty-five (22).[12] Then, on his twenty-fifth birthday, he learns of a purported source of eternal youth and beauty, and these three unlikely adventurers set out for Africa in search of the "rolling Pillar of Life" (31). Specifically, they travel to a land inhabited by the Amahaggar people, who are ruled by *She-who-must-be-obeyed*, a queen "having knowledge of all things, and life and loveliness that does not die" (30).

In her article "Rider Haggard's Heart of Darkness," Sandra Gilbert makes much of the fact that the Amahaggar society is matriarchal. As Holly explains:

> [W]omen among the Amahaggar live upon conditions of perfect equality with the men, and are not held to them by any binding ties. Descent is traced only through the line of the mother, and while individuals are as proud of a long and superior female ancestry as we are of our families in Europe, they

never pay attention to, or even acknowledge, any man as their father, even
when male parentage is perfectly well known. (81)

Gilbert sees this land as a place where "relations between its men and
women inhabitants are exactly antithetical to those that prevail in normal
civilized societies" and thus "a realm where what patriarchal culture defines
as misrule has become rule" (126).[13] Specifically, she describes an early episode in which the Englishmen's Arab companion, Mahomed, almost falls
victim to the customary Amahaggar mode of execution (placing a red-hot
earthen pot on the heads of strangers) as "grotesquely sexual in its elabora-
tion of the ways in which female misrule can cause a vessel associated with
female domesticity to become as deadly as female anatomy" (126).

A cross-examination of Holly's testimony concerning women's roles
in this society, however, reveals that, in reality, the women do not rule,
and that Holly's claim of equality between Amahaggar men and women
simply is not substantiated by the facts. Each tribe of about seven thousand
people is governed by an elected ruler known as a Father, and, as Holly
clarifies, there "is but one titular *male* parent of each tribe" (81; emphasis
added). In Haggard's fantasy, the language is unambiguous—women cannot
be Fathers. As the Amahaggars have no written laws, this rule (like the
common law) is based on custom; however, there is little chance that this
established precedent will be challenged, for anyone who offends against
custom will be "put to death by order of the Father" (90)—thus *ensuring*
uninterrupted acquiescence in the law.

Men are also the only armed members of the society, and in almost
every description of an Amahaggar man, he either is holding his spear
or has it nearby. Moreover, the men use these weapons to "control" the
women. Billali, one of the Amahaggar Fathers, describes the position of
women as follows: "'We worship them . . . up to a certain point, till at last
they get unbearable, which,' he added, 'they do about every second generation'" (114). At this point, he explains, "we rise, and kill the old ones as an
example to the young ones, and to show them that we are the strongest"
(114). While women in Britain also were "dying" (or at least suffering) on
their pedestals, the Amahaggar women more literally suffered their fate of
being "worshipped," while remaining powerless.[14]

Not surprisingly, in this world of male fantasy, the only power we see
an Amahaggar woman exercising is the ability to make sexual advances to
the man of her choice. Leo, for example, is embraced almost immediately
by the beautiful Ustane, and while the moral and prudish Job "ejaculated,
'The hussy—well, I never!'" (88), Leo warmly returns Ustane's embrace.
According to Amahaggar custom, this exchange is akin to a marriage cer-

emony, although the arrangement continues only until one of the partners wearies of it. While the Amahaggar women do maintain some control over their private lives, their actual power appears to be mere fancy.

The Queen of the Amahaggars, however, as Queen Victoria was described in the *Jex-Blake* case, is an "illustrious and solitary" exception to this power structure. While the men rise up and kill *other* older women, the 2000-year-old She or Ayesha (as she prefers to be called by Holly) has ruled over both Amahaggar men and women for generations. In fact, she shares much in common with Britain's real "Great White Queen" Victoria.[15] Queen Victoria similarly was "above the law" in that she was exempt from the rules of coverture. As the monarch, Victoria was unique among married women. She was not obliged to take her husband's name or to hand over her property to him after their marriage; she could enter into independent contracts and dispose freely of her own possessions (D. Thompson 120). While Victoria did not support the efforts of nineteenth-century women to reform the laws of coverture, she maintained an identity, including a legal one, of her own.[16]

In what Adrienne Munich identifies as "a revealing fantasy of Haggard who had never known another monarch than Victoria and who was only six years old when Prince Albert died" (272), both Ayesha and Victoria enjoy very long reigns and suffer extensive periods of mourning for their male lovers. Also, Ayesha tells Holly that her "empire is of the imagination" (175), which seems an apt description of the immense symbolic power Victoria wielded, especially in connection with "her" Empire. As Dorothy Thompson explains, "Disraeli's move in creating the title of Empress of India for the queen in 1876, and the celebrations of her golden jubilee in 1887 and diamond jubilee a decade later, meant that there was a grand royal event in each of the last three decades of the century—events that highlight the growing imperial power of Britain" (117). Moreover, a diary entry of one of her granddaughter's friends provides a glimpse of the personal hold Victoria had on the country's imagination. Visiting Windsor Castle and seeing the light of the Queen's lamp "glowing late into the night," Helene Vacaresco wrote that thinking of that "frail little old lady working there and holding in her hands the threads of . . . her vast Empire" filled her "with something like awe" (qtd. in Mullen and Munson 136).[17] Victoria's "awesome" power, however, exceeded the realm of the imaginary: "[B]y the time of her death, the need of a figure on which to focus the idea of Britain had become so deeply part of the political scene that even republican political leaders feared to challenge it" (D. Thompson 125). For the sake of Empire, the political nature of the Queen's very public role had to be acknowledged.[18]

In the novel, when Holly first comes into Ayesha's presence, he is filled with a nameless terror when he feels "the gaze of the unknown being seeking through and through me" (141) from behind a curtain. When he turns his gaze upon her, he finds himself linguistically impotent: "I have heard of the beauty of celestial beings, now I saw it; only this beauty, with all its awful loveliness and purity, was *evil*—at least, at the time, it struck me as evil. How am I to describe it? I cannot—simply, I cannot! The man does not live whose pen could convey a sense of what I saw" (155). In its ambiguity, this is typical of almost all of Holly's descriptions of Ayesha. He tries to capture the multiplicity of meanings that she implies, but language fails him. He describes her in contradictory terms or qualifies his assessments as he does with the afterthought, "at least, at the time, it struck me as evil." His reference to "at the time" foregrounds the fact that he is remembering. So has he changed his mind, deciding that she is not evil? It is as if he wants to emphasize his own trouble in coming to terms with the powerful woman that She is and the possibilities that She represents.

After Holly has spent hours discussing classical languages and history with a charming, witty, and flirtatious Ayesha, she gives a little sob when she is reminded of Kallikrates, the man she had loved and murdered two thousand years ago in a jealous rage and for whose return she has been waiting since that time. Holly comments, "I saw that after all she was *only* a woman, although she might be a very old one" (157; emphasis added). When she is *only* a woman, acting in an acceptable womanly way, he is no longer terrified.

His assessment of her changes, however, when he sees her the next day, not as a languishing beauty, but as a powerful woman presiding over a court of law. He is commanded to appear in her courtroom, and there witnesses a sight "as strange as any I ever saw, even in that unholy land" (173). As he stands near the back of the room, taking in the crowd of gloomy looking spectators, there is a cry of "Hiya! Hiya!" (meaning She! She!), which may have sounded to Holly reminiscent of, but profoundly different from, the familiar call to order of "Hear ye! Hear ye!" The crowd then immediately falls upon the ground in a degrading inversion of "All rise." Ayesha enters the courtroom, following a long procession of guards and male and female mutes, and then tells Holly to come sit at her feet and see her do justice.

What follows is a formal court proceeding.[19] The prisoners are summoned; Ayesha asks Holly to identify the men who attacked him and his companions and then has him testify concerning the attempted murders. Holly recounts "the history of the cannibal feast, and of the attempted torture of our poor servant [Mahomed]" (172). When he finishes, Ayesha calls upon Billali to verify Holly's testimony. After the case for the prosecu-

Figure 3 "'Curse Her! May She Be Everlastingly Accursed!'" Illustration by Maurice Greiffenhagen taken from the 1919 Longman's edition of *She*.

tion has been presented, Ayesha asks if any of the accused would like to speak in their own defense. One man asks for mercy, explaining that the attack had been made in a sudden fury and that they deeply regretted their actions. An intense silence follows this plea, and Holly is struck by the strangeness of this entire scene. He finds Ayesha particularly remarkable:

> Then, seated in her barbaric chair above them all, with myself at her feet, was the veiled white woman, whose loveliness and awesome power seemed to visibly shine about her like a halo, or rather like the glow from some unseen light. Never have I seen her veiled shape look more terrible than it did *in that space*, while she gathered herself up for vengeance. (174; emphasis added)

Figure 4   "I Saw The Fire Run Up Her Form." Illustration
by Maurice Greiffenhagen taken from the 1919 Longman's edition of *She*.

There are many spectacularly awful scenes in the novel—Holly witnesses
Ayesha ritually curse the Egyptian wife of Kallikrates, controlling a flame of
fire with the movements of her body. (See figure 3.) Later she will actually
bathe in the fire of the Pillar of Life. (See figure 4.) But it is in a court of
law, where "She" sits in judgment, that Holly finds Ayesha most terrifying.

Ironically, it is in that same space that Ayesha appears to stand in for
"civilized" white society, in contradistinction to the cannibalistic and savage
Amahaggars. This scene emphasizes Ayesha's whiteness. (See figure 5.) In
fact, swathed as she is from head to foot, whiteness is her only identifi-
able feature. Ayesha's pose is thoughtful and reflective, while the multitude
before her are described as groveling upon their stomachs. (Those standing
in the illustration are her guards—appropriately also dressed in white—and

Figure 5 "Ayesha Gives Judgment." Illustration taken from
the 1919 Longman's edition of *She* (by Maurice Greiffenhagen
or Charles H. M. Kerr).

the prisoners whom she has commanded to stand.) In this formal legal
proceeding, with evidence given and corroborated and the defendants
given an opportunity to speak, the chaos of the earlier scene governed by
Amahaggar custom (the attempted hot-potting and following mayhem) is
disciplined.

While Ayesha's judgment is harsh (the men are condemned to death),
this outcome should not be all that troubling to Holly, who describes the
defendants as "would-be murderers" and considers them responsible for
the death of Mahomed. Also, while it is true that the men will be tortured,
Holly has emphasized their attempted torture of Mahomed in his own testimony. In fact, while Holly professes to make a plea for mercy for the prisoners, his narrative suggests that he takes more interest in the particular
fall of Ayesha's Greek accent than in the plight of the "knots of evil-doers"
(173). Soon after the prisoners are taken away, he joins Ayesha on a sight-
seeing tour of the caves of Kôr. So what is it that made her so terrible to
Holly in that space?

Upon cross-examination, Holly's horror of Ayesha in the courtroom seems to have nothing to do with the fate of the Amahaggars and everything to do with her position "above them all." From the time of Holly's first acquaintance with Ayesha, he has refused to bow to her authority. He is indignant when Billali tells him that he must crawl on his hands and knees when in her presence: "I was an Englishman, and why, I asked myself, should I creep into the presence of some savage woman? If once I began to creep upon my knees I should always have to do so, and it would be patent acknowledgement of inferiority" (140). As an Englishman, he is confident of his superiority to both Billali, who *does* creep, and to his "savage dusky queen" (138).[20] Similarly, in the courtroom scene, when Ayesha enters and everyone falls to the ground, Holly recounts that he was left standing "like some solitary survivor of a massacre" (171).

Thus, when this white *woman* sits as judge, the seat of judgment becomes barbaric and Holly cannot emphasize enough (he tells us three times in the course of this short narrative) that he sat "at her feet." Unlike the scenes in which Ayesha unveils for Holly, when all of her power is sexual, her power in the courtroom is of a very different nature. Although her garb is a bit peculiar, she too closely resembles those "shes" seeking power in law and society back in England for her position above Holly to be regarded as anything short of terrible.

A reading that focuses only on issues of women and power in this novel, however, would fail to examine what Laura Chrisman describes in her article, "The imperial unconscious? Representations of imperial discourse," as "the multiple dynamics within the text, of gender, 'race,' and a variety of social science discourses, whose intersections are overdetermined by the dictates of a highly problematic imperialism" (42). Edward Said, describing imperialist "structures of attitude and reference," notes the widespread (virtually unanimous, Said argues) nineteenth-century beliefs inherent in cultural discourses that "subject races should be ruled, that they *are* subject races, that one race deserves and has consistently earned the right to be considered the race whose main mission is to expand beyond its own domain" (53). In this context, it is important to explore on cross-examination the meanings of Ayesha not only in her role as a powerful ruling judge and queen, but more specifically in her role as an imperial and *white* ruler.

It is clear that Ayesha is white from the first pages of the novel because the letter from Leo's father that Leo opens on his twenty-fifth birthday emphasizes this point: "[T]he people there [in the land of the Amahaggars] speak a dialect of Arabic, and are ruled over by a *beautiful white woman* who is seldom seen by them, but who is reported to have power over all things living and dead" (28). When Holly first appears before Ayesha, the first thing he sees is "a most beautiful white hand (white as snow)" (142).

Her body is wrapped in a soft, white gauzy material and "one could distinctly see the gleam of the pink flesh beneath [these wrappings]" (142). This white queen rules over a people of a different race, a darker race. Holly describes the Amahaggars as too dark, or rather too yellow, to be Arabs. As one critic comments, "the Amahaggar are portrayed as a bastard race, a degenerate survival from the golden age of Kôr" (Bunn 21). The travelers learn that Ayesha intervenes to stop wars among the Amahaggar tribes. In this way, the text suggests that, like the colonies of England, the Amahaggar tribes benefit from the rule of their queen.

The confrontation between the imperial She and the Amahaggar Ustane provides a rich context in which to explore the complex dynamics of gender, race, and imperialism in the text. When Ayesha hears of the attachment between Ustane and Leo (who Ayesha believes is the reincarnation of her long-lost love Kallikrates), she announces that Ustane must die: "No other woman shall dwell in my Lord's thoughts; my empire shall be my own" (202). Holly, however, persuades Ayesha to spare Ustane's life. When Ustane explains to Ayesha that Leo is her husband—"I took him according to the custom of our country" (205)—Ayesha responds that she has done evil; Ustane has married a man not of her own race, which invalidates the custom. As the Amahaggars are a bastardized race, there clearly is no truth to this statement. It is yet another example of a made-up rule.

And, like Alice, Ustane defies authority and refuses to leave, boldly daring Ayesha, "Destroy me, then, if thou hast the power!" (206). In a rage, Ayesha strikes Ustane on the head, leaving three finger-marks across her bronze tresses, and the marks were "white as snow" (206). Holly staggers back in horror and the marks strike terror in Ustane's heart: "Utterly awed and broken down, the poor creature rose, and, marked with that awful mark, crept from the room sobbing bitterly" (207). While this scene may be read as two women fighting over a man, the emphasis on customs and rights in their exchange suggests that much more is at stake. Ustane is standing up for the integrity of her customs; moreover, she is refusing to let Ayesha deny her the only power that she has been granted as a woman in her society—the power to choose a husband. But the "civilized" Ayesha has no respect for "savage" ways, and when an Amahaggar stands up for her customs and rights, this imperial queen blasts her into submission with a fierce display of white power. A few pages later, when Ustane returns again to claim Leo, Ayesha murders her in cold blood.

While Ustane is presented heroically in this imperial romance, it is simply shocking the way the Englishmen so easily accept her death. Leo and Holly witness the murder, and while Leo immediately springs at Ayesha in a rage, moments later, "with the corpse of his dead love [Ustane] for an altar, did Leo Vincey plight his troth to her red-handed murdress—plight it for ever and a day" (230). That evening, racked with remorse over Ustane's murder, Leo admits an insatiable desire for Ayesha, and Holly comments that Leo, despite his shame and grief, would have been mad "to entertain the idea of running away from his extraordinary fortune" in being the object of Ayesha's devotion (243).[21] In his article "Victorians and Africans: The Genealogy of the Myth of the Dark Continent," Patrick Brantlinger discusses late-nineteenth-century scientific justifications offered by eugenicists and social Darwinists, not only for imperialism, but also for genocide. Arguing that these two ideas were inseparable, Brantlinger comments that "whereas imperialism could be lavishly praised in public, open support for the liquidation of 'inferior' races was another matter" (205).[22] In the novel, Ustane's murder represents this unspeakable side of imperialism, and a troubling footnote that Holly adds to his manuscript months after he has completed it enacts the justifications of genocide that were the subtext of the social discourse of Empire.

In Holly's manuscript, after recounting Ustane's murder and describing Ayesha as "a mysterious creature of evil tendencies," Holly adds:

> After some months of consideration of this statement I am bound to confess that I am not quite satisfied of its truth. It is perfectly true that Ayesha committed a murder, but I shrewdly suspect that, were we endowed with the same absolute power, and if we had the same tremendous interest at stake, we should be very apt to do likewise in parallel circumstances. (242)

Ayesha's "tremendous interest" was her empire, both Kallikrates ("my empire shall be my own") and her African empire (202). Months later, back in England and far removed from the dead body of Ustane, Holly recharacterizes Ayesha as justified (she had so much at stake) rather than evil. Edward Said sees in British literature a "consistency of concern . . . that fixes socially desirable, empowered space in metropolitan England or Europe and connects it by design, motive, and developments to distant or peripheral worlds (Ireland, Venice, Africa, Jamaica), conceived of as desirable but subordinate. And with these meticulously maintained references come attitudes—about rule, control, profit and enhancement and suitability . . ." (52). One wonders what structures of attitude and reference become culturally encoded when murders of "subject races" are so readily excused in the name of the tremendous interest of empire.[23]

Near the end of the novel, Ayesha says that they must travel to England to "live as it becometh us to live" (254). They shall overthrow Queen Victoria and destroy any tyrants who will stand in the way of Kallikrates' (and her own) rule. Holly informs her that "in England 'blasting' was not an amusement that could be indulged in with impunity, and that any such attempt would meet with the consideration of the law and probably end upon a scaffold" (255). She responds, laughing with scorn, "The law . . . the law! Canst thou not understand, oh Holly, that I am above the law, and so shall my Kallikrates be also?" (255). While confessing that it made him "absolutely shudder to think what would be the result of her arrival there [in England]," Holly ultimately concludes that an all-powerful British Empire would be worth the great cost, including, it seems, the "terrible sacrifice of life" that the text has rehearsed in Ayesha's blasting of Ustane:

> In the end she would, I had little doubt, assume absolute rule over the British dominions, and probably over the whole earth, and, though I was sure that she would speedily make ours the most glorious and prosperous empire that the world has ever seen, it would be at the cost of a terrible sacrifice of life. . . . What was the meaning of it all? After much thinking I could only conclude that this wonderful creature . . . was now about to be used by Providence as a means to change the order of the world, and possibly, by the building up of a power that could no more be rebelled against or questioned than the decrees of Fate, to change it materially for the better. (256)

But while Holly's (Britain's) unbridled lust for power may be acceptable (the desire to "make *ours* the most glorious and prosperous empire that the world has ever seen" [256; emphasis added]), an all-powerful She is not. As Gilbert explains, Ayesha had to be destroyed by the Pillar of Life, the "fiery signifier whose eternal thundering return speaks the inexorability of the patriarchal Law She has violated in her satanically overreaching ambition" (130). As figuratively played out in the courtroom scene, where She sat above them all, Ayesha's opposition to "the eternal [patriarchal] Law" had to be foreclosed (295). Even in the context of Empire, She was too much of an exception. And with Ayesha's devolution at the end of the novel from "the loveliest, noblest, most splendid woman the world has ever seen" (294) into literally a "hideous little monkey frame" (295), the text spectacularly clarifies that, ultimately, "She" is not a "person."

Mary Slessor

White Queen of the Okoyong

It seems a sudden shift from a raven-haired beauty with serpent-like grace, sharing fruit and conversation with an English gentleman, to a red-headed missionary making her way barefoot through the African bush; from the imaginary land of imperial Kôr and the Amahaggars, to the real world of imperial England and the Okoyong; from the pages of an eroticized imperial romance to accounts of the life of a missionary and magistrate. However, the fictional Ayesha and the real-life Mary Slessor both ruled in Africa as "white queens" and judges, their rules in flagrant violation of the rules about women in public, political, and legal roles that were being so vehemently defended and enforced back in Britain. Representations of Slessor, like those of Ayesha and other exceptional "shes," were overdetermined and inherently contradictory. A cross-examination of the accounts of Slessor's real-life experiences, especially in her capacity as an appointed magistrate of the British government, brings to light compelling additional testimony concerning women, law, and power in the late nineteenth century.

In 1876, Slessor sailed from Scotland, leaving behind a childhood clouded by extreme poverty and violence, to become a missionary in the Calabar region of Eastern Nigeria. It had been a dream of Slessor's mother that one of her sons be a missionary in Africa, but when all of her sons died, she supported Mary's desire to follow in the footsteps of Dr. David Livingstone, hero to both mother and daughter. After serving for twelve years in the base missionaries in Duke Town, Old Town, and Creek Town, Slessor was transferred inland, at her request, to live with the Okoyong. It took more than two years for her to persuade the mission officials to let her live with the Okoyong tribe, where it was rumored that "old customs when women were flogged to death for trivial offenses, branded with smouldering sticks like cattle, and dragged screaming to be buried with a chief" still prevailed (Buchan 82). Slessor's friends were "horrified" and tried to dissuade her, as did a group of traders who claimed the Okoyong were more in need of a gun-boat than a missionary (Buchan 87).

All such reports must be read within the context of the imperialist structures of attitude and reference that informed them, and with the understanding that with no writing back from the Okoyong, we have only one-sided accounts. While we cannot assess the actual threat to Slessor's safety, if any, posed by the Okoyong, we do know that Slessor's move—a woman going alone to live with an African tribe—was unprecedented.

Slessor lived with the Okoyong from 1888 to 1902.[24] During that time, she gained a reputation that was legendary in the Calabar region, and her fame soon spread to Britain. Mary Kingsley, who made a special trip to meet her, wrote the following in her 1897 travel narrative *Travels in West Africa:*

> Her great abilities, both physical and intellectual, have given her among the
> savage tribe an unique position, and won her, from white and black who

know her, a profound esteem. Her knowledge of the native, his language, his ways of thought, his diseases, his difficulties, and all that is his, is extraordinary, and the amount of good she has done, no man can fully estimate. (19)

While many tales of Slessor and the Okoyong circulated, I would like to focus on two particular narratives: the first is an account of Slessor in her position as Her Majesty's Vice-Consul and District Magistrate; the second comes from Kingsley's *Travels in West Africa*.[25]

In 1890, Sir Claude Macdonald was appointed Her Majesty's Special Commissioner and Consul-General and, in an effort to expand the authority of the British government in the Calabar region, he began to appoint vice-consuls to supervise native courts. Because of her knowledge of the customs and laws of the Okoyong, Macdonald sought to appoint Slessor as vice-consul and district magistrate. This was not a popular decision. Slessor's missionary colleagues criticized her for being so involved with government affairs; moreover, Caroline Oliver remarks that her colleagues "were shocked at her involving herself in anything so heathen and sometimes obscene as native customs" (120). Some members of the government were not too pleased either. Oliver reports that Sir Clement Hill at the Foreign Office "was outraged at the idea of a woman holding such a office . . ." (120).

Nevertheless, Slessor was offered and accepted the appointment and presided over the local Okoyong courts within the context of the Doctrine of Repugnancy, which "recognized native law and custom except insofar as they were repugnant to civilised standards of natural law and justice" (Oliver 120). A well-known account of Slessor is T. D. Maxwell's description of her presiding over the Okoyong court. He was the Chief Magistrate at Calabar and was visiting in an official capacity. He relates the following first impression of Slessor:

> What sort of woman I expected to see I hardly know; certainly not what I did. A little frail old lady with a lace or lace-like shawl over her head and shoulders (that must, I think, have been a concession to a stranger, for I never saw the thing again), swaying herself in a rocking-chair and crooning to a black baby in her arms. (qtd. in Livingstone, *Mary Slessor of Calabar* 129)[26]

Maxwell had traveled to see the first woman in the British Empire to be appointed a magistrate, a lay position that carried an enormous amount of real legal power, especially in the colonies. A woman in her position must have been almost impossible for him to imagine, as he makes clear. As with Holly's description of Ayesha in the courtroom, Maxwell cannot imagine a woman "in that space."

The rest of Maxwell's description is his attempt to negotiate the cultural paradox of Slessor as magistrate, and to do so he calls on various images of women. In the end, however, these representations do not add up to any coherent picture. At first, he describes her as a "little frail old lady" in a rocker (much like Helene Vacaresco's description of Queen Victoria). This is a very strange description of a woman in her early forties who, pictures show, had not aged prematurely. He also, however, presents her as a mother figure; she is crooning to a baby in her arms. Later, the queen/mother image conflates as he describes Slessor taking her position at the front of the court, "surrounded by several ladies- and babies-in-waiting" (129).

Then the description abruptly shifts; there is a change in both the tone of the passage and the presentation of Slessor. Maxwell reports as follows:

> Suddenly she jumped up with an angry growl: her shawl fell off, the baby was hurriedly transferred to some one [*sic*] qualified to hold it, and with a few trenchant words she made for the door where a hulking, overdressed native stood. In a moment she seized him by the scruff of the neck, boxed his ears, and hustled him out into the yard. . . . (130)

This is the same "little frail old lady" he was describing only a few sentences before; now she is manhandling a hulking "local monarch of sorts" (130). It is as if Maxwell suddenly remembers that he is describing a vice-consul of the British Crown. As such, neither an old woman nor a mother seems appropriate. Instead, he needs to show her as a powerful representative of the British government who is capable of using whatever means necessary to keep order; she is commended for using violence against one who had "defied her orders" (130).

But only a few lines later, he is again undercutting Slessor's authority by suggesting that her court and her brand of justice are outside the "real" realm of law. Beginning with what sounds like high praise ("I have had a good deal of experience of Nigerian Courts of various kinds, but have never met one which better deserves to be termed a Court of Justice than that over which she presided"), he then comments that the "litigants emphatically got justice—sometimes, perhaps, like Shylock, 'more than they desired'—and it was essential justice unhampered by legal technicalities" (130). Of course, Shylock's justice came at the hands of Portia, suggesting that Maxwell's assessment is influenced by the gender of this particular magistrate. In any event, it is certainly peculiar for a chief magistrate (one who handles appeals) to seem unconcerned that one of the courts under his jurisdiction is "unhampered by legal technicalities." Either the fact that the litigants are members of the Okoyong tribe or the fact that the magistrate is a woman (or, most likely, some combination of the two) led him to consider this amazing admission of little consequence.

In many respects, Maxwell seems unable to take Slessor or the business of her court seriously. In another example he provides of one of Slessor's judicial decisions, he portrays her more like a mother resolving a squabble among children than a magistrate settling disputes among litigants:

> A sued B for a small debt. B admitted owing the money, and the Court (that is "Ma") ordered him to pay accordingly: but she added, "A is a rascal. He treats his mother shamefully, he neglects his children, only the other day he beat one of his wives with quite unnecessary vehemence, yes and she was B's sister too, his farm is a disgrace, he seldom washes. . . . On the other hand, B was thrifty and respectable, so before B paid the amount due he would give A a good sound caning in the presence of everybody." (130)

Unfortunately, we do not know A's or B's side of the story or how the "local monarch of sorts" felt about Slessor's adjudicative style or British justice in general. A cross-examination of Maxwell's testimony, however, does illuminate the fact that a high-ranking official in the British government viewed the Okoyong people as unruly children, undeserving of names, and as sources of comic relief. Both Slessor and the Okoyong are demeaned by this testimony because, by suggesting that she is not a "real" judge, it also implies that the problems of the Okoyong are not of sufficient import to require one. Of course, it is important to acknowledge that A, B, and the local monarch were not given the choice of rejecting all forms of British judgment and authority. Also, apparently uncomfortable designating Slessor as "the Court," Maxwell inserts the parenthetical "that is 'Ma,'" which works to enhance the image of mother and children playing law.

While she was often referred to as "Ma," another of Slessor's familiar titles was the "White Queen of the Okoyong." Working both to negotiate and obscure the complexity of Slessor's position (in terms of gender, race, and power), this name was particularly popular among the white men's clubs in Africa (Oliver 135–36).[27] Much more acceptable as "Ma," a "pioneer missionary," or even "a white queen," Slessor's identity as a woman with real legal power was effectively *un*represented.[28]

As a final comment on Slessor, it is interesting to see what another atypical nineteenth-century woman had to say about her. Mary Kingsley, who traveled through Africa "as a lone she-wolf," provides an account of Slessor that serves in certain respects as a cross-examination of Maxwell's account (Huxley 5).[29] Kingsley is most interested in Slessor's work in saving twin babies, who, she explains, were believed to be evil.[30] Visiting after Maxwell, she describes the following incident that took place while she was with Slessor:

> Miss Slessor had heard of the twins' arrival and had started off, barefooted and bareheaded, at that pace she can go down a bush path. By the time she had gone four miles she met the procession, the [mother] coming to her and all the rest of the village yelling and howling behind her. On the top of her head was the gin-case, into which the children had been stuffed. . . . Needless to say, on arriving Miss Slessor took charge of affairs, relieving the unfortunate, weak, staggering woman from her load and carrying it herself, for no one else would touch it, or anything belonging to those awful twin things. . . . (189)

In this account, Slessor is no frail woman in a rocker, but a woman able to race more than four miles through a bush path, barefooted, and then take on a heavy load and walk back. Kingsley reports that, on the way home, Slessor waited while the villagers cut a new path to her house because she knew that if she took the twins down the main market road it would never be used again (189–90). While much can be said about Slessor's "interference" with tribal laws and customs, Kingsley's representation does work to discredit any implication in Maxwell's testimony that Slessor does not take the Okoyong people and their beliefs seriously.

Kingsley does not mention that Slessor is a magistrate (however, she also does not mention that she is a missionary). Rather than referring to her as "Ma" or a "white queen," she claims that Slessor "rules" the Okoyong "as a white chief" (19). While the idea of white superiority is very prevalent in Kingsley's account, it is interesting that she represents Slessor in a male role. Kingsley concludes her narrative on Slessor by noting, "This instance of what one white can do would give many important lessons in West Coast administration and development. Only the sort of *man* Miss Slessor represents is rare" (19; emphasis added).

In the nineteenth century, figures like Miss Slessor were difficult to represent. The identities available to women were not adequate to represent women in politically powerful positions. In an effort not to diminish what she saw as the importance of Slessor's work and accomplishments—her *real* power—Kingsley apparently decides that the only way to imply the true nature of Slessor's power is to refer to her as a "man."

Women in the Legal Profession

"She" Makes It

While Slessor was handing out justice a continent away, women in Britain were still trying to get a foot in the door. In 1903, Bertha Cave applied to be called to the Bar of Gray's Inn. When the Benchers of the Inn refused her admission, she appealed their decision. It took a special tribunal (composed of the Lord Chancellor, the Lord Chief Justice, and five other justices) just five minutes to determine that there was no precedent for ladies being called to the English Bar and to aver their unwillingness to establish one (*The Law Times* 107).[31]

In December of 1912 Miss Bebb, after completing her studies at Oxford University, submitted notice to the Law Society of her intention to sit for their February examination and enclosed the required fee. As had happened in the late 1870s, the Law Society told her not to present herself for examination, "giving the reason that she was a woman" (*Bebb v. Law Society* 286). However, much had changed since those earlier petitions. Women in Britain had been actively fighting for greater rights and powers under the law, and in 1913, Bebb's case was championed and supported by several feminist groups.[32] Bebb brought a lawsuit against the Law Society in 1914, asking the court to declare that she was a "person" within the meaning of the 1843 Solicitors Act (6 & 7 Vict., c. 73) and therefore should be allowed to practice law.

The arguments in this case will sound familiar. Bebb's attorney offered examples of many public offices held by women—Keeper of the Great Seal, Constable of England, Marshal and Great Chamberlain, governess of a workhouse, sexton, churchwarden—and, of course, "there have been Queens of England" (287). He also offered specific evidence that women, in England in the past, had acted as attorneys.[33] Finally, he quoted the Solicitors Act itself, which provided that any "person" complying with specified conditions was entitled to be admitted as a solicitor—Bebb met all of the qualifications and thus was such a person. The Solicitors Act even included a provision stating that words importing the masculine gender also were to apply to a female unless "there be something in the subject or context repugnant to such construction" (s. 48).

Arguing that "[e]ver since attorneys have been established as a profession, women have been deemed disqualified to act as attorneys," the defense did find it repugnant to construe the statute to include Bebb as a "person" (*Bebb* 290). And, of course, they confidently invoked that popular refrain, "The practice which has been followed for hundreds of years is a conclusive answer to the appellant's claim" (289).

The Court of Appeals agreed with the defense, citing the unimpeachable Lord Coke as its primary authority: "Lord Coke . . . 300 years ago said that a woman is not allowed to be an attorney. . . . [A]nd the opinion of Lord Coke on the question of what or what is not the common law is one which requires no sanction from anybody else" (*Bebb*, Cozens-Hardy opinion 293–94). In light of this common-law tradition, the judge dismissed the examples offered by Bebb's attorney of the many public offices that women had held in the past as "a most interesting discussion as to what women can do" but "beside the mark" (294). One of the other appellate judges, quoting *Chorlton* as quoted in *Jex-Blake*, reiterated the passage about exceptional instances being of "comparatively little weight, as opposed to uninterrupted usage to the contrary for several centuries" (*Bebb*, Swinfen opinion 296).

Finally, Judge Phillimore, after paying due homage to Coke—"He is only a witness, no doubt, as to the common law, but he is a witness of the highest authority" (298)—"explained" away the exceptions to uninterrupted usage offered by Bebb's attorney as follows: "The cases as to women holding certain parochial offices have been distinguished, on the very occasions when the possibility of their holding them has been upheld, on the ground of there being offices which, in the view of the Courts, were suitable to women" (298–99). Statements such as this clarify the role that judges could play in reinforcing and tailoring cultural gender roles. For, Phillimore acknowledged, uninterrupted usage has been interrupted—not only through legislative initiatives, but also by judges—but *only* when the exceptions have been judged "suitable." Stuttering over his own written words, Phillimore fumbled through the rest of this discussion ("I do not say . . . what I say is . . ."), at last resorting to a common and "safe" legal out: "The cases as to parochial offices may stand on their own merits; they have really no bearing on this case" (299). Thus, the evidence that called into question the common-law tradition was dismissed as irrelevant.

After Bebb was denied status as a "person" under the Solicitors Act, a Committee for the Admission of Women to the Solicitors' Profession enlisted the support of the Lord Chancellor and the government, and a bill was introduced to enable women to become solicitors. The Law Society opposed this legislation, but the outbreak of World War I put the issue temporarily on hold (Birks 277).

In both 1917 and 1918, Lord Buckmaster introduced bills to admit women to the legal profession, but the bills were opposed by both the Law Society and the Bar. After women's substantial contributions to the war effort, however, there was wide support for feminist initiatives, and when in 1919 it became clear that there was strong government backing for opening up the legal profession to women, the Law Society voted to remove all obstacles that kept women from practicing (Abel-Smith and Stevens 193). Later that same year, the Sex Disqualification (Removal) Act (9 & 10 Geo. 5, c. 71) was passed, expressly permitting women who had received a law degree, or whose studies entitled them to one, to serve articles and be admitted and enrolled as solicitors. This Act further provided that

> A person shall not be disqualified by sex or marriage from the exercise of any public function, or from being appointed to or holding any civil or judicial office or post, or from entering or assuming or carrying on any civil profession or vocation, or for admission to any incorporated society . . . and a person shall not be exempted by sex or marriage from the liability to serve as juror. (s. 1)

Thus, women also were admitted to the Inns of Court.[34]

Carrie Morrison became the first woman to be admitted as a solicitor in 1922.[35] In that same year, Ivy Williams became the first woman called to the Bar.[36] Cornelia Sorabji, an Indian woman who studied law at Somerville College, Oxford from 1889–92, also qualified for the bar in 1922. By the 1930s, she was an internationally known barrister (Burton 4).[37] As discussed in the Introduction, Helena Florence Normanton was the first woman barrister to practice in England, being briefed at the High Court of Justice in 1922 and the Old Bailey (Central Criminal Court) in 1924 (Lang 166). In the political realm, the 1918 Representation of the People Act (7 & 8 Geo. 5, c. 64) gave women over thirty who either were householders or wives of householders, or had an university education, the right to vote.[38] The 1918 Parliament (Qualification of Women) Act (8 & 9 Geo. 5, c. 47) granted women the right to be elected, sit, and vote as a member of the Commons House of Parliament.[39] In 1919, Nancy Astor became the first woman to sit in the House of Commons. Women were not granted the right to sit in the House of Lords until 1958.[40] Margaret Bondfield became the first woman Cabinet member when she was appointed Minister of Labour in 1929. In 1962, Elizabeth Lane became the first woman appointed as judge in Britain when Lord Chancellor Dilhorne appointed her to the County Court Bench. In 1965, she was appointed to the High Court Bench.[41] Lane tells her own story in *Hear the Other Side: The Autobiography of England's First Woman Judge* (1985). At long last, women in powerful legal and political roles were able to judge for themselves how they might best be represented.[42]

When Holly is first brought into Ayesha's apartments and feels her gaze sinking through and through him from behind the curtain, he ponders: "Who could be behind it?—some naked savage queen, a languishing Oriental beauty, or a nineteenth-century young lady, drinking afternoon tea? I had not the slightest idea, and should not have been astonished at seeing any of the three" (Haggard, *She* 141). Similarly, T. D. Maxwell had no idea what to expect of Slessor: "What sort of woman I expected to see I hardly know" (Livingstone, *Mary Slessor of Calabar* 129). In the late nineteenth century, because women allegedly had no "public functions," because women under laws conferring power were not "persons," it is no surprise that Holly and Maxwell had no idea what to expect when about to come face to face with these "exceptional" women.

Munich has argued that the "cultural paradox of Queen Victoria's specific kind of monarchy—the apparent contradiction of a devoted wife, prolific mother, and extravagant widow who is also Queen of an Empire upon which the sun never sets" (265) resulted in "a fragmentation of symbolization, representations in which all possibilities are entertained . . . the representation of excess or the excess of representation" (268–69). Similarly, in trying to represent Ayesha and Slessor, their narrators respond with a plethora of often contradictory images. Holly, over the course of his narrative, presents Ayesha as all of the possibilities he had imagined. She is, at various times, naked, savage, a queen, languishing, Oriental (in Saidian terms), a beauty, young (or at least young-looking), and a lady. What a cross-examination of Holly's narrative testimony illuminates is the importance of context to his choice of representations. When he is alone and flirting with Ayesha, she "is the incarnation of lovely tempting womanhood" (189); moreover, nakedness does not imply savagery. When she mourns Kallikrates, she is "only a woman" (157). But when Ayesha is presiding over a court of law, exercising the "cold *power* of judgment," She becomes "icily terrible" (189; emphasis added).

Maxwell also responds to the unorthodox Slessor with a superfluity of representations. In the space of two pages, he presents her as young and old, fierce and docile, maternal and childish. Ultimately, taking into account the context of his visit, which was to review the performance of one of the British government's appointed magistrates, he opts for presenting a maternal image, "the Court (that is 'Ma')" presiding over infantalized Africans (possibly drawing on the strength of that image from the anomalous royal Court of Queen Victoria).

In the "person" cases, Lord Coke was the star witness, bearing testimony over the centuries as to women's uninterrupted and thus "rightfully" continued exclusion from public, political, and professional roles. Reading these legal decisions through the lens of feminist jurisprudence—which tells us to question everything, especially received doctrine—we can see clearly that the judges, while literally sitting in judgment, were also very much passing judgment upon those "shes" whom they believed to be overreaching in their ambitions. Other legal and literary texts present similar judgments of exceptional women like Ayesha and Slessor. A cross-examination of the testimony of Victorian witnesses like Holly and Maxwell reveals chaotic attempts at the level of narrative to control these increasingly threatening, oversized Alices.

CHAPTER 5

Appealing Women

Late-Century Publication of Private Wrongs

appeal

3.a. The transference of a case from an inferior to a higher court or tribunal, in the hope of reversing or modifying the decision of the former . . . 5. A call for help of any kind, or for a favour; an earnest request; an entreaty. . . . 6.a. Language specifically addressed *to*, or adopted to exert influence *upon*, some particular principle of conduct, mental faculty, or class of persons. . . .

—*Oxford English Dictionary*

"For heavens sake do move Heaven and Earth to get the Lunacy Laws reformed" is the desperate appeal that Georgina Weldon wrote to Prime Minister Gladstone on April 15, 1878. Barricaded in a room in her own home, she was trying to keep from being forcibly removed to an asylum for the insane. As she goes on to explain to Gladstone:

> Mrs. Lowe (the secretary for the Lunacy Law Commission) was sent on to me in consequence of a letter I had written W. Harrison the Editor of the *Spiritualist*, she is here, she has barricaded me in and is I hope going to take the lot off to Hunter St. Police station!—But *do* for God's sake, W. Gladstone, have this seen to at once . . . It appears the Law affords me no protection, that any spiteful person who will bribe two blackguard Doctors to swear I am mad may procure a warrant and come in my own home and carry me off. . . . (Weldon, Letter to Gladstone)

Weldon was certainly right about the state of the law in 1878, and were it not for her indomitable pluck and loud public protests, she might very well have spent the rest of her years behind closed doors—her appeals forever silenced.

In this chapter, I present several Victorian women like Weldon who engaged in what today we would call consciousness-raising, a feminist legal method that emphasizes the importance of publicizing private wrongs. Legal scholar Leslie Bender describes consciousness-raising as "a process of educating and exposing one another to the subtleties and harms of patriarchy," a process by which "[w]hat were experienced as personal hurts individually suffered reveal themselves as a collective experience of oppression" (9). This feminist legal method "offers a means of testing the validity of accepted legal principles through the lens of the personal experience of those directly affected by those principles" (Bartlett, "Feminist Legal Methods" 837) The consciousness-raising championed by Catharine MacKinnon in the 1970s involved the sharing of unspoken and hitherto unspeakable details of women's private lives in small groups (airing the Gothic). To be most effective, however, Bender contends that this "subversive and transformative" practice also must include "bearing witness to evidences of patriarchy as they occur, through unremitting dialogues with and challenges to the patriarchs, and through the popular media, the arts, politics, lobbying, and even litigation" (10). The women I discuss in this chapter pled their cases in this wide array of forums, calling for the reversal and modification of court decisions, earnestly requesting opportunities to testify on their own behalf, and using language in such a way as to create knowledge and understanding of women's perspectives on legal matters. They performed feminist jurisprudence with appeals that were both subversive and transformative.

"A sort of legal *Donna Quixote*"

Georgina Weldon's Multiple Appeals

Georgina Weldon was soon to learn that her husband Harry was responsible for her near-abduction by the asylum attendants. Harry, from whom she had been separated for three years, had requested his old friend Sir Henry de Bathe to sign an order under the Lunacy Acts to commit her to a private asylum run by Doctors Winn and Winslow. There was a real financial benefit to Harry of putting Weldon away. Their separation arrangement at the time gave her £1000 per year and possession of Tavistock House. The costs to Harry of keeping her in Winslow's institution would have been

$400 a year. Winslow later testified that he had suggested to Harry that it might be best for Weldon to be cared for by a companion, but that Harry had thought institutionalization would be best ("Weldon v. Semple," 12 July 1884, 6). While Harry signed a statement of facts describing behavior that was supposed to support her commitment, he could not sign the actual order because he had not seen her within the past month. At Harry's request, de Bathe, who previously had not seen Weldon for more than a year, stopped by her home to visit her for about an hour and then signed the commitment order.

Also, on April 14, 1878, Weldon had been visited by Winn and Winslow, who had introduced themselves as Mr. Shell and Mr. Stewart and claimed to be spiritualists who were interested in placing some children in the orphanage that Weldon operated.[1] They spoke to her for about thirty minutes. Later that same day, two other men who claimed to be from Shell and Stewart (who turned out to be Drs. Rutherford and Semple) also visited Weldon. The law required two certificates, each signed by a different doctor, to commit someone to an asylum. Based on a short conversation with her, Rutherford and Semple each certified to her insanity, making her husband's attempt to institutionalize her perfectly legal.

The next day a man and two women from Winslow's asylum came to Weldon's home, and the two women, in response to the man's cry, "Take her," grabbed Weldon and tried to remove her physically from the house. That was when she broke loose, ran to her room, and locked herself in. These attendants from the asylum remained in her house for almost five hours. Finally, after they had gone, with the help of Mrs. Lowe and faithful servants, Weldon escaped from her home and took refuge with friends. Before coming out into the open (she waited one month until the order had expired), she wisely had herself examined by two doctors who declared her perfectly sane. And thus with characteristic panache, Weldon catapulted herself to the forefront of the campaign to reform the lunacy laws.[2]

For the next four years, she told her story to anyone who would listen. In 1879, she published *How I Escaped the Mad Doctors;* she was a popular lecturer for the Lunacy Law Amendment Society; and every Tuesday afternoon and Wednesday evening she held widely publicized "at homes" at Tavistock House to raise money for Lunacy Law reform.[3] At these "intimate entertainments," Weldon read from *How I Escaped the Mad Doctors* and provided musical entertainment (Grierson 176). On the back of the tickets to these public meetings, she clarified their purpose: "Mrs. Weldon gives these Lectures on the principle that 'a drop of water will wear away a stone.' Although her room can hold but 250 persons, still she hopes that her limited public may unite with her in doing all they can towards LUNACY

LAW REFORM . . ." (Grierson 176). In this way, Weldon sought to make public this hitherto private issue, and she relentlessly pursued this campaign in spite of numerous threats and attempts literally to shut her up.

A chilling letter written by one of Harry's legal advisors one month after the failed attempt to institutionalize Weldon is evidence of the immense power the law gave husbands to silence troublesome wives. On May 15, 1878, Harry was offered the following legal insights:

> I suggest that . . . an offer should be made to Mrs. Weldon that if she would go quietly to Tavistock House and remain there, she should not be sent to an asylum, and that she should have the children [the orphans] sent for from France to be with her, but she would be required to submit to some conditions; in particular that she must abstain from writing to the papers or circulating defamatory statements or initiating any legal proceedings or prosecutions, except they were sanctioned by you. . . .
>
> I think it would not be at all desirable to enter at all with Mrs. Weldon into the question of personal restraint. She would probably be ignorant, and her chief advisor, Mrs. Lowe, is also apparently ignorant, that it is quite within your legal power to apply any means of restraint that might be necessary in your own house without any papers, and therefore she would perhaps be satisfied with the pledge that she should not be taken to an asylum; and if she once returned to Tavistock House and you retained possession, you would be free to apply restraint if needful. . . . (qtd. in Treherne 69–70)

In short, the legal position was that if Weldon would not agree to return to her proper sphere ("to go back quietly to Tavistock House and remain there") and role (to care for the children), and to keep quiet, her husband could threaten and, if need be, force her into submission (although it was prudent not to publicize or even speak of such tactics). Unlike many Victorian women who effectively were restrained in word and action by such threats, Weldon "escaped" and proceeded to do all that Harry and his legal advisor feared she might.[4]

She wrote to the papers, the first installment of "Our Lunacy Laws: The Story of Mrs. Weldon, written by Herself" appearing in the London *Figaro* in December of 1878. In response, Harry and de Bathe sued James Mortimer, the publisher of the *Figaro*, for libel. The newspaper clarified its reason for publishing Weldon's narrative as follows:

> [O]ur sole object in publishing Mrs. Weldon's story had been, and is, to permit a defenceless woman whom we sincerely believe to have been cruelly misrepresented and ill-used an opportunity of vindicating herself before

the public . . . We utterly disclaim all malice in the publication, and we are
actuated solely and exclusively by a sense of public duty, and the conviction
that great wrongs are perpetrated under the present Lunacy Laws of England. (qtd. in Treherne 81)

Despite this defense, Mortimer was sentenced to three months' imprisonment in Holloway Gaol. Weldon would have much preferred to be sued
herself because, in her opinion, the trial received far too little publicity.
She wrote in her diary the day after the trial was held, "Astonished beyond
measure to find that the *Figaro* trial took place yesterday. Of course it went
as I prophesied it would. All hushed up" (Treherne 83). Weldon understood
that hushing up private wrongs suffered by women perpetuated women's
oppression. Undaunted by the law's threats or its punishments, Weldon
herself was imprisoned for libel—twice. Determined to have her say, she
spent five weeks in Newgate prison in 1880 (Treherne 86), and six months
at Holloway Gaol in 1885 (Grierson 241).

Weldon wanted to change the lunacy laws to keep others from suffering the fate from which she had so narrowly escaped; she also, however, wanted to have those people who had accused her of being insane
judged—and judged wrong. Although a vitriolic critic of the legal system,
Weldon wanted the law—with its public and authoritative claim to "truth"—
to pronounce her perfectly sane; she wanted her day in court. While she
tried many times to initiate precisely the type of legal proceedings that
Weldon's lawyer had sought to forestall, the government would not prosecute. The *London Times* reports on October 7, 1878 that Mrs. Weldon
"appealed to Mr. Flowers [the magistrate] to assist her, by granting sum-
monses for conspiracy or otherwise, in getting a public inquiry into the
circumstances which led to her being nearly arrested and forcibly taken to
a lunatic asylum . . ." ("Police" 12). Seven days later, the *Times* reports that,
upon reviewing a written statement that he had asked Weldon to prepare,
Flowers had informed her that "it would be better to place the matter in
the hands of her legal advisers" ("Police," 14 Oct. 1878, 12). Of course, as
a married woman under coverture, she was unable to bring the kind of
civil suit that Flowers was suggesting (it would be absurd to suggest that
Harry would bring a suit on her behalf in this matter). The magistrate thus
presented her with no legal remedy.

It also became apparent that, despite her urgent and compelling appeal
to Gladstone, she would not be receiving any help from high places.
On November 6, 1878, the *Times* published two letters that Weldon had
received from Gladstone (which she probably provided the newspaper in
yet another attempt to gain publicity for her cause). In the first of these let-

ters, dated April 27, 1878, most likely written in response to her missive on the night of Harry's thwarted plot, Gladstone wrote, "I am afraid the only good office I could offer would be to bring any statement under the notice of the Lunacy Commission. The alteration of the laws would be a task for which my antecedent experience has given me no qualifications; and perhaps I ought to add that I do not gather distinctly in what points they ought to be amended" ("Lunacy Laws" 9).[5] The second note, dated June 29, 1878, clarified that she could expect no help from the Lunacy Commission on this issue:

> I forwarded your statement to Lord Shaftesbury personally, and I am assured that it will be duly considered. It seemed to me doubtful whether most of the statements it contained would fall within the domain of the Commissioners, and the answer I received last night was to this effect. It does not appear that they are able to found upon it any suggestion for the amendment of the Lunacy Law. ("Lunacy Laws" 9)[6]

Weldon's narrative of her own experiences, her recounting of the real-life effects of the law, fell outside the purview of the government body commissioned to administer the law; the harm she suffered suggested no need for reform.

By August of 1879, the *Times* reported the following incident:

> Mrs. Weldon attended before Mr. Mansfield [a magistrate] and made a statement about certain grievances. She said she would, if the magistrate wished it, go into a full statement of the matter, her object being to get the magistrate's advice. Mr. Mansfield said the best advice he could give the applicant was *to keep herself as quiet as she possibly could.* ("Police" 12; emphasis added)

The law was tired of listening to her story, and living under coverture, she could bring no legal action on her own.

Then the Married Women's Property Act of 1882 was passed, giving a married woman the right to sue on her own behalf. The law came into effect in January of 1883, and in September of that same year, Weldon sued Drs. Winslow, Rutherford, and Semple, Harry Weldon and his solicitor Neal, and Sir Henry de Bathe. She also sued several newspapers for libel. Serving as her own attorney, she soon had initiated seventeen separate actions. She rented an office in Red Lion Court, near the Royal Courts of Justice, and hired a retired solicitor, Mr. W. Chaffers, to help her draw up the pleadings (Grierson 204). Brian Thompson reports that "from 1883 until the end of the century, she brought over a hundred cases before the courts" (258). As Edward Grierson notes, that she handled all of these proceedings, all but single-handedly, was amazing. But, he reports, "she thrived on them, and it is as a lawyer that she chiefly deserves to be remembered: not the first but certainly the most effective woman advocate before the coming of the professional . . ." (226).[7] Indeed, when Helena Normanton was admitted to Middle Temple in 1919, the *Evening News* in describing other women legal pioneers reported, "Among other litigants who have moved pudges [*sic*] and juries, the name of Mrs. Weldon stands out. She won verdict after verdict in the 'eighties'" ("Sister Buzfuz").

Just as twentieth-century feminist legal scholars and litigators struggled to raise awareness of the real harm of sexual harassment, Weldon worked to publicize injustices under the lunacy laws. First in her writing and speaking, and then in her courtroom appearances, she "gave formerly private and hidden experience a public dimension and so legitimized it as a subject of public discourse" (Schneider 643). A closer look at two of the lawsuits she tried in 1884, her suit against Dr. Forbes Winslow and her suit against Dr. Semple, shows how she used her own experiences to raise consciousness of injustices facilitated by the laws on lunacy.

On March 13, 1884, her case against Winslow began. She sued him to recover damages for alleged libel, assault, trespass, and false imprisonment. She made clear in her opening statement "that one of her principal objects in bringing this action was to expose the abuses of the Lunacy Laws" ("Weldon v. Winslow," 14 Mar. 1884, 3), and in this endeavor she was most successful. The newspapers carried extensive coverage of the trial, and in summing up the case, the judge (Baron Huddleston) stated that he was "astonished that a person could be confined in an asylum on the statement of anybody, providing that certain formalities were gone through . . . [I]t was positively shocking that such a state of things should exist" (qtd. in K. Jones 198). However, he then proceeded to nonsuit Weldon, declining to send the case to the jury on the basis that there were no issues of fact for them to decide. Huddleston held that the order signed by de Bathe constituted a defense to the actions of Winslow and his associates (the alleged trespass, assault, and false imprisonment), that the alleged libels were privileged information, and that there was no evidence of malice to interrupt that privilege ("Weldon v. Winslow," 19 Mar. 1884, 4). While the judge was critical of the lunacy laws in some of his dicta (what he said on the side), his actual decision in the case reflected his belief that these English gentlemen (Harry Weldon and de Bathe) could not possibly have been acting in the malicious way that Weldon suggested, and while he did think the proceedings in this case had been "strangely precipitate," "he could not doubt that all the parties in the present case had acted conscientiously" (4). All evidence aside, the "fiction" that middle-class English husbands acted, if nothing else, gentlemanly toward their wives, had to be maintained.

If Weldon had not been doing the legal work herself, the nonsuit most likely would have concluded her tale; the legal expenses would have prohibited further proceedings. But because she dared to take on this most unladylike role of lawyer, to play Portia for real (and without any disguise), the public exposure of the abuses of the lunacy laws continued. Weldon appealed Huddleston's ruling to the Divisional Court, where Judge Manisty strongly disagreed with Huddleston's finding that there were no issues for the jury in this case. Manisty particularly was outraged that Winslow, as proprietor of the asylum to which Weldon was to be sent, had arranged to have the two doctors sent over to her house and had drawn up the statement of facts signed by Harry Weldon:

> That the registered proprietor of a lunatic asylum should interfere in any
> way in selecting the medical men who are to give the certificates and in get-
> ting the particulars of the "statement," a most important document, required
> by the Legislature for the protection of persons supposed to be insane—
> when he should have nothing to do with it and it ought to be perfectly inde-
> pendent and absolutely free from all suspicion of his interference—is most
> improper. ("Weldon v. Winslow," 9 Apr. 1884, 4)

Calling the case "one of the most important that has come into court for many years," he declared that "there must be a new trial" (4).[8]

The new Winslow trial was set for November of 1884, and while Weldon was preparing for the beginning of her July trial against Semple, there was a debate in the House of Lords on the lunacy laws, specifically precipitated by the *Weldon v. Winslow* litigation. On May 5, 1884, Lord Milltown moved to pass the following resolution: "That in the opinion of this House the existing state of the Lunacy Laws is eminently unsatisfactory, and constitutes a serious danger to the liberty of the subject" (*Parliamentary Debates* 1270). An aged Earl of Shaftesbury appeared in defense of the Lunacy Laws, urging great caution in disturbing, not perfect, but greatly improved, legislation. Calling on his over fifty years of experience on the Lunacy Commission, he argued the need to keep these matters as private as possible to encourage early treatment of mental illness. While he refused to speak about the Weldon case because it was still ongoing, his biographer reports that he referred to Georgina as "that awful woman, Mrs. Weldon" (Battiscombe 329).

Speeches following Shaftesbury's by the Lord Chief Justice, the Lord Chancellor, and others, however, made clear that the Lords agreed that the laws needed to be changed. The Marquess of Salisbury specifically addressed the privacy issue, claiming that "[f]rom the point of view of those who were concerned in maintaining freedom, the defect in the administration of these laws was in the utter absence of publicity" (*Parliamentary Debates* 1290). Noting that people might want to rid themselves of "inconvenient" relatives in order to secure property, or that parties to a domestic relationship might desire that the other party no longer have his or her freedom, Salisbury acknowledged that "[m]otives of that kind were familiar enough in fiction, and he was afraid they were not altogether strange to real life" (1290). Milltown withdrew his motion based on the Government's agreement to introduce specific legislation. Weldon's tenacious storytelling had moved the narratives of the abuses of the lunacy laws from the pages of earlier sensation novels such as Wilkie Collins' *The Woman in White* (1860), Mary Elizabeth Braddon's *Lady Audley's Secret* (1862), and Charles Reade's *Hard Cash* (1863), to the pages of the leading newspapers, to a parliamentary debate that was the initial step to actual legal reform.

Weldon's stranger-than-fiction factual narrative continued to unfold with the Semple trial that began on July 9, 1884. Semple was one of the two doctors who had certified Weldon as insane, and she sued him for unlawful entry and for writing a false and malicious medical certificate that had caused her great harm. This was a highly publicized case, with the major newspapers devoting columns and columns to the testimony given at the trial. The *Times* reported, "The trial appears to excite great interest, the court is crowded, ladies are present, and in the course of the day Lord Tennyson came into court, and stayed a short time" ("Weldon v. Semple," 12 July 1884, 5).

The main issue in this case came down to whether the certificates signed by the doctors were prepared in accordance with the spirit of the protections provided in the Lunacy Act (the relevant Act being The Lunacy Amendment Act 1853 [16 and 17 Vict., c. 96]). Section 4 of this Act provided as follows:

> [N]o person shall be received as a lunatic into any licensed house or hospital without an order . . . together with such statement of particulars . . . nor without the medical certificates . . . of two persons, each of whom shall be a physician, surgeon, or apothecary, and shall not be in partnership with or an assistant to the other, and each of whom shall separately from the other have personally examined the person to whom the certificate signed by him relates not more than seven clear days previously to the reception of such person into such house or hospital. . . .

Section 10 provided that the person signing such certificates must "specify therein the facts upon which he has formed his opinions . . . and distinguish in such certificate facts observed by himself from facts communicated to him by others."

There was much conflicting testimony about the interview between Weldon and the doctors, and the jury (as the triers of fact) were to determine which story they believed to be true. Semple argued that he had satisfied the terms of the statute. He had seen Weldon separately (when Rutherford stepped out into the hall) for, he said, about a quarter of an hour (a number that makes reference to a ten-minute interview by the certifying doctor in Braddon's *Lady Audley's Secret* startlingly realistic). Semple said Weldon had talked "incessantly" and related several "delusions," which he listed in his certificate. Weldon swore that Semple was alone with her for no more than five minutes and had only asked her about her singing (he had seen her once in concert). She denied ever making certain of the statements set out in the certificate, clarified what she had meant by others, and claimed they were made in the presence of both doctors, not in their separate examinations.

When Semple testified, he kept emphasizing that he was simply doing his job, and that he bore no ill will against Weldon. Fortunately, Weldon herself served as a constant reminder of what could have been the very real consequences of actions he considered routine—an obviously sane woman would have been wasting away in a lunatic asylum. What may have been business as usual for him had dire consequences that he did not seem sufficiently to take into account. The judge in this case stressed how inappropriate it was that Winslow had showed Harry's statement of facts to Semple before he had interviewed Weldon. Harry's statement, among other things, suggested that there was hereditary insanity in Georgina's family. The judge also commented that "[a]nything more calculated to excite suspicion could not be supposed than both the doctors meeting and going together" ("Weldon v. Semple," 29 July 1884, 3). Judge Hawkins then set out the following standard by which Semple's actions were to be considered by the jury: "He was only responsible if he signed the certificate without using due care . . . that is, without making due inquiries, such as it was in his power to make—and thus was guilty of gross and culpable negligence" (3).

The jury found him guilty of that level of negligence. In the jury's answers to specific questions of fact presented to them by the judge, Weldon achieved the public "certification" of her sanity that she had desired for so long. Among the seventeen questions and answers read aloud in court and published in newspapers were the following:

1. Was the plaintiff, Georgina Weldon, in fact a person of unsound mind when she was seen by the defendant, Dr. Semple, and when he signed the

certificate on the 14th of April, 1878? No, she was not. . . .

3a. Or was such examination as he made a mere colourable examination, made, not with a view to discover from such examination her real mental condition, but for the mere purpose of satisfying the letter of the statute without complying with its substance, and with a view to ascertain the truth?—It was a colourable examination to satisfy the statute without complying with its substance, and not to investigate with a view to ascertain the truth. ("Weldon v. Semple," 29 July 1884, 4)

From the tone of the summing up and the wording of the questions put to the jury, it is obvious that the judge in this case was sympathetic toward Weldon. Aside from his comments about Semple, he offered the following pronouncements from the bench. His harshest criticism was directed at Harry Weldon and de Bathe, as he rewrote the earlier narrative of Huddleston:

[I]t seemed almost incredible that two English gentlemen, in a country where liberty was boasted of, and not even a criminal could be incarcerated without the order of a magistrate or some one in authority—it seemed almost incredible that two English gentlemen who had not seen her for a year, or for three years, should have given an order to confine her as a lunatic. ("Weldon v. Semple," 29 July 1884, 3)

He also commented, "He hoped the law upon the subject would be altered; it was not for him to say in what way, but he did say that the law, in the state in which it was, must be calculated to fill everybody who contemplated it with terror and alarm" (3). As I discussed at length in the preceding chapter, the judge's perspectives on a case can really matter. Fortunately for Weldon and lunacy law reform, Judge Hawkins was ardently on their side.

Arguing that "[t]he verdict, and Mr. Justice Hawkins' indictment of the state of the Lunacy Laws as they then existed, did more towards effecting the alteration of a crying evil than all the slowly-moving machinery of the House of Lords or Commons" (Treherne 107), Weldon's 1923 biographer called the Semple case, "the undoing of the Lunacy Laws" (Treherne 97). Evidence from contemporary newspapers and journals corroborates this conclusion. The *Times*, for instance, wrote the following in a lead article that was published at the end of the trial: "The real importance of the case is that it secures the triumph of the agitation against the lunacy laws in their present shape. Their reform is henceforth only a question of time" ("Weldon v. Semple," 29 July 1884, 9). The article on Georgina that was published in the August 1884 issue of the periodical *Life* offered the following comments about this modern Portia:

Figure 6   "Mrs. Weldon." Illustration taken from the August
1884 issue of *Life*.

Her manner and bearing are fascinating, and it is certain that she will never
rest until she has brought her self-appointed task to a completion. If so, we
shall have to thank her for an immense reform, and her name will deserve
to rank with those of Howard, Mrs. Fry, and Florence Nightingale. She is still
in the prime of life; she enjoys marvellous energy and self-possession; she
is an accomplished advocate, and she has a remarkable business aptitude.
("Mrs. Weldon" 163)

The article also commended Weldon's legal skills: "she has sufficiently proved
the thorough soundness and clearness of her mind by arguing difficult points
of law in a manner which has won her the highest compliments from the

judges, and which will cause her name to be handed down in the law reports together with those of the greatest lawyers now practising" (163).[9]

Quite the character, Weldon is described in this article as a self-made "legal *Donna Quixote*" (163), and the accompanying illustration shows her dressed up as Dickens's famous lawyer from *The Pickwick Papers* (1837)—Serjeant Buzfuz. (See figure 6.) While Weldon was highly praised for her courtroom skills, her approach to law was anything but traditional. One of her lawyer friends, also drawing on the Quixote image, commented on her philosophy of law as follows:

> She saw the world moving round and round like some vast piece of machinery, and she saw that in the course of its motion were worked numberless acts of infinite oppression and wrong. It was useless to tell her that the machinery as a whole worked admirably. Her attitude was that of the old knight-errant, who did not trouble herself about the abstract principles of law or justice, but rode out to discover individual cases of oppression, and to decide them on her own authority and to redress them according to her own judgment. (qtd. in Treherne 51)[10]

Much more concerned with women's real-life experiences than the law's abstract "truths," too familiar with legal injustices to accept that all was well with the system, Georgina set out *really* to make things right. Not surprisingly, her perspective on law and justice was viewed as quixotic or, in more feminine terms, eccentric.

Rather than letting comic representations detract from the seriousness of her endeavors, Georgina made them work *for* her. Her behavior of appearing in court as a plaintiff-in-person (and winning) was eccentric, but the publicity associated with her legal adventures meant that wide audiences were reading the representation in *Life* that "the thorough soundness and clearness of her mind" had been proven (163). The Buzfuz portrait accompanying the *Life* article was of Weldon as she appeared in public readings she gave from *The Pickwick Papers*. Making the most of the crossovers between the discursive fields of law and literature, Weldon knew that her "performances" as a lawyer were winning her the publicity that was so vital to the success of her causes. Of course, when she argued her cases in court, she was not permitted to wear a wig and gown, the professional attire of an attorney. The *Life* illustration, however, in which she is dressed as Buzfuz but which has a caption reading only "Mrs. Weldon," blurs the lines between fiction and reality.[11] She looks like the real thing. When Weldon's 1959 biographer comments that "[t]he Semple case confirmed Georgina's position as the most admired badgerer of lawyers since the death of

Dickens," he touches on a key point about Georgina (Grierson 223). More than a character, she was the *author* of her own legal story. In the courtroom, in her writing, in her public performances—she *always* was representing herself.

The gains for her own reputation and lunacy reform that resulted from her successful suit against Semple were further bolstered in November 1884 when she won her new trial against Winslow. In 1887, a Lunacy Acts Amendment bill was introduced. Among other provisions, it included a clause requiring that an order from a judicial authority be obtained before certification could take place. A bill containing this clause became law in 1889 (52 and 53 Vict., c. 41) and a bill consolidating the governing 1845 Act with all subsequent legislation was passed in 1890, becoming the Lunacy Act 1890 (53 and 54 Vict., c. 5).[12]

While Weldon's feminist jurisprudence in connection with lunacy law reform was most intentional, one of her legal losses also proved a tremendous gain for many women. In 1880, in an attempt to make Harry provide her with a house (after the mad doctor affair, Harry had sold Tavistock House and reduced Georgina's annual allowance from £1000 to £500), and to redeem her character (by ensuring access to Harry as a witness to deny "all the vile lies he has insinuated against me" ["Mrs. Weldon on Conjugal Rights," Jan. 1884, 3]), Weldon filed a petition against her husband Harry for restitution of conjugal rights. In 1882 she won this case (she was represented by counsel), and Harry was ordered to live under the same roof as Georgina. He refused to do so, and in 1883, Georgina (this time representing herself) appealed to the President of the Probate, Divorce, and Admiralty Division for an order of attachment, which was granted. Pursuant to this order, Harry would be imprisoned if he did not return to Georgina. Illustrating the power of the law and its representatives to protect the "reasonable" man, Parliament passed the Matrimonial Causes Act of 1884, popularly known as "The Weldon Relief Act," that abolished attachment as a remedy for failure to comply with an order for restitution of conjugal rights. Instead, failure to comply was made equivalent to desertion (Grierson viii). It was not lost upon Georgina that this amendment in the law was not intended to benefit women. She writes in *Social Salvation*, the journal she edited, as follows:

> After centuries of cruel oppression towards the female sex, in the shape of a law which forced a woman against her will to submit to the repulsive embraces of a male to whom Religion and Law had bound her by a solemn farce at the Altar of the Christian Creed; the Lord Chancellor, in the year 1884, brought in *a bill to amend the Law relating to the Restitution*

of Conjugal Rights. . . . [T]he Lord Chancellor has not been inspired to present this Bill for the purpose of saving from prison or exile a poor delicate woman, who shrinks from the contact of a violent, drunken, dissolute, spendthrift . . . but with the view of sparing the "gentleman," of whose conduct the public will, at last, be given the chance of obtaining a clear conception . . . when certain pending actions she [his wife] has brought against her persecutors will have been tried. ("Mrs. Weldon on Conjugal Rights," Jan. 1884, 2)

Georgina, against whom all of this legislative power had been garnered, was justifiably outraged, "Can it be possible that a man who refuses to live with his wife without assigning any reason whatever for his conduct is encouraged by Legislators to abandon, libel, and rob her, and that Parliament itself is put into motion for the purpose of baulking the wife of her rights after she has been grudgingly accorded them?" ("Mrs. Weldon on Conjugal Rights," Feb. 1884, 2).[13] For other women, however, this change proved extremely beneficial by enabling them more easily to prove desertion on the part of their husbands and thus obtain certain protections under the law (e.g., the ability to keep their own earnings). Henry Fenn, legal reporter and author of *Thirty-Five Years in the Divorce Court*, commented that the amendment "has been taken advantage of to such a large extent it is difficult to estimate . . . [I]ts benefits cannot be too strongly dwelt upon . . . and numberless ladies owe this redoubtable champion of women's rights [Weldon] a deep debt of gratitude for her action in the matter" (198).[14] Thus, in trying to thwart Georgina (or protect Harry), the lawmakers inadvertently provided a much needed remedy to many deserted wives.

Weldon summed up her legal strategy as follows: "The principal aim of my opponents is to gain time, and to obtain adjournments and delays; they do their best to confuse me with an inextricable labyrinth of law, trying to get rid of me at any price; but I stand up to them, and I appeal, and appeal, and appeal" (qtd. in Treherne 98). In other words, she never gave in to the conspiratorial desire to keep her quiet. Thus, her private wrongs became public wrongs—opening up the possibility for the publication of women's "collective experience of oppression" (Bender 9).

In the next section of this chapter, I turn to another sensational case, *Queen v. Jackson* (1891). The heroine of this real-life tale is Emily Jackson, a woman who indeed suffered "personal restraint" of the kind mentioned by Harry Weldon's legal counsel. Proving the wisdom of the lawyer's advice to keep restraint a private matter, the public attention brought to the *Jackson* case changed the law of coverture forever.

The Clitheroe Case

Appealing to Public Opinion

In March 1891, the British public was treated to a real-life sensation story, "the Clitheroe Abduction case."[15] On a Sunday morning, two men seized Emily Jackson as she was coming out of church and forced her into a waiting carriage—one of these men was her husband. Following the abduction, the carriage drove to her husband's place of residence in Blackburn, where all of the occupants went inside and the doors were locked. Emily's sisters and brother-in-law soon tracked her and demanded admittance to the house. When they were refused, Emily's brother-in-law asked the police to "break into the house and rescue the lady" ("Remarkable" 8). Once the police realized that Mr. Jackson had obtained a decree for restitution of conjugal rights (which Emily had ignored), they "declined to interfere" ("Remarkable" 8).

The *Times* reported that there was "considerable romance in the affair" ("Remarkable" 8) and, for ten days, the more dramatic details of the case filled the pages of the newspapers. On the morning after the abduction, "milk and the papers were taken in by means of a string let down from one of the bedroom windows, and, later on, all kinds of provisions were obtained in the same way. At noon a box of cigars was hoisted up to the garrison" ("Remarkable" 8). Crowds thronged the streets "in spite of the snow and a bitter wind," and police were on hand to keep order ("Clitheroe Abduction," 11 Mar. 1891, 8). Then, on March 11, 1891, Mr. Jackson was finally forced to leave the Blackburn house. He had to respond to assault charges filed against him by Emily's sister for injuries she had sustained while trying to hold onto Emily during the abduction. However, before he left the house, "a dozen men armed with picking sticks . . . filed into the yard" and when Jackson unbarred the door and came out, six of these armed men proceeded into the house and took possession of it "to prevent anybody opposed to Mr. Jackson's interest from getting into the place" ("Clitheroe Abduction," 12 Mar. 1891, 12).

On March 16, 1891, the Queen's Bench Division of the High Court rejected an application for a writ of *habeas corpus* filed by Emily's family, stating that "though generally the forcible detention of a subject by another is *prima facie* illegal, yet where the relation is that of husband and wife the detention is not illegal" ("Law Report," 17 Mar. 1891, 3). On appeal, however, Mr. Jackson's arguments that he had a common-law right to custody of his wife were rejected, with the Court of Appeal (composed of the Lord Chancellor, Lord Esher, and Justice Fry) claiming that such an idea derived from "absurd and obsolete *dicta*" that could not be considered authoritative "in a court of justice, in this or any other civilized country" ("Queen v. Jackson" 679). The Court was also much influenced by the legislated change in the 1884 Matrimonial Causes Act (the Weldon Relief Act). As the *Times* reports:

> It has to be remembered that in 1884 an Act was passed abolishing the power of the Court to imprison a husband or wife for refusing to give those "conjugal rights," which, by a strange anomaly, the Court may still grant, and which it had granted Mr. Jackson. This weighed with all the Judges, and it is hard to see how we are to escape Lord Justice Fry's conclusion that the passing of such an Act finally extinguishes any such pretensions as those which the husband here attempted to put forward. ("Clitheroe Abduction," 20 Mar. 1891, 9)

As a result of this decision, which many found surprising and the legal world found shocking, Mrs. Jackson was free to return to her family. The *Standard* reported, "Marriage, in fact, without a note of warning, has, by this single decision of the Appeal Court, been placed upon an entirely new footing. The judgment has sprung a mine upon society, and destroyed at one blow the prescription of ages" (qtd. in Haughton Jackson 41). The *Solicitors' Journal,* calling the decision a "rude shock" to the common law ("Husband and Wife" 357), expressed great surprise at the Lord Chancellor's decision "to declare, *for the first time*" the following (359; emphasis added):

> that, according to English law, a wife is at liberty, immediately after going through the ceremony of marriage in church, to desert her husband, and without any excuse to condemn him to a life of celibacy; that the continuance of the marriage relation is perfectly voluntary, and that a husband may, for no fault of his own, be deprived of a home and the prospect of children to inherit his name. (359)

Far from objective, this "legal conclusion" was in keeping with much of the publicly expressed sentiment. It was reported that Mr. Jackson received many sympathetic cards and letters and that a fund had been established to help him take his case to the House of Lords ("Clitheroe Case," 1 Apr. 1891, 5). In contrast, Mrs. Jackson, upon returning to Clitheroe, was mobbed by a hostile crowd: "Groans, hisses, and yells were given for Mrs. Jackson, and cheers, with the singing of 'He's a jolly good fellow,' for her husband. The midnight scene was an extremely stormy and threatening one, the police being hard pressed to prevent violence" ("Clitheroe Case," 28 Mar. 1891, 5).

The next night "hundreds of persons assembled" to burn an effigy of Mrs. Jackson. Ultimately, the effigy was not burned, but there was a serious riot, with stones being thrown at the houses of both Mrs. Jackson's sisters ("Clitheroe Abduction," 30 Mar. 1891, 4).

Mr. Jackson did not appeal the decision to the House of Lords, but in mid-April the Lord Chancellor and Lord Esher were questioned about the decision in a parliamentary session. In defending the decision, Esher made the following telling comment:

> Those intelligent people who have declared that the judgment is wrong must be prepared to maintain the converse—namely, that if a wife disobeys her husband he may lawfully beat her; and if she refuses him a restitution of conjugal rights he may imprison her, it was urged, in the cellar or in the cupboard, or, if the house is large, in the house by locking her in it and blocking the windows. ("Clitheroe Case," 17 Apr. 1891, 6)

As evidenced by the letter from Harry Weldon's lawyer, personal restraint was a private matter that the law preferred not to talk about. With the *Jackson* case, however, lawful domestic violence that was an unspoken "disability" of coverture was brought into broad daylight. When Emily Jackson filed for a writ of *habeas corpus*, she gave the court two choices: either publicly articulate the law's acceptance of brute force or set her free. As the Court of Appeal's decision makes clear, the thought of explicitly acknowledging such a "truth" compelled the court to say it wasn't so.

Emily Jackson's voice is completely missing from the official legal record of this case. The published opinion includes detailed discussions of legal authorities and precedents relating to a husband's right to beat, confine, and imprison his wife. It also presents certain facts specific to this case based on affidavits that were filed on both sides. However, "the wife had no opportunity of making any affidavit," as she was locked up in her husband's house ("Queen v. Jackson" 672). The affidavits on her side were not hers, but rather filed on her behalf. The published opinion also notes that the judges spoke with Mrs. Jackson and determined that she was acting as a free agent and not under the undue influence of her relatives. There is no legal record, however, of what Emily Jackson said.

Emily Jackson's voice, perspectives, and experiences, however, are documented in an outlaw text. Free from her husband, but not from public censure, Emily Jackson decided that it was time to tell her side of the story. On April 17, 1891, she published a "Vindication" in the *Lancashire Evening Post* (which was reprinted in the *Times*). Like Weldon, Norton and others, Emily Jackson presented, in the court of public opinion, "private" details that are missing from the legal record. In the newspapers' first installment of the "Vindication," she explained: "I wish simply to appeal to my countrymen, and especially to my countrywomen, against the opinions which in many directions have been formed against me without hearing my side of the case" (Emily Jackson, 18 Apr. 1891, 14); she laments that she has been "condemned unheard" (14). While her legal appeal had been successful in a court of law, she hoped that her narrative appeal would vindicate her in the court of public opinion.

An analysis of Emily Jackson's story makes clear that she is speaking to a "jury of her peers," presenting facts that have been omitted that she believes will clarify her motives and actions. As in Susan Glaspell's 1917 short story of that name ("A Jury of Her Peers"), Jackson emphasizes what, in the case of the law or "objective" newspaper articles, might be deemed trifles.[16] Just as Wollstonecraft's novel includes Maria's memoirs, which presents to her daughter (and the reader) the context of Maria's life from her own perspective, Jackson's "Vindication" narrates details of her experiences that she knows, for some readers, will illuminate a very different story. Specifically she publicizes disillusionment and fear, rewriting the "romance" that the *Times* alluded to in the early days of the abduction from the perspective of the damsel for whom marriage represented only increasing distress.

Emily married Haughton Jackson when she was 46. They married speedily, just before Haughton sailed to Australia to commence farming. Her family was surprised to learn of the marriage and disapproved, although she published a letter from her sister to Haughton suggesting that her family had become reconciled to the marriage. Upon reflection, Emily felt that her constitution was not sufficiently strong to endure the strenuous life of a colonial settler, so she wrote Haughton asking him not to buy land or to begin to build a house in Australia. Instead, she expressed her desire for them to settle in England. She also told him that she did not expect him to return for six months or so, and that he should make the most of his journey. In response to this request, she received a package including two letters from Haughton: one "public" letter, written in affectionate terms, speaking of his voyage and his illness on the journey; the other, which she was to keep private, asking her to send £100 for the return fare of Haughton and his friend Dixon Robinson. As Haughton and Robinson had had no time to spend the capital Emily believed they had both taken out to begin their farming operations, she was shocked that they had no money to pay their return fare. Moreover, the letter also suggested to Emily that Haughton wanted to use Emily's money to set up "a sort of joint home" with his sister and Dixon Robinson (Emily Jackson, 20 Apr. 1891, 12). Emily published the actual letters to leave "anyone to judge of the effect which they were calculated to have upon me" (12).

Feeling that she had been much deceived, that she had been married for her money and not for herself, she lamented, "How I felt any woman can best understand who has ever trusted as I had trusted, and with such a result" (21 Apr. 1891, 12). Disillusioned with her marriage, Emily wrote Haughton an indignant response, a letter expressing the sentiments of someone who is used to managing her own affairs. In the letter he wrote back, the hitherto tacit threat that marriage had posed to Emily's happiness and her ability to have any say in her own future was made manifest. Haughton wrote:

> As you justly say, everything between husband and wife should be sacred, yet you have dared to tell your people what I have written you. Do not make any mistake; there shall be a perfect understanding between us, but I will make it, not you. It is most ridiculous for you to say you will have this or that; it depends upon whether I approve or no. . . . (21 Apr. 1891, 12)

Based on this letter, Emily decided that it was impossible for them to live together. With the help of a supportive family, she managed for a while to enforce her decision, refusing even to see Haughton when he returned to England. She recounted a violent altercation between Haughton and her sister and brother-in-law when he stormed into their home, demanding to see his wife. She reprinted a letter she wrote to him the following day:

> Sir,—I was on the staircase and heard the violent way you forced yourself into my sister's house last evening, and also your abuse of everybody and especially abominable language to my sister on her quietly requesting you to leave the house. Your insulting and unmanly letter to me of the 28th of May opened my eyes to your real character, and your behaviour last night only more fully confirms me in the determination I then formed—to have nothing more to do with you. (22 Apr. 1891, 12)

When she finally did agree to meet with him on January 16, 1889, after he had applied for a writ of restitution of conjugal rights, she explicitly told him that she was afraid to live with him. She described how he raised his voice considerably and characterized himself as having "just a little bit of temper" (23 Apr. 1891, 12). While there are contested facts in the *Jackson* case, Haughton Jackson's undisputed abduction of Emily on that Sunday morning proves that her fears were justified. Exhibiting classic batterer behavior, he was determined to have her—by any and all means.[17]

In her vindication, Emily documents her terror inside the carriage: "Mr. Jackson was very excited, and shook his fist in my face in a menacing manner. I was faint and sick and breathless, and all I could say was, 'You surely are not going to hurt me?'" (23 Apr. 1891, 12). She further explains that "[f]rom the rough handling I received in the struggle I felt sore all over my body for several days; my chest was very painful, my arms were very much bruised and swollen, and were black and blue from the shoulders to the elbows and discoloured, and finger marks and swelling were seen by the doctor a month afterwards" (12). But her most persuasive evidence of the violence of this episode comes in her detailed description of "the bonnet incident."

It was admitted by all parties that, upon arriving at the Blackburn House, Mr. Jackson had ordered Emily to remove her bonnet, and when she refused, he had thrown it into the fire. The *Times* treated this incident as comical: "Unless it was an extremely unbecoming bonnet, this was outrageous on the part of Mr. Jackson. A man may show his determination that a lady shall not leave him without burning her bonnet" ("Clitheroe Abduction," 20 Mar. 1891, 9). In Mrs. Jackson's account, there was nothing funny about it:

> He was very violent and furious, and seemed quite beside himself with passion. After he had abused me in this way [applied opprobrious epithets to her and her sisters] he ordered me to take off my bonnet. I said I would not do so, and then he seized it with great violence and tore it off my head. It was fastened in my hair with two long pins 6 in. long, while two other pins quite 4 in. long fastened my veil. The strings of the bonnet were tied securely under my chin and the bows pinned down. He dragged it savagely away from those fastenings, and the strings caught my neck and hurt me so much that I managed to push the knot forward from under my chin. My neck was very much hurt and very sore for some time afterwards. When he had torn it off he placed it on the fire and burnt it, grinning at me with rage all the while. I was most frightened and indignant at this, and said, "Are you aware, Mr. Jackson, that you have assaulted me?" When this happened Mr. Dixon Robinson said to him, "You are going beyond bounds." Mr. Jackson then seized me most violently by the shoulders and pushed me on a sofa, saying, "Sit there until I tell you to move, and if you don't do as I tell you I will screw your neck round like a chicken's." (Emily Jackson, 23 Apr. 1891, 12)

The violence of this act would not be lost on or dismissed as funny or irrelevant by those who were intimately familiar with those six-inch pins and tightly secured fastenings.

Resisting the role of the silenced wife, Emily (like Georgina Weldon) represented herself in her narrative, appearing in print "in person." Feeling compelled to respond, Haughton answered Emily's vindication in a pamphlet entitled *The True Story of the Clitheroe Abduction; or, Why I Ran Away With My Wife*, which is framed by "objective" editorial comment that advocates on Haughton's behalf. While the Introduction claims that the publishers are not going to suggest "whether Mr. Jackson is right or Mrs. Jackson is an injured woman," its biases are patently obvious (5). A brief analysis of the style and substance of Haughton Jackson's defense illuminates ideas about the patriarchal and private nature of marriage that the Clitheroe decision exploded.

As the title suggests and the introduction clarifies, Mr. Jackson's narrative will be the "true" facts. Mrs. Jackson's side of the story is her side of the story; his is *the* story. In explaining why they believe this case has been in the press for so many months, the publishers explain, "Marriage is a social institution which is vital to our well-being, and apparently the last decision in the Courts has robbed it of every semblance of reality: the wife would seem to incur no obligation when she goes to the altar, and the man to obtain no rights" (5). The wording shows the reality of the institution of marriage; it means rights for husbands and duties for wives. The pamphlet hopes that "Mr. Jackson's artless tale will 'catch on'" and lead to the reversal of this "travesty of justice" (5).

The pamphlet itself is composed of many letters, with brief explanations by Haughton Jackson concerning his courtship, marriage, and fallout with Emily. Melodramatic in its presentation, it includes large-print section headlines such as "What a Charming Fellow Dixon Is" introducing one of Emily's letters, and "'Come Back, Come Back!' she cried in grief" introducing another. Editorial comments appear in brackets throughout the forty-eight-page pamphlet, with one of the more interesting suggesting that a lack of sexual urgency on the part of both parties was a big part of the problem: "Indeed, this strange courtship is a forcible argument for early marriages. As Hamlet says, after a certain age the hey-dey [*sic*] of the blood is lost, sentiment does not exert its force, the fires of ardour burn lower, the will is less powerful, and the man or the woman know themselves less as purely sexual entities" (16). In the editor's opinion, this "romance" began too late to follow the well-known marriage plot. Another reading of this same story, however, is that the woman's will was more powerful, and that she did not let sentiment overrule what her mind suggested to her was not fair and not right.

That Emily would have a mind of her own seems impossible for Haughton to grasp. As was rehearsed over and over again throughout the century, one interpretation of her lack of "appropriate" wifely sentiment was madness ("I considered my wife to be the victim of some strange hallucination") (22). Another was that her family unacceptably was interfering in the private affairs of husband and wife ("I conceived her to be under an undue restraint on the part of her relatives") (22). In speaking of the abduction, Haughton says that he had been planning it for weeks. Apparently receiving advice similar to Mr. Weldon about dealing with a recalcitrant wife, Haughton makes clear: "I was legally advised what my rights and powers were" (26). While he states that he shrank from the sensational abduction, he feels that he had no other choice. In his defense, he states the following:

> At the outset, I believed that when she saw me her professed love for me would change her point of view, and let her come away with me without the slightest use of force. This I hoped and believed. Having determined upon such a scheme, I also wished to spare my wife all possible publicity, notoriety, or discomfort; and, I may say that if there was any "scene" at Clitheroe at the time of her "abduction," she and her relatives and friends made it. (26)

In providing such an explanation for his behavior, Haughton unintentionally reveals character traits of an abuser. As Waits explains, "Batterers are quite remarkable in their ability to externalize and rationalize their acts. The most obvious and frequent target of blame is, of course, his victim. . . . Even when the batterer does not blame his wife, he attributes his behavior to other forces" (194). Haughton's own account of what happened scripts his belief that the violence on his part was fully justified by the intolerably inciting behavior of Emily and her family.

Haughton's language testifies to his determination to take his rightful possession of Emily: "Was I going quietly to submit to the extraordinary course which she had elected to take? No!" (26). Throughout these proceedings, Emily Jackson is spoken of as a misplaced possession. She belongs to her husband, but her family refuses to turn her over to her rightful owner. The law's role (prior to the decision of the Court of Appeal) in supporting this view is obvious in Justice Cave's words when he first denied Emily's application for a writ of *habeas corpus:* "He [Haughton] was right to re-take possession of her from those who were endeavoring equally by force to restrain him having the custody of her" (qtd. in Haughton Jackson 31–32).

Haughton Jackson's purpose in speaking out, he asserts, is to clear up matters that are obscure, and while his story does raise questions of fact concerning, for instance, what Emily should have realized about his limited financial means, his "defense" reads as a justification rather than a denial. In fact, his testimony is self-incriminating because it corroborates the fear and violence that Emily documented. For example, he claims that his behavior at Emily's sister's house was ungentlemanly, but provoked. The story is told under the headline, "I go to Claim my Wife," and concludes with his rhetorical question and response, "What married man would have behaved less violently under similar circumstances? I wonder now I did not strike at those who stood between me and my wife" (34).

In speaking of the abduction itself, he relates that when they arrived at the Blackburn house "she [Emily] was rather obstreperous, and would not say anything. When her relations came I wanted her to go upstairs but she would not, so I took her up, in the same way as you would carry a bundle. . . . She appeared to be under the impression that I contemplated doing her some injury" (30).[18] He also admits to making several attempts to be intimate with her, with his account saying, "I am afraid I cannot say that she gave me any real sign herself of returning affection" (30). To his proposals that they consummate the marriage, "she always refused" (31). Of course, it would have been perfectly within his legal rights to force her compliance, marital rape not being a crime in England until 1991.[19] Because the case had become a public spectacle, however, the Jacksons were not accorded the level of privacy that so easily accommodated this lawful crime in other marriages.

Haughton's conclusion clarifies his ideas of marriage that Emily so clearly did not live up to: "Good wives before now in thousands have given up all to be true and loyal to the man of their choice. She has given up nothing. She has made no sacrifice. Her marriage vow remains as false as a dicer's oath. I will not believe that she realises the enormity of the offense she has committed" (45). In his eyes, he has done nothing wrong, and he appeals to the British public to condone his justified acts: "However our joint stories have gone forth to the world. She writes a Vindication. I make no apology. The world already thinks the woman doth protest too much. Instead of a Vindication she has given forth a most pathetic and voluminous exposition of feelings mainly based upon imaginary situations" (45). In other words, the more vehement her protest, the less reliable her story. But as Emily Jackson and others published real and fictional accounts of violent and unhappy marriages, it became increasingly difficult simply to accept the husband's story as true and dismiss the wife's as imaginary.

With the *Jackson* decision, Elizabeth Wolstenholme Elmy declared that "'Coverture' is dead and buried."[20] She viewed this decision as, at long last, rewriting the Gothic reality of marriage that Wollstonecraft had decried a century before—one in which wives could be locked up and chastised with impunity. As Elmy wrote in a letter to *The Manchester Guardian*, marriage would be constituted in and on new terms:

Of the momentous character of this judgment there can be no question whatever. It is a declaration of law which is epoch-making in its immediate consequences, and its ultimate results reach far into the future, involving indeed the establishment of a higher morality of marriage, and the substitution, in the relation of husband and wife, of the ethics of justice and equality for the old and worn-out code of master and slave. (4)

In her study *Marriage, Wife-Beating and the Law in Victorian England* (1992), legal historian Maeve Doggett disagrees with Elmy's claim that the decision altered the nature of the marital relationship (142). While acknowledging *Jackson* as a "legal landmark" and a "significant change in the law" (142), she argues that the male judges and parliamentarians ultimately responsible for the changes in the laws regarding divorce, married women's property, child custody, and wife-beating were motivated by a sense of gallantry and by a desire to punish deviations from what were viewed as middle-class family values, rather than by any interest in increasing women's civil liberties. Even if that is true, however, I believe that many legal reform efforts such as the sixteen-year campaign to repeal the Contagious Diseases Acts, as well as the continuing work of late-century New Women literary reformers to break down the public/private barrier, did much, from the point of view of women, to alter the marital relationship. Reading the *Jackson* decision in the social contexts of these boundary-breaking efforts emphasizes the radical *repositioning* it articulated and constituted. Drawing on increasingly changing cultural perceptions of marriage, the *Jackson* decision further bolstered them by actually making it illegal (and thus to an even greater number of people morally wrong) to force women to stay within what many still considered their properly designated private sphere.

Narrative Appeals in New Woman Novels

With unhappy wives like Weldon and Jackson publicizing their stories, the wrongs of marriage (the aptly named disabilities of coverture) were "uncovered" and openly debated in public and in print. One of the more popular forums for the interrogation of the institution of marriage was the New Woman novel that came of age in the 1890s.[21] As Teresa Mangum argues, New Woman writers like Sarah Grand "saw the novel as a concrete and immediate, if fictional, structure within which to begin, at least imaginatively, the transformation they wanted to effect in the public world" (13).

Revising the conventional marriage plot, New Woman novelists took up the story where most romances ended, narrating the tragedy of "ever after" for wives who lived in fear and danger, as well as those who could not live happily in such an unequal relationship. In her study of New Woman novels, Ann Ardis explains, "Because their authors choose *not* to view art as a sphere of cultural activity separate from the realm of politics and history, these narratives refuse to be discrete. They do not want to be read singly or separately; moreover, they choose not to be silent about the intertextual debate in which they participate" (4). Openly engaging with "present-day reality" (Bakhtin, "Epic and Novel" 39), New Woman novels were political and unapologetically so.

While many New Woman novels end tragically, I am looking at a different sampling—New Woman novels that explore the topic of marriage but offer some hope for further revision of what was still a defining social text for women.[22] The three New Woman novels that I discuss in this chapter explore marriage and other issues central to women's emancipation in the larger contexts of feminist writing, activism, history, and law. Sarah Grand's *The Beth Book* (1898) explicitly examines the closely related roles of women writers and political activists in ongoing efforts to bring about legal reform. George Paston's 1899 *A Writer of Books* probes a woman writer's relationships to law and history. I conclude with *Gloriana; or The Revolution of 1900* (1890), Florence Dixie's tale of societal transformation through feminist jurisprudence.

THE BETH BOOK: "LITERARY WOMAN" AND THE LAW

While *The Beth Book* shares the bildungsroman qualities of novels such as Charlotte Brontë's *Jane Eyre* (1847) and is reminiscent of George Eliot's *Mill on the Floss* (1860) in its engaging portrait of young girlhood, the changes in law and literature that took place in the 1880s and 1890s fundamentally changed the identities that women were able to acknowledge publicly and claim as their own. Thus, *The Beth Book* is a coming-of-age story for a progressive age. The conflation of literary woman and political activist is actualized in the character Beth, whose book appears to be (until the final pages) the fictional biography of a writer. It is only in the final pages, when Beth becomes a public speaker (encouraged by her women friends who are political activists), that it becomes clear that signifying beneath Sarah Grand's literary heroine is a woman like the heroine of Grand's childhood, Josephine Butler.[23] Butler was the energetic and seemingly tireless leader of one of the most sustained women's legal movements of the late century, the Movement to Repeal the Contagious Diseases Acts. Although written in 1898, *The Beth Book* is set in the 1870s and 1880s, a time period during which the Contagious Diseases Acts were in effect. The novel portrays the feminist activism that resulted in the repeal of the Acts and is an example of Bakhtin's "ambivalence of writing" in the way that it "implies the insertion of history (society) into a text and of this text into history" (Kristeva, "Word, Dialogue and Novel" 39). The novel draws on, responds to, and furthers the social texts and contexts of this movement. The novel also illustrates the ways in which the ideology that underwrites coverture—that women are to be subordinate to men—affects the treatment of all women under the law. Before turning to a specific discussion of *The Beth Book*, however, I briefly will introduce the campaign to repeal the Contagious Diseases Acts that so informs this outlaw novel.

Literary Politics in the Movement to Repeal the Contagious Diseases Acts

Sarah Grand's *The Beth Book* intertextually engages with the reform movement to repeal the Contagious Diseases Acts, and, thus, an understanding of this legal context enriches and highlights much of the feminist jurisprudence performed in this outlaw novel. The first of these Acts were passed by Parliament in 1864 and 1866 as sanitation measures. The Acts, "designed to control the spread of venereal disease among enlisted men," provided that plainclothes "medical police" could apprehend any woman suspected of being a common prostitute and order her to submit to a genital examination to determine if she were infected (Walkowitz, *Prostitution* 71–72, 78).[24] If a woman refused to be examined, she was taken to a magistrate who could order her to submit to the examination under threat of imprisonment for her failure to comply. Women who were found to be diseased were subject to involuntary confinement in Lock hospitals until they were cured. When released, they were presented with certificates verifying their status as disease-free women.[25] When women were excluded from the first meeting of The National Association for the Repeal of the Contagious Diseases Acts on the basis that men's control of women's bodies need not concern them, they formed the Ladies' National Association for the Repeal of the Contagious Diseases Acts (LNA) and chose Butler as their leader. While arguing on a practical level that the Contagious Diseases Acts were not effective in controlling venereal disease, the central argument of these feminist repealers was that the Acts evidenced the state's acceptance and sanction of the sexual subordination of *all* women to men. As Butler argued, the definitions of women embodied in the Acts categorized women on the basis of their sexual relationships to men (pure or fallen), and were used not only to justify a "slave class of women for the supposed benefit of licentious men," but also to keep "pure" women safely enslaved within the home.[26] Butler stressed the importance of leveling distinctions among women.

In discussing the twentieth-century law and literature movement, legal theorist Robin West introduces a new character, one she calls "literary woman." She contrasts this character, who has emerged from a literary analysis of the law, with "that abstract character who has emerged from the economic analysis of the law: 'economic man'" ("Economic Man" 867).[27] West argues that "literary woman" is necessary to any meaningful justice because she is able to take context and marginal perspectives into account; she provides a "bridge that facilitates empathetic understanding" (874).[28] Through narrative and metaphor, "literary woman" gains insight into different experiences and perspectives:

> Metaphor and narrative are the means by which we come to understand what was initially foreign. Narrative is the communication that facilitates the profoundly difficult "intersubjective comparison of utility" [empathy] when more ordinary means fail. In political contexts, we rely on metaphor when our differences leave us desperate, when nothing else works and we have no other choice. (874)[29]

Butler and her fellow repealers understood this power and, employing a literary politics, they used metaphor and narrative to bridge the gulf between public and private women.[30] Examinations with the speculum were decried as "instrumental rape" (Walkowitz, *Prostitution* 109). Walkowitz comments that in "highly colored language, LNA literature denounced the examination as a surgical outrage, an 'espionage of enslaved wombs.' The examination was depicted as an unnatural, voyeuristic intrusion into the womb that degraded any female, whether she be a private patient or a public prostitute" (*Prostitution* 129–30). Stories of women who were tracked down and captured, victims of a "medical lust of handling and dominating women" and a "police lust of hunting and persecuting women," were published in pamphlets such as J. J. Garth Wilkinson's *The Forcible Introspection of the Women for the Army and Navy by the Oligarchy Considered Physically*[31] and the LNA's journal *The Shield*. Personal testimonies were narrated and retold in speeches made throughout the country. Walkowitz summarizes the power of this narrative advocacy:

> Stories of instrumental rape, false entrapment, and pitiful suicides had the virtue of appealing to all supporters of repeal—to working-class radicals

and middle-class nonconformists alike. These accounts tended to depict registered women as innocent victims of male lust and medical and police tyranny; as such, the women remained appropriate objects of solicitude, even for middle-class moralists who chiefly condemned the acts for making "vice" safe. (*Prostitution* 110)

Stories of Butler's own victimization since she had become a "public woman," speaking out against the Acts and in defense of prostitutes, also circulated widely. For example, in Pontefract, in 1872, Butler was planning to speak in a hayloft, having been turned away from all other locations in town. When she arrived, she discovered the floor of the loft covered with cayenne peppers, which made it almost impossible to breathe, let alone speak. After a group of women had gathered in the loft, the bundles of hay below were set on fire. Butler recounts the following:

Then, to our horror, looking down the room to the trap-door entrance, we saw appearing head after head of men with countenances full of fury; man after man came in, until they crowded the place. There was no possible exit for us, the windows being too high above the ground, and we women were gathered into one end of the room like a flock of sheep surrounded by wolves. . . . Their language was hideous. They shook their fists in our faces, with volleys of oaths. . . . We understood from their language that certain among them had a personal and vested interest in the evil thing we were opposing [prostitution].[32]

In another incident in Manchester, Butler "was covered with flour and excrement, her clothes had been torn off her body, her face was discoloured and stiff with dried blood and she was so bruised that she could hardly move" (Petrie 139). Kent comments that these incidents "suggest that women who left the private sphere and ventured into the public arena were perceived by men to be public women—prostitutes—and deserving of the same treatment" (73). Not an epic heroine, but rather one very much in contact with everyday realities, Butler was a proto–New Woman; stories of women like her would be told in novels.

Women's Writing/Women's Activism: The Connections

In *The Beth Book*, Beth's literary proclivities are apparent at an early age. As a young girl, she is constantly making up elaborate stories, oftentimes living the fantasy life she creates. Beth composes her first poem for a neighborhood boy Sammy, who at the age of eleven is the love of her life. Having earlier informed her that "[m]en write books . . . not women, let alone gels," Sammy refuses to believe that Beth has written the poem (172). Beth, who suffers many of the "anxieties of authorship" that Gilbert and Gubar have identified as common to nineteenth-century women writers, responds indignantly: "I made it myself, every word of it. I tell you it came to me. It's my own. *You've got to believe it*" (183).[33] At this point in her life, while she asserts the power of her pen, she feels a pressing need for Sammy's validation; she is struggling with what it might mean "to be a woman writer in a culture whose fundamental definitions of literary authority are . . . both overtly and covertly patriarchal" (Gilbert and Gubar 45–46).

At sixteen, Beth marries Dr. Dan Maclure. Like Wollstonecraft's Maria, Beth sees marriage as an escape from an oppressive home life, but all too soon she "began to realize what the law of man was with regard to her person" (345). She comments about her husband, "one would think he had bought me" (345). Maclure is a selfish, crude, and thoughtless man who has married Beth for her social position and small inheritance from her great-aunt. The descriptions of her life with Maclure are strikingly similar to those of Maria's everyday existence with Venables. In Maclure's role as husband, he controls and spends all of their money, opens her letters, and allows her no privacy at all. Desperate to find a place of refuge from his overbearing presence, she searches the house and literally discovers what Virginia Woolf years later would write was essential for a woman writer— "a room of her own" in the attic, "a secret spot, sacred to herself, where she would be safe from intrusion" (347).

It is in this room that Beth begins to write seriously. Despite the constant insults of Maclure (who knows she writes but not where), who protests that "[l]iterature is men's work" (366), Beth perseveres. Now, rather than seeking support from unlikely sources such as Sammy and Maclure, she turns to women writers of the past: "As she read of those who had gone before, she felt a strange kindred with them; she entered into their sorrows, understood their difficulties, was uplifted by their aspirations, and gloried in their successes" (370). After suffering her own marital sorrows and difficulties, she achieves success as an author when her book is critically acclaimed and she is described as "a new light of extraordinary promise on the literary horizon" (518).

The study of Beth's life, however, does not conclude on this bright note. Instead, Beth finds that she has no desire to begin writing again. She expresses her concerns to her friend Angelica, who consoles her by suggesting that her writing may have been a necessary precursor to some other vocation. Angelica assures Beth that "versatile people make mistakes sometimes. They do not always begin with the work they are best able to do; but there is no time lost, for one thing helps another—one thing is necessary to another, I *should* say, perhaps. Your writing may have helped to perfect you in some other form of expression" (520). In other words, this literary woman could be an advocate of a different kind.

But some other form of expression? What work is Beth best able to do? In the end, it turns out to be the kind of work that Josephine Butler did. Throughout this book, I have been discussing women who were "literary women" in the sense of Robin West's figure—women who made connections between law and literature, between storytelling and justice. Over the course of the century, many women authors had been doing much more than writing entertaining books; they had been collecting and publicizing stories of oppression—using them, just as reformers like Butler did, to advocate for change in women's lives. *The Beth Book* highlights these connections in the way it startles us—with its sudden shift in direction—into looking again and anew at the nineteenth-century woman writer.

A revisionary look at *The Beth Book* illuminates that Beth's sudden shift at the end is an evolution that makes perfect sense. As readers, we have witnessed her protesting in the face of injustice from the day of her birth. The novel, in fact, opens on that day with a poignant portrait of Beth's mother, Mrs. Caldwell, another example of a nineteenth-century woman overburdened by a large family:

> She was weak and ill and anxious, the mother of six children already, and about to produce a seventh on an income that would have been insufficient for four. It was a reckless thing for a delicate woman to do, but she never thought of that. She lived in the days when no one thought of the waste of women in this respect, and they had not begun to think for themselves. (1)

Beth's mother is presented as a self-sacrificing woman who puts all of her husband's needs before any of her own. On this night, ignoring her own weariness and backache, she frets about the small amount of whiskey left in the bottle. Brightening at the very sound of her husband's footsteps, she is forced to endure his angry mood, his criticism of her appearance, and his insults about her uselessness. Later in the evening, he leaves her to meet his mistress on the beach. Beth arrives that night, "unassisted and without welcome, and sent up a wail of protest" (9).[34]

Beth's mother is also a portrait in conformity, unquestioning in her respect for the epic discourses of law, medicine, and religion. She is trapped in an architecture of patriarchy in which "every effort was made to mould the characters of women as the homes of the period were built, on lines of ghastly uniformity" (124):

[A]ny discussion even of social problems, would not only have been a flying in the face of Providence, but a most indecent proceeding. She knew that there was crime and disease in the world, but there were judges and juries to pursue criminals, doctors to deal with disease, and the clergy to speak a word in the season to all, from the murderer on the scaffold to the maid who has misconducted herself. There was nothing eccentric about Mrs. Caldwell; she accepted the world just as she found it, and was satisfied to know that effects were being dealt with. Causes she never considered, because she knew nothing about them. (2)

From a very early age, it is clear that Beth *is* concerned with causes and that she will not be molded to conform to the idea of womanhood that her mother represents. Instead, Beth emulates women like Josephine Butler, taking special note of and speaking openly about injustices to women. For example, when Beth would pass a house on her way to school in which a man had murdered his wife, "beaten her brains out with a poker" (18), Beth would always expect to see a slender stream of blood running beneath the door. To her, women's oppression is very *real*. One of the family servants Harriet, herself a gifted storyteller, once told Beth about a woman who had dreamt that her husband's fishing boat didn't come home and so the next morning wouldn't let her husband leave. Harriet recounts as follows: "'e was that mad 'e struck 'er an' knocked 'er down an' broke 'er arm, an' then, needs must, 'e 'ad to fetch the doctor to set it, an' by the time that was done, the boat 'ad gone wi'out 'im. The other men thought 'e was drunk—'e often was—an' they wouldn't wait. Well, that boat never came back" (126). Beth's only response to this story is a question: "And did he beat his wife again?" (126). She cannot refrain from the "indecent" discussion of women's legal and social problems.

Things change drastically, however, when Beth becomes a wife. In its critique of women's subordination in marriage, the novel engages with important late-century topics for feminist reformers such as wife abuse and marital rape. While Beth is never actually struck by her husband, the verbal and emotional abuse in the relationship is constant. For example, in response to her comment that she prefers "to look like what I am," her husband responds, "So you do. . . . You look like a silly little idiot" (342). Maclure also regularly undermines her self-confidence:

If anything were amiss in her dress or appearance, he told her of it in the offensive manner of an ill-conditioned under-bred man, generally speaking when they were out of doors, or in some house where she could do nothing to put herself right, as if it were some satisfaction to him to make her feel ill at ease; and if she were complimented by any one else about anything, he had usually something derogatory to say on the subject afterwards. (359–60)

The Beth Book also explores the implications of a husband's absolute right of access to his wife's person. Desperate for some measure of privacy, one day Beth locks herself in her bedroom. Her husband's irate reaction to this small act emphasizes how central his complete and ready access to her body is to his conception of marriage: "I cannot understand a wife locking her husband out of her room, and what's more, you've no business to do it. I've a legal right to come here whenever I choose" (345). It was then that "Beth began to realise what the law of man was with regard to her person" (345).

This novel also daringly presents a woman's perspective on conjugal rights. Beth is not presented as at all passionless, but rather her sexual desire is turned off by dutiful (forced) sexual responsiveness:

> But he had satiated her once and for all, and she never recovered any zest for his caresses. She found no charm or freshness in them, especially after she perceived that they were for his own gratification, irrespective of hers. The privileges of love are not to be wrested from us with impunity. Habits of dutiful submission destroy the power to respond, and all that they leave to survive of the warm reality of love at last is a cold pretense. By degrees, as Beth felt forced to be dutiful, she ceased to be affectionate. (343–44)

Her sense of isolation as a married woman is exacerbated by the fact that Beth is shunned by the women in her town with whom she shares common interests because (unbeknownst to her) Dan is a doctor in a Lock hospital who examines and treats women brought in under the Contagious Diseases Acts. Dan has "protected" Beth from knowledge of the nature of his work. As she struggles to perform her wifely duties in spite of Dan's increasingly intolerable behavior (fits of jealous rage, relationships with other women, vivisecting a dog in their home), Beth begins to lose her sense of self:

> Since her marriage she had given up her free, wild, wandering habits. She would go into town to order things at the shops in the morning, and take a solitary walk out into the country in the afternoon perhaps, but without any keen enjoyment. Her natural zest for the woods and fields was suspended. She had lost touch with nature. Instead of looking about her observantly, as had been her wont, she walked now, as a rule, with her eyes fixed on the ground, thinking deeply. (354)

As a result of her condition of coverture ("since her marriage"), it was not just Beth's legal existence that had been suspended, but her very nature. For Beth, the everyday effects of being under coverture (without "free, wild, wandering habits") resulted in a loss of vitality. Moreover, this vivacious young woman, who had been always observant, always speaking her mind, was now required ("as a rule") to keep her thoughts and ideas to herself.

Rather than celebrating the merging of two into one, the novel graphically details "the awful oppression of [Beth's] married life; the inevitable degradation of intimate association with such a man as her husband" (418). Countering the comforting image in Blackstone's definition of a woman's position "under wing, cover, and protection," the novel notes: "The tragedy of such a marriage consists in the effect of the man's mind upon the woman's, shut up with him in the closest intimacy day and night, and all the time imbibing his poisoned thoughts" (356). In the novel, Beth is not "under wing," but rather "shut up" with her husband. Reminiscent of the critique of marriage in *Maria*, Beth's marriage also is Gothic in the way that it shows her literally losing herself in Dan's way of thinking, and thus almost succumbing to madness.

Beth's eyes begin to open to her own degradation in her marriage, however, as she befriends a group of activists who, in the novel, are working toward repeal of the Contagious Diseases Acts. The fictional group of reformers in *The Beth Book* understood, just as feminist activists do today, that it is crucial for women to get together and tell their stories. When Beth first comes among these women, she is told, "I hope you are prepared to discuss any and every thing . . . for that is what you will find yourself called upon to do among us" (412). This activist explains the reason for this as follows: "The peculiarity of man is that he will do the most atrocious things without compunction, but would be shocked if he were called upon to discuss them. Do what you like, is his principle, but don't mention it; people form their opinions in discussion, and opinions are apt to be adverse. Our principle is very much the opposite" (412). Beth is in complete agreement, "I have just begun to know the necessity for open discussion. . . . I do not see how we can arrive at happiness in life if we do not try to discover the sources of misery" (412). With the help of these women, she rejects her unhealthy and maddening condition under coverture: "She had recovered her self-possession, her own point of view. . . . During that dreadful phase she had seen with Dan's suspicious eyes. . . . Now, however, she had recovered herself" (433). Emphasizing its importance, the phrase "she had recovered her self-possession" is almost identically repeated two sentences later, "she had recovered herself." Beth once again becomes an acting subject.

Over the course of the novel, the Contagious Diseases Acts are, in fact, repealed, and Beth separates from the husband who has been so cruel. While changes in the laws regarding married women's property have made it possible for Beth to support herself and to have complete access to her inheritance, she is unable to obtain a divorce ("the acute mental suffering her husband had caused her had merely injured her health and endangered her reason, which does not amount to cruelty in the estimation of the law" [518]). In this novel that is concerned with how things *should* be, however, Beth is not fated to a life alone. The reappearance near the end of the novel of Arthur Brock, a man with whom Beth had fallen in love after she had left her husband, suggests new possibilities for this New Woman.

Having taken steps to alleviate her own suffering, Beth is called to speak to others. The following description of the crowd's reaction to a political speech Beth delivers echoes the enthusiastic responses to reformers like Butler:

> For she had spoken that night as few have spoken—spoken to a hostile audience and fascinated them by the power of her personality, the mesmeric power which is part of the endowment of an orator, and had so moved them that they rose at last and cheered her for her eloquence, whether they held her opinions or not. (525)

Beth's reaction to this discovery of her true calling is complex. In certain respects, she resembles her self-sacrificing mother—only Beth is sacrificing herself for the cause of women. While disheartening, there is no doubt much truth in this portrayal. While a great achievement, Josephine Butler's all-consuming, sixteen-year campaign to repeal the Contagious Diseases Acts was also exhausting and frightening. Many times she must have felt that her life was not her own. Similarly, Sarah Grand's biographer relates that Grand suffered acute depression because she "yearned to escape and yet felt bound by what she saw as her vocation" (Kersley 81). Beth describes her feelings as follows:

> She was cowering from the recollection of a great crowd that rose with deafening shouts and seemed to be rushing at her—cowering, too, from the inevitable which she had been forced to recognise—her vocation—discovered by accident, and with dismay, for it was not what she would have chosen for herself in any way had it occurred to her that she had any choice in the matter. . . . Beth could not have lived for herself had she tried. So that now, when the call had come, and the way in which she could best live for others was made plain to her, she had no thought but to pursue it. (524)

An early dream of Beth's may have foreshadowed this move onto the public stage as an advocate for women. As a young girl, she had dreamt that she was in a cave, a cave located, oddly enough, beneath the stage of a theatre. Trapped in this cave, which was filling with smoke (reminiscent of Josephine Butler's well-publicized incident in the Pontefract hayloft), Beth awakens. It is telling, however, that if the dream had continued, Beth's only way out of the cave (not a womb-like safe place but an increasingly dangerous place of confinement) would have been *through* the theatre—out into that quintessentially public sphere.

In the 1890s, after the campaign to repeal the Contagious Diseases Acts made "public" many hitherto "private" women, after the decision in *Queen v. Jackson* un*Lock*ed women on an even broader scale, Beth has more options than Wollstonecraft's Maria. Maria *must* critique the law in writing; Beth can speak out publicly. Whereas Wollstonecraft figures her feminist jurisprudence as Maria writing against the wrongs of woman, Sarah Grand, with her representation of Beth speaking to a great crowd as an advocate for women's legal rights, testifies to the reforming possibilities that literary women throughout the nineteenth century helped to engender.

A WRITER OF BOOKS: LITERARY HISTORIANS

There is no sudden change in career path at the end of George Paston's 1899 *A Writer of Books*, and the eponymous character, Cosima Chudleigh, remains just that through the final pages of the novel. However, this book also explores the connections between literary women and feminist activism, focusing on the role of the woman writer, as a writer, at the end of the nineteenth century. While Beth's childhood accounts for more than half of *The Beth Book*, Cosima's desire to write is explained in a few pages by her book-filled, secluded upbringing by her father, a small town librarian. When he dies, she moves to London to gain more experience of real life, taking the manuscript of her first book with her.

Like Gissing's *New Grub Street* (1891), this book critiques the pressures that writers felt in the 1890s to sacrifice their art to create bestsellers. Cosima's publisher, for example, tells her she must "stow the jaw" (78), cut out "all the dissertations and all the dialogue that doesn't advance the action of the story" (79). He explains that his readers read for the plot; she must change her story to have a happy ending, specifically a wedding. As this is her first novel, and she desperately wants to gain a hearing, she agrees: "During the next few days Cosima was occupied in slashing and mutilating the offspring of her brain, and soon began to feel as if she were up to her elbows in gore" (81). Her aborted first attempt to tell her own kind of story, however, does not discourage her from trying again.

One evening, "as Cosima was at work upon her [second] book" (49), she is disrupted by muffled sobbing coming from the boarding house room adjoining hers, occupied by Mr. and Mrs. Barton. Knocking on the door, she discovers Mrs. Barton, alone and in tears, and asks if she can be of any use. The unhappy woman despairingly responds: "You! No; how should you be of any use? . . . You're only a woman, and women are powerless to help themselves or each other" (49). Rather than leaving her to suffer in private, Cosima encourages Mrs. Barton to tell her story.

Mrs. Barton's narrative illustrates the cruelty of child custody laws that still permitted the involuntary separation of a mother from her children. Unlike Caroline Norton (who thirty years earlier had gained limited rights for mothers who were separated from their husbands), Mrs. Barton still lives with her husband. But he is a man with sensitive nerves; he dislikes noise and has sent their young son away to school. Mrs. Barton, who her husband felt was too lenient with the child, is allowed to see the boy once a month. When Cosima asks her why she did not refuse to let him go, she explains that even at this time, "[a]ccording to our laws, children belong solely to the father as long as he has done nothing to forfeit his rights over them" (51). The cruelty of taking away her child is not something "that the law takes cognisance of" (51). Far from seeing herself as under the protective wing of her husband, Mrs. Barton compares herself to a mother thrush whose nest and young birds had been destroyed: "Morning after morning, I used to hear the unhappy mother [thrush] searching for her children. She would fly round and round the spot, uttering one long piercing note, the most heartwringing sound I ever heard . . . It made me feel so wretched that I had to change my room at last for one where I couldn't hear it" (50).

Upon hearing Mrs. Barton's real-life tragedy, Cosima indignantly responds, "I wish I were a man—a member of Parliament or a great lawyer. I would never rest until I had changed such an infamous law" (51). Cosima's desire to be a man is only a desire to be in a position to change the law; she now understands the significance of Mrs. Barton's observation that she is only a woman. But she has been of some use; Mrs. Barton is a little calmer after this late-night telling. Cosima, a writer of books, leaves with the knowledge that a well-told story has the power to evoke a pressing need for change.

In yet another example of women's maddening circumstances, Mrs. Barton later starts to imagine that her son is with her, and she croons to a bundled sofa cushion. When the child actually dies, Mrs. Barton is sent to a private asylum and Mr. Barton moves away. Cosima views the entire tragedy as a "deliberate crime" (86), but a woman doctor who also lives in the boarding house assures her that the law will take no notice:

> The laws are supposed to be framed to protect the weak? Oh, I know that's a pleasant legal fiction. The laws are framed by the strong, and naturally they are framed for the benefit of the strong. That's why women, children and animals have such a poor time of it generally. I can remember a time when I used to be hot and fierce and rebellious over the wrongs of the weak, but now I take all that as a matter of course. It is the natural and logical result of our lopsided system of government, a government by one sex only. (86)

While Cosima's writing is interrupted for one evening by Mrs. Barton's legal wrongs, this literary woman's life is forever altered when she becomes a wife herself. When her childhood friend Tom asks her to marry him, she is shocked; she loves him only as a brother. But when he persists with his entreaties, certain that she will learn to love him, she weighs the pros and cons of marriage in a most deliberate and unromantic manner. She ultimately decides that the marriage plot is one she must explore: "If . . . she were to resolve never to marry until she fell passionately in love, it seemed likely that she would be doomed to remain a spinster all her life, and so lose an experience that must be valuable to any woman, and practically indispensable to a novelist" (110). Shortly after she accepts this proposal, she meets Quentin Mallory, a man who cares about what she cares about and is interested in her ideas and opinions. She begins to have serious doubts about her upcoming marriage but feels that she cannot disgrace Tom by backing out. Much is made of the fact that they have acquired a flat and furniture, and human suffering is thus discounted and considered largely irrelevant when weighed against social trappings and expectations.

As one of the New Woman novels to rewrite the marriage plot, *The Writer of Books* details Cosima's misery from the fateful day of her wedding. Immediately after the ceremony, she laments her unalterable mistake: "She was no longer one; she had ceased to belong to herself. Her freedom and independence were gone forever . . . She was seized by a sudden, almost uncontrollable impulse to shriek aloud that she had made a mistake, that she did not wish to be married, that she took back all the dreadful vows she had uttered so mechanically" (139). Too late, Cosima understands the dreadful condition of coverture—she is "no longer one." Her new knowledge makes her want to "shriek," affiliating her with women activists like Butler, who had been dubbed the "shrieking sisterhood."[35]

Just as Sue Bridehead shrank from the sexual attentions of Phillotson,

Tom's attentions and embraces twisted Cosima's life story into a "squalid kind of tragedy" (140). After she gives birth to a stillborn child, she is at last free from Tom's undesired embraces and she begins to write again. But when Tom's former passion for her revives, "[h]er short-lived happiness was changed to misery, her newborn beauty faded, the light died out of her face, and a strained hunted expression came into her eyes" (238). Cosima is tortured because she loves Mallory but feels she must be true to Tom. She permits herself to leave her husband, however, when her friend Bess presents her with a packet of love letters that Tom has sent to Bess. As Bess knowingly warns, however, "You can't divorce your husband on that sort of evidence, not even get a legal separation" (242). But Cosima replies with a radical revision of the meaning of the law in her life: "I no longer have a husband—I am free to follow my own inclinations. If the law doesn't allow me to dissolve my marriage, why then, I'll be a law unto myself. No woman has ever had a voice in making the laws, and therefore no woman is bound to obey them" (242). She then goes to Mallory and her words echo those of Wollstonecraft's Maria: "The law does not give me freedom, but I acknowledge no law except my own. I divorce myself by my own law, and I shall marry again by my own law if it seems good to me" (245). But Mallory refuses to be the cause of her social ruin. More conventional regarding the possibility of a relationship outside of marriage than *The Beth Book*, *The Writer of Books* does not hold out much promise that Cosima and Mallory will be together. The ending, however, is hopeful in that Cosima realizes that she has important and fulfilling work to do:

> Love may once have been a woman's whole existence, but that was when a skein of embroidery silk was the only other string in her bow. In the life of the modern woman, blessed with an almost inexhaustible supply of strings, love is no less episodic than in the life of a man. It may be eagerly longed for, it may be tenderly cherished, but it has been deposed forever from its proud position of "lord of all." (257)

As she nurtures her pain with a pen, the novel's ending holds out the promise of a fulfilling future (259).

The relationship between Cosima and Mallory, however, is much more than a thwarted romance. Mallory is a well-known historian, and his conversations with Cosima and their shared goals and motivations testify to the connections between literature and history explored in the novel. Mallory speaks of reading novels as part of an historian's business: "Novels, plays, letters, and memoirs are the modern historian's bricks and mortar. . . . It is the life and thought and manners of a people that he desires to portray, the *vie intime* of a country and period. If he cannot reproduce the spirit, the very atmosphere of the age, he has failed . . ." (123). Encouraging Cosima to write from a woman's point of view, not to try to write like a man, he tells her how important that will be for history:

> We have plenty of opportunity of getting the masculine point of view, but it is only in comparatively recent times, that we have had female writers who possessed ideas of their own, and dared to express them. We laugh sometimes at their grammar and their logic, but it mustn't be forgotten that the work of those who thought for themselves will be invaluable documents for the social historian of the future. We, of the present day, would give our ears if the past were lighted up for us in the way the nineteenth century will be for him. We can follow the development of thought of man from the first dawn of history, but the thoughts of woman are buried in her grave. (144)

When Cosima presses him, "And whose fault is that?" he responds that it is the fault of our fathers, "who held that the pen was no less unfeminine a weapon than the sword. But prejudices never go unpunished, and the penalty of that prejudice is that we have lost half the history of the human race" (144). In the interest of future historians, Mallory wants Cosima with her writing to "[t]ell us what you and your sisters think and feel, what you have seen and suffered" (145).

That is, in fact, what Paston does in (and as) *A Writer of Books*. While Cosima is honing her craft, real life is happening around her, interrupting and becoming part of her work and, according to Mallory, the historical record. There is the story of the Bartons, the tale of a seduced young girl who commits suicide, and the trial of Cosima's friend Bess, who stabs a man to ward off his unwanted sexual advances. There is the story of Cosima's own marriage, which is literally and figuratively set beside the genuinely happy union of Tom and Cosima's neighbors, the Mackays. Mrs. Mackay, another fine storyteller who collects the "private histories and domestic affairs" (176) of the neighbors, has accumulated much wisdom about the institution of marriage and articulates some very feminist ideas about birth control.

When Cosima asks her if she wants children, she replies, "Lord no . . . [a] man's quite child enough for any reasonable woman" (176). She says the idea of maternal instinct is all man's doing: "The men are always prating about the wonderful things every true woman ought to feel, and we have to pretend we do so as not to get left. There may be a woman here and there who wishes to have one child, but there are none who wish for half a dozen" (176). She admits that she would never say that if a man were around though, "Wouldn't he think me a little monster for saying what I really thought?"

(176). Here on the pages of this novel, however, this woman's unspeakable thoughts are recorded. Cosima, a New Woman who is aware of the debates on the issue of birth control, comments, "Some of the modern sociologists think that equality and economical independence for women would be the best solution to the population problem. You seem to have arrived at very much the same conclusion" (176). Mrs. Mackay speaks with the authority of someone who watches the world around her, who collects the stories of the everyday: "Of course, there would never be too many children in the world if the women were free to please themselves. . . . Even silly people like me who have never studied sociology know as much as that" (176).

All of these stories become "the story" as the novel narrates what Cosima and her women friends and contemporaries think and feel, what they have seen and suffered. Earlier in the novel, Cosima had explained to Mallory that she was not, like her friend Bess, a feminist reformer:

> I feel that I was born to paint them [the times], not to set them right. . . . It is much more amusing to live in a transitional age, when the fighting is at its height. Though I may only play the part of war correspondent, I like to smell the powder and hear the whizz of the bullets about my ears. I expect that in the history books of the future, the nineteenth century will be spoken of as another Hundred Years' War, the war for freedom. All the great movements have been in the direction of freedom, the freedom of knowledge and religion, of trades and slaves, and even of women and children. (225)

Mallory is surprised that she is content to "stand aside and observe and criticise" (225). He tells her, "Your attitude reminds me of that sensible housewife, whose husband insists on managing the kitchen, the nursery and the school-room as well as the garden, the stable and the farm. She smiles at his blunders and bides her time . . ." (225–26). At the time that Cosima made this comment, she desperately was trying to be that sensible housewife, to fulfill her proper role out of a sense of obligation. But that was before she realized that her role of wife would again include her sexual "duty" ("a terror that she had never foreseen" [238]), before she learned that Mallory loved her too, before Tom expected her to accept and forgive his feelings for Bess but, like Hardy's Angel Clare (in *Tess of the D'Urbervilles*), refused to live with her after learning of her feelings for Mallory, before she was forced to accept the injustice that her reputation (as a woman, as a writer of books) would be forfeited if she followed her heart.

In the last scene of the novel, Cosima heads toward her writing-table "to prepare the materials of war"; she is ready to begin her "campaign" (259). Rather than naming herself a war correspondent, she sees her writing as playing a much more active role in the war for freedom than she had earlier acknowledged. While we aren't told what kind of novel she is sitting down to write, she has just won critical acclaim for a novel that was published by a top-rate firm after being rejected by her plot-oriented publisher for being "as dull as real life" (232). Presumably her next novel also will be based on real life, influenced by her historical muse Mallory for whom her "love was as true and as strong, though her suffering was considerably less, because, instead of saturating her pillow with useless tears, or consuming her heart in vain regrets, she was already beginning to think seriously about her next book" (257). She hopes her campaign will help her "to conquer heart-sickness and win forgetfulness and peace" (259); maybe this will be by imagining or working to re-create a world in which "crimes" that result from unjust laws and social rules, such as those that kept Mrs. Barton from her child and Cosima from Mallory, are written out of the plot.

Arnold Bennett wrote in a review of Paston's novels, "We do her no injustice when we say that she is not primarily interested in fiction. It happens to be the accepted vehicle for thought, and so she uses it—and uses it very cleverly. . . . What does interest 'George Paston' is the question of 'women's rights'—the inequality of women with men before the law and social custom" ("George Paston" 520).[36] Maybe Cosima will write books like Paston, books that the critic Bennett characterized as "the best women's rights pamphlets ever written" ("George Paston" 520).

GLORIANA; OR, THE REVOLUTION OF 1900: REVOLUTIONARY POLITICS

While *The Beth Book* and *A Writer of Books* end with their heroines beginning new and promising lives after they have left unhappy marriages, Florence Dixie's novel *Gloriana; or, The Revolution of 1900* is a novel that pleads a case for, and presents as a reality, the possibility of true equality for women and, thus, better lives for all. Having a philosophy similar to Clapperton's, Dixie believes that human beings consciously can better their own lot—but her specific solution is through a change in women's place in society, a change ultimately brought about by women taking their rightful place in the world of law.[37]

Unlike some of the more subtle literary calls to action, *Gloriana* radically presents a revolution—the real kind—and Dixie is aware that her controversial topic will enrage certain readers and critics. Anticipating such a response, she meets the charge head on in her preface:

Many critics, like the rest of humanity, are apt to be unfair. They take up a book, and when they find that it does not accord with their sentiments, they attempt to wreck it by ridicule and petty spiteful criticism. They forget to ask themselves, "Why is this book written?" They altogether omit to go to the root of the author's purpose; and the result is, that false testimony is often borne against principles which, though drastic, are pure, which, though sharp as the surgeon's knife, are yet humane; for it is genuine sympathy with humanity that arouses them. (x)

In her opening statement, Dixie defends her novel against unfair charges like those launched against Frances Trollope's *Jessie Phillips*, Jane Clapperton's *Margaret Dunmore*, and other novels with a purpose. Challenging the contemporary critical perspective (and hence its judgment), she identifies the critics' lack of analysis of a book's purpose as a major failing on *their* part. Also, defending herself against accusations of malicious intent, she comments, "There may be some, who reading 'Gloriana,' will feel shocked, and be apt to misjudge the author. There are others who will understand, appreciate, and sympathize" (x). Through this novelistic appeal, Dixie hopes to find and increase the jury of readers who will fit in the latter category, who will justly judge her motivations and the merit of her literary work.

While Dixie speaks on behalf of herself and *Gloriana* in the preface, she sees the novel itself as the advocate; it is pleading the cause she espouses:

"Gloriana" pleads woman's cause, pleads for her freedom, for the just acknowledgement of her rights. It pleads that her equal humanity with man shall be recognized, and therefore that her claim to share with what he has arrogated to himself shall be considered. "Gloriana" pleads that in women's degradation man shall no longer be debased, that in her elevation he shall be upraised and ennobled. (xi)

She concludes with an explicit statement of the novel's purpose: "If therefore, the following story should help men to be generous and just, should awaken the sluggards amongst women to a sense of their position, and should thus lead to a rapid revolution, it will not have been written in vain" (xii). Dixie fully acknowledges that her intention is to incite.

The heroine of the story, Gloria de Lara, has a vision when she is twelve that she is to be the leader of a great revolution to right the wrongs of women. At this age, as she is coming into womanhood, she realizes that she does not want to become a woman on the terms that her society offers.

The next time the reader sees her, she is twenty-two and a man, at least to all the world. Gloria, as Hector D'Estrange, has attended Eton, taken high honors at Oxford, and written a very provocative article entitled "Essay on Woman's Position" that is the talk of London. Like the novel *Gloriana*, this article is published in 1890. It gets people of all classes talking about women's position in society in much the same way that Dixie hopes her novel will. Among other ideas set forth in Hector's article is the question, "Why should the professions which men have arrogated to themselves be entirely monopolized by their sex, to the exclusion of women? . . . I do not see that we should be a whit less badly governed if we had a woman Prime Minister or a mixed Cabinet, or if women occupied seats in the Houses of Parliament or on the bench in the Courts of Justice" (22).

Four years after publication of this article, Hector runs for and wins a seat in Parliament. The primary action of the novel begins four years later in 1898. Hector has become a shining political star: "His eloquence and debating power are the wonder of all who hear him, and his practical, sympathetic knowledge of the social questions of the day has made him the idol of the masses. He has just succeeded in carrying his Woman's Suffrage Bill by a large majority, thereby conferring on women, married or unmarried, in this respect, identical rights with men" (69–70). Another of Hector's crowning achievements at this time is the opening of a Hall of Liberty, a vast hall funded from conscriptions of women that was built "to accommodate women students from all parts of the world, who may wish to take part in the physical drill or educational advantages afforded by this great central institute for the training of womankind" (71). While on a much grander scale, Dixie's Hall of Liberty is similar to Clapperton's lecture hall. In each of these forward-looking novels, there is a structure that stands for and as a new and public "place" for women in society.

Hector also is very much an advocate for the working classes. Unlike most late-century socialists, however, Hector believes that gender equality is the first step toward equality of all kinds. In his speech to the huge crowds at the opening of the Hall of Liberty, he sets forth this position:

> You boast of a civilization unparalleled in the world's history. Yet is it so? Side by side with wealth, appalling in its magnitude, stalks poverty, misery, and wrong, more appalling still. I aver that this poverty, misery, and wrong is, in a great measure, due to the false and unnatural position awarded to woman; nor will justice, reparation, and perfection be attained until she takes her place *in all things* as the equal of man. (78)[38]

Hector's immense popularity results in his being elected Prime Minister in 1900.

Behind this great political success, a private tragedy is brewing. Gloria's mother, Speranza de Lara—one of the most modern mothers portrayed in nineteenth-century literature—has been stalked by her ex-husband Lord Westray. When Speranza was seventeen, she was forced to marry Westray, who was her stepbrother, in order to keep her two brothers from being stripped of their only source of funds:

> Sold by the law which declares that however brutally a man may treat his wife, so that he does not strike her, she has no power to free herself from him; sold by the law which declares her to be that man's slave, this woman, bright with the glory of a high intellect, perfect in Nature's health and strength, was committed to the keeping of a man whom Fashion courted and patted on the back, whilst declaring him at the same time to be the veriest rogue in London. (13–14)

Exposed by her husband's infidelities to the risks of syphilis ("he was free to do everything including poison her" [13]), and treated brutally for six years of marriage, Speranza fell in love and ran away with Captain Harry Kintore: "And when at length he [Kintore] bade her fly with him beyond the reach of so much misery and cruelty, was it a wonder that she succumbed, and flew in the face of the law that bound her to the contrary?" (15). But her flight from the "protective wing" of her husband was doomed; Westray followed the couple and shot Kintore dead.

While we are given no details, we know that Speranza and Westray divorced, and that Speranza stayed abroad and bore Gloria, Kintore's child. After all these years, Westray is again after Speranza; typical of an abuser, he needs to control her. First, he approaches her after she has returned to England with the audacious proposal that they remarry. When she rebukes him, "[h]e grinds his teeth with rage . . . racking his brain for a means of overcoming her, and forcing her once more to obey his will. The fact that she defies him, hates him, loathes him, has refused him, only arouses in him more madly than ever the desire to become possessed of her once again" (37–38). Like Haughton Jackson, Westray opted for kidnapping. This abduction took place before Hector is elected Prime Minister, and what the reader knows is that Hector and his good friend Evie, the Duke of Ravensdale, learn of Westray's capture of Speranza from a loyal servant, Rita Vernon. When they discover Westray and Speranza in a house of ill repute, the first section of the novel ends with "a loud cry as a shot rings through the silent house" (96); the reader is not told what else transpires on that evening.

Two years later, as Prime Minister, Hector introduces a bill into Parliament that would legislate absolute equality for women. Described as "a free and unfettered charter of liberty," the bill is "a final and decisive declaration that women are not man's inferiors, but have as clear and inalienable a right as he to share the government of their country, and to adopt the professions hitherto arrogated by men solely to themselves" (100). Hector expects that the bill will be defeated in Parliament, but his plan is, after the defeat, to appeal to the people: "I shall be defeated on it without a doubt, but it will be before the country, and I can appeal to the country upon it" (98). For Hector, the law should be the will of the people.

In the speech that accompanies his introduction of this bill, delivered to a standing-room-only crowd with thousands more people gathered outside the House of Commons, Hector voices many of the concerns and proposals that feminist writers and other advocates had been presenting to the public for years. Specifically, he calls for educating men and women together, with an emphasis on the need for sex education. He also argues for opening all of the professions to women and making women eligible to hold all political offices, including seats in Parliament. Alluding to the Sandhurst case, Hector states, "It is now eleven years since County Councils were established. At the very first elections women were chosen as representatives, but on appeal to the law they were ousted from their seats" (113). He poses the rhetorical question, "What is there preposterous and appalling in the suggestion that women should become Members of Parliament, and when, by genius or talents, they can attain to such, assume Cabinet rank, and claim the right to carry on the affairs of their country?" (113), and then responds that it "'is merely custom that now debars them'" (113). Hector is determined to legislate away that custom—the custom that, as was discussed in chapter 4, is the common-law tradition of excluding women from public offices.

In anticipating objections to the bill, Hector admits that the number of marriages probably will diminish, but he presents this as one of the benefits of the bill:

> Thousands of miserable unions are yearly effected in consequence of women's unnatural and one-sided position in Society. In all these cases she does not marry because, with a knowledge of the subject, with every profession thrown open to her and chance to get on equal to men, she is satisfied that she prefers married life. No. In the cases referred to, she marries for money, and for position, or to escape the restraints of home, or because she has no

chance of making her way in the world, and the result is that these marriages are miserable failures. . . . (114)

He also emphasizes the population question: "There is a problem creeping gradually forward upon us, a problem that will have to be solved in time, and that is the steady increase of population" (114). Hector believes that the emancipation of women is the immediate and necessary first step in addressing this growing concern. The bill, as Hector and his fellow D'Estrangites expected, is defeated. Unexpected, however, is the appearance of an officer who arrests Hector for the murder of Lord Westray.

Gloria, as Hector, represents herself at this trial, and while (like a true modern Portia) she is in the guise of a man, in *Gloriana* we have one of the first representations of a woman acting as an attorney in British fiction. At this trial, like that of Hetty in *Adam Bede*, the reader does not know whether Hector is guilty or innocent. But the narrative voice in this novel (which has celebrated Hector's character throughout) continues with its advocacy on Hector's behalf: "None, looking at the beautiful face, with its clear, radiant complexion, magnificent eyes, and high, pale, thoughtful brow, around which the old-gold curls lovingly cluster, could bring themselves to believe that that man is a murderer" (119). The reader cannot either—but for reasons that go beyond Hector's angelic appearance. Specifically, the reader knows that the premise of the prosecution's case is wrong. The state is trying to establish a secret affair between Speranza and Westray and characterize Hector as Speranza's jealous lover. The reader therefore immediately is suspicious of the witnesses whose testimony corroborates these misinterpreted relationships. Also, the reader is aware that Westray and one of the prosecution's star witnesses have previously schemed together. (It turns out that Westray is not really dead and that the entire murder charge is a set-up.) Therefore, the reader dismisses incriminating evidence in a way that the fictional jury cannot.

When Hector opens his defense, he explains his intimacy with Speranza by acknowledging her as his mother (although he doesn't say that he is her *daughter*). He also admits to the jury (and to the reader) that he did shoot Westray that night, but explains that Westray suffered only a superficial wound and emphatically did not wish Hector to report the incident to the police. Hector then proceeds to call witnesses to support his side of the story.

One of the many ways in which this novel performs feminist jurisprudence is in its highlighting of the manner in which women and their testimony are misrepresented in legal discourse. For example, when Speranza narrates her abduction by two men hired by Westray (they attack her while she is out walking alone and rush at her with knives when she resists), the prosecutor "smiles superciliously. 'Hallucination,' he mutters audibly. 'Many women are subject to it'" (132–33). He again mutters "hallucination" at Rita Vernon's testimony; she is an eyewitness to the attack. To emphasize for the reader the truth of Speranza's and Rita's testimony, the narrator does not have them recount what had happened. The narrator simply states that Speranza "tells the facts as we have described them in a former chapter" (132) and Rita "gives in simple, unaffected, language the story of the attack on Speranza and the part she played in it" (133). Thus, there are absolutely no discrepancies between these women's testimony and what the reader knows to be the narrative truth. That the law, as represented by the state, is reading the facts all wrong is emphasized when the prosecutor tells the jury, "And, gentlemen, as against this very clear and circumstantial evidence, we are asked by Mrs. de Lara and Rita Vernon to accept a romance which all sane men can only regard in the light of hallucination, if not, as I regret to believe, downright deliberate falsehood. We are asked to believe. . . ." (137); he then recounts in detail the "story" of the kidnapping that the reader knows is exactly what happened. Interestingly, when Evie Rosendale tells his story, even though it is favorable to Hector, there is no cross-examination. As a man, his word is more credible, not so easily dismissed as hallucination.

When the prosecutor needs to discredit the testimony that is damaging to his case, he draws on the familiar connection between women and madness to do so. Also, as happened when women were accused of "unnatural" crimes such as infanticide, the prosecutor disparages Speranza's character with his rendition of her personal history, that she "broke faith with her husband, whom in wedding she had sworn to love, honor, and obey, and shamelessly fled with her lover, Harry Kintore" (135). Rita's past life as a prostitute (Evie Rosendale had rescued her from this fate) also becomes part of the case against Hector. Speranza's and Rita's sexual histories made them improper women and hence unreliable witnesses.

At the end of the trial, the jury, apparently composed of sane men who could only regard these women's stories as hallucination, rejected their testimony and found Hector guilty. The prosecutor's more familiar story of revenge, a jealous Hector tracking down Westray with the intent to commit murder, was a much more believable story. Not even Hector's revelation that he is a woman (which he offers to clear up confusion that arises when a doctor testifies that Speranza gave birth to a daughter not a son) can save him. Hector is found guilty and sentenced to death.

It is then that the revolution begins. Flora Desmond, leader of a regiment of women that has been formed under the leadership of D'Estrange, encouraged by thousands of people gathered outside the courthouse, leads her guards in an attack on the prison van. Once Hector is released, he addresses the crowd:

> I have been unjustly accused and unjustly condemned. If it were not so, I would not accept the rescue brought me by my faithful women guards, aided by your kindly and generous devotion. . . . There are bad laws which must be done away with, good ones which must be set up to accomplish social reform. . . . And now, my friends, we are on the eve of a great revolution. If the people will stand by me, I will stand by them. Let us loyally determine to carry this great question to a successful issue, nor rest till it has been accomplished. (149)

She then announces her true sex to the crowd: "I am a woman! Henceforth I am no longer Hector D'Estrange, but Gloria de Lara" (150). Whisked away by the White Guards, she is protected by the crowd at the cost of many lives as the government's Blue Guards try to recapture her. This scene, with British soldiers charging on horseback through a large crowd of working-class men and women, echoes the tragedy of Peterloo.[39] The laws passed suppressing public meetings to keep Gloria from spreading her radical philosophies also hearken back to efforts a century earlier to stave revolutionary action.[40] Showing contempt for any law "which has not been ratified by the people's approval" (180), Gloria addresses large crowds throughout the country, "vanishing as quickly and mysteriously as she appears" (180). Gloria views the law as a problem, not herself as an outlaw.

The covert machinations of Westray continue, until Gloria finds herself tricked and held captive on his boat. In a violent storm at sea, Westray really does die (his body is found this time) and Gloria is believed dead. Hope wanes (even for the reader) that Gloria may have survived, as Evie Rosendale (who loves Gloria) and Flora Desmond bring her great plans for the future to fruition. Upon learning of Westray's plot against Gloria, the people have chosen D'Estrangeism and Evie has formed a Ministry known as the second D'Estrangeite Cabinet. Evie brings Gloria's legislation to a vote again: "I appeal to you to show on this occasion a true courage worthy of men, and abolish forever from the Statute Book those disabilities under which women are deprived of rights to which they are entitled by reason of their common humanity with man" (263). Evie concludes by invoking Gloria's name and work for the "suffering and slaving classes" (265): "In her name I appeal for justice, and I confidently believe that I shall not appeal in vain" (263).

And he doesn't. The bill passes as "the peers obey the country's mandate, and acknowledge the people's will as law" (266). The celebratory tone continues through the end of the novel as the country and the reader discover that Gloria did indeed survive the shipwreck. She had been rescued by a ship sailing to South America, and the captain, having recognized her and knowing that she was a fugitive from the law, loyally had protected her from recognition. Gloria returns to England to find that she has been re-elected to Parliament (as a woman this time) and that she is to be joined by several other women lawmakers. She becomes, upon Evie's resignation, England's first woman Prime Minister.

In the final chapter of *Gloriana*, titled "1999," a stranger and his guide are flying over London in a balloon. From this bird's eye view, they see "a London vastly changed from the London of 1900" (282); it is immaculately clean, and poverty is a condition of the past. From the guide, the stranger hears the history of the great Gloria of Ravensdale. Gloria had married Evie, although she certainly was never "covered" by him. Achieving equality in marriage, they now lie side by side in a grave overlooking the Atlantic Ocean. Giving up all of their personal wealth, they had devoted their lives to achieving greater equality for all. Gloria served as Prime Minister for years, followed by Flora Desmond. The guide of the future testifies to and the land itself is proof of the great progress made under their leadership: "As we pass across it [the country] you will see evidence of peace and contentment, and plenty everywhere. We owe it all to the glorious reforms of Gloria of Ravensdale" (283). Such was the vision that inspired the feminist jurisprudence of *Gloriana*.

AFTERWORD

More than a century ago, Florence Dixie imagined her utopian worldview of the time and social landscape that we inhabit today. An overview in this first decade of the twenty-first century showcases that pollution, poverty, and inequality, relating not only to the gender and class issues that Dixie examined but also, for example, to discrimination based on race and sexual orientation, remain very much a part of the scene.[1]

In the final pages of *Gloriana*, the stranger in the balloon wants to know the story of the past in order to understand what he sees in the present. From the "history" the guide recounts, the reader learns the future of the novel's characters. In this way, the novel highlights the perspective that history offers, not only on what has and has not been accomplished, but also on where the future might lead. As historian Gerda Lerner explains, "In preserving the collective past and reinterpreting it to the present, human beings define their potential and explore the limits of the possibilities" (221).

This study of women writers in nineteenth-century law and literature is also very much about legal history. As I have argued elsewhere,[2] an examination of only those legal narratives of the past that are included in "official" legal texts—legislative histories, statutes, judicial opinions—perpetuates the myth of "women as marginal to civilization and as the victim of historical process" (Lerner 223).[3] This, in turn, has devastating future effects because with "no precedent for significant action, heroism, or liberating example," women "cannot imagine alternatives to existing conditions" (Lerner 222–23). A critical challenge of feminist jurisprudence is the uncovering of evidence of women's significant and active role in legal history. In discussing the narrative advocacy of women writers (in real-life courtrooms, in the court of public opinion, and in the legal forum provided by the novel form), it has been my aim to bring to light, impress on the historical record, and hence submit to the court of critical opinion a range of heretofore suppressed evidence of nineteenth-century women's feminist jurisprudence.

Similarly, *In Contempt: Nineteenth-Century Women, Law, and Literature* also introduces "new evidence" to consider in evaluating the cultural role of the nineteenth-century novel. In analyzing the mutually constitutive relationship between culture and law, Naomi Mezey suggests employing the ethnographic method of "thick description . . . in an effort to locate the slippage and elision between the two, directing us not so much to a singular explanation as to neglected questions and revealing juxtapositions" (38). The outlaw novels discussed in this study are sites of this kind of slippage and elision. They challenge and resist a singular explanation of the novel as serving a policing role in society. They bring to light new and different questions about gender and the law, and they create new knowledge when juxtaposed to more canonical texts on which prior judgments about the cultural work that the novel performs have been based.

Finally, I hope that this study will energize, enrich, and expand the field of law and literature, addressing issues that have kept it from producing "the excitement that it is capable of generating" (Baron, "Law," 1060–61). Specifically, Jane Baron has identified a need in this field for a more thoughtful approach to interdisciplinarity and a more critical analysis of "how we categorize knowledge and why" (1061).[4] Similarly, Julie Stone Peters has suggested that the field of law and literature has "tended to exaggerate disciplinarity, caricaturing disciplinary difference through each discipline's longing for something it imagined the other to possess" (449). Also of concern is the fact that the law and literature movement has been slow to acknowledge the contributions of literary women and the significance of gender, with Judith Resnik characterizing women as "almost invisible" in this field (349).[5]

Feminist theory and methods question and break down limiting categories. They also ensure the relevance of women's experiences and stories. Disciplinary boundaries, as well as traditional ideas about which texts should be the objects of study, have resulted in the suppression of much of the women's writing presented in this book. With its emphasis on the role of women writers as advocates and its explorations of the performance of feminist jurisprudence in their publications, this study is intended to bridge texts and disciplines in transformative ways. *In Contempt: Nineteenth-Century Women, Law, and Literature* advocates for explorations at the intersections of law, literature, history, and feminism, specifically ones that take into account the important legal and literary precedents that are "outlaw texts."

TABLE OF ACTS

Poor Law Amendment Act 1834 (4 & 5 Will 4, c. 76): 13, 47–48

Prisoners' Counsel Act 1836 (6 & 7 Will 4, c. 114): 29

Qualification of Women Act 1907 (7 Edw 7, c. 33): 200n4

Representation of the People Act 1867 (30 & 31 Vict, c. 102): 98

Representation of the People Act 1918 (7& 8 Geo 5, c. 64): 120

Representation of the People (Equal Franchise) Act 1928 (18 & 19 Geo 5, c. 12): 204n38

Sex Disqualification (Removal) Act 1919 (9 & 10 Geo 5, c. 71): 120, 204n34

Solicitors Act 1843 (6 & 7 Vict, c. 73): 118–19

NOTES

Introduction

1. This Act made it possible for a Court of Chancery to award mothers custody of their children under the age of seven and access to children under sixteen. Norton was responsible for the introduction of this legislation, and her efforts have been acknowledged as very influential in getting this Act passed. See Shanley 25.

2. Norton claimed to have no problem with the law treating husband and wife as "one" so long as they were living together amicably, but when they were "living alienated and in a state of separation" the results were "unjust, unfit, and unnatural" (*Laws* 167). Quite conservative in her published views, Norton asserts, "What I write, is written in no spirit of rebellion; it puts forward no absurd claim of equality; it is simply an appeal for protection" (*Laws* 2). However, as Poovey has argued, the act of making a public appeal was very radical at the time, and her transformation "from the silent sufferer of private wrongs into an articulate spokesperson in the public sphere" worked to challenge "the entire ideological order that the legal and sexual double standard supported" (*Uneven Developments* 64–65).

3. Norton created a great stir with the publication of her *A Letter to the Queen on Lord Chancellor Cranworth's Marriage and Divorce Bill* (1855). Critiquing provisions of the proposed bill that allowed men to divorce adulterous wives but only allowed women to separate from adulterous husbands, Norton highlighted the injustice of this unequal treatment with scathing irony:

> "[I]t is not good for MAN to be alone,"—but extremely good for woman. Hard that a husband should not divorce an adulterous wife! Hard that he should not form a "purer connection!" Hard (though *he* has a career and occupations out of his own home), that a second chance of domestic happiness should not again greet him!—But not the least hard that his weaker partner, elevated, according to Mr. Gladstone, to an equality with him, since the Christian advent,—she, who if she has not a home has nothing—

should be left stranded and wrecked on the barren sands, at the foot of the world's impassive and impassable rocks. (58)

Parkes and Howitt joined Smith in her efforts to amend married women's property laws; they became involved in divorce reform when the legal issues were linked in the parliamentary debates of 1856 and 1857. See Shanley 32–35.

4. The 1857 Act did include certain provisions that helped women escape the strictures of coverture. For example, if a woman was granted a separation decree, she was treated as a *feme sole* with respect to her property and contracts. Also, if she was deserted by her husband, she could go before a local magistrate and receive an order to control her earnings as a *feme sole*. Also in 1857, Smith, Parkes, Anna Murphy, and Anna Jameson started *The Englishwoman's Journal*, which became the official paper of the burgeoning women's movement (St. John-Stevas 261).

5. Under the 1870 Act, a wife was entitled to keep her own wages and earnings made after marriage and passage of this law. Property belonging to her prior to marriage, however, was her separate property only if so agreed to by her husband in writing. She was entitled to keep any personal property as one of the next of kin of an intestate and specific bequests of money (but only up to £200). The law did not address at all the limitations on a married woman's own testamentary powers. See Holcombe 166–83 for a discussion of the legislative history of this Act, as well as why it was declared a "legislative abortion" in its final form (179). Under the much broader 1882 Act, a married woman was considered to have the rights of a *feme sole* with respect to acquiring, holding, and disposing by will or otherwise her separate property. Her separate property included all real and personal property that belonged to her prior to marriage, as well as her wages and earnings acquired after marriage. Married women were also granted the right to enter into contracts and to sue on their own behalf. See Holcombe 184–205 for the legislative history of the 1882 Act. Also, see Dorothy Stetson's book, *A Woman's Issue: The Politics of Family Law Reform in England*, for a study of "the political influence of feminists on the development of divorce and matrimonial property law in England" (15).

6. See Mitchell, *Cobbe*, for a discussion of Cobbe's central role in the inclusion of provisions relating to protection from domestic abuse in the Matrimonial Causes Act of 1878, specifically the impact of her writings such as "Wife-Torture in England," published in the *Contemporary Review* while the legislation was pending. See Mitchell generally for a biographical account of Cobbe, one of the most influential women writer advocates in the nineteenth century.

7. The Contagious Diseases Acts and Butler's seventeen-year campaign are discussed in detail in chapter 5.

8. Thomas Talfourd introduced the bill that became the Infant Custody Act in 1839 (Shanley 25); Richard Monkton Milnes was supportive on many women's issues including reform of married women's property laws (34); Lords Brougham and Lyndhurst advocated for women's rights during the debates on reform of divorce and property laws (35, 40); and John Stuart Mill, Jacob Bright, and George Shaw Lefevre (who introduced the married women's property bill in 1868) agreed with Wollstoneholme, Butler, and Cobbe on the need to rethink substantially the institution of marriage (67).

9. Women's efforts to influence the law more directly are discussed in detail in chapter 4.

10. As Patricia Smith explains in the introduction to a collection of essays representing the wide spectrum of approaches to and focuses of feminist jurisprudence, "This analysis and critique manifests itself in a variety of ways, owing partly to the range of issues it covers and partly to the divergence among feminists on virtually all points other than the rejection of patriarchy" (3). Far from limiting its scope to the fields of equal protection, reproductive freedom, rape, sexual harassment, spousal abuse, prostitution, and pornography, "the issues covered by feminist jurisprudence are as wide ranging as the areas covered by law" (4). Martha Chamallas identifies "the central core of feminist legal theory" as "the exploration of women's subordination through the law," with subordination "meant to convey the systemic nature of women's inequality" (xx). For helpful introductions to this field, see Chamallas; Dowd and Jacobs; Scales; Smart, *Feminism and the Power of the Law* 66–89; Cain; Smith, Introduction; and Bartlett, "Perspectives in Feminist Jurisprudence." For collections of essays on feminist jurisprudence and feminist legal theory, see Bartlett and Kennedy; Smith, *Feminist Jurisprudence;* D. K. Weisberg; Wing; Barnett; and Taylor, Rush, and Munro. In this book, I draw on the work of a wide array of feminist legal theorists.

11. Richard Delgado, in the context of law, describes an "outgroup" as "any group whose consciousness is other than that of the dominant one" (2412).

12. One of the purposes of Sedgwick's study of Gothic conventions was to make meaningful the critical gesture of writing "Gothic" in the margins of a text. I hope that this book will make "feminist jurisprudence" an increasingly common and critically significant marginal note.

13. In her article "Victorian Narrative Jurisprudence," Krueger persuasively makes the case that if literary historians contributed to studies of narrative jurisprudence and lawyers engaged with literary history then "the goals of narrative jurisprudence are better served, the significance of narrative evidence made more clear, and therefore its defence more robust" (438). This is because there would be attention paid to "an historical process of social formation carried out by fusing aesthetics and rationalism" (438). For an excellent discussion of Victorian feminist narrative jurisprudence, see 456–60.

14. Krueger focuses primarily on gender and feminist jurisprudence but also suggests "how literary history might contribute to other forms of 'outsider jurisprudence,' which advocate for justice for legally disadvantaged sexual, racial, ethnic, and religious groups" (3).

15. As I discuss more fully in chapter 1, I also focus primarily on novels written by women that have been outside the consideration of many studies on nineteenth-century law and literature. In *A Critical Introduction to Law and Literature,* for example, Kieran Dolin explores "border crossing" between the two disciplines across centuries, focusing his discussion of the nineteenth century around "the debate about the legal and political position of women in Victorian England" (16). While there is excellent discussion of Caroline Norton (122–26) and reform efforts by literary women (126–30), the novelist that Dolin focuses on in this chapter is Charles Dickens. This chapter also discusses the fictionalization of the Norton case in William Thackeray's *The Newcomes* (1853–55) and George Meredith's *Diana of the Crossways* (1885) (Dolin 130–33).

16. For details of the Waters case, see Bentley 202–5. See Shanley 87–93 for a discussion of the legal discourse surrounding the baby farmer cases, as well as for

a discussion of the feminist response to the law's "truths" about infant mortality. Moore's story depicts many of the feminist arguments such as that poverty and male irresponsibility were significant aspects of the problem of high infant mortality. His introduction of the baby farmer Mrs. Spires's murderous husband stresses that men also are implicated in the "business" of infanticide. So too, Moore's novel argues, are the upper classes who willingly sacrifice the children of their wet nurses for their own. As there is no mention of the husband of Mrs. Rivers, the woman who hires Esther to feed her child, all the blame of the class issue is translated into the selfishness of this wealthy woman.

17. The actress Helen Faucit believed that the quick and intelligent Portia had discovered the problem in the wording of the bond almost immediately upon hearing it, which would explain her light-hearted mood as she sets off to meet with Bellario (Foulkes 31). Ellen Terry later in the century played the part as if Portia has an inspiration near the end of her dialogue with Shylock in the courtroom when she remarks, "'Tarry a little; there is something else'" (4.1.304). Terry herself realized that this allowed Portia only nine lines to look up the specifics in the law books (Foulkes 33). Critics like William Winter, however, thought Portia never could have come up with the winning legal argument herself. He concludes that the "line and plan of *Antonio's* defence have been thoroughly worked out by Bellario." See William Winter, *Shakespeare on Stage* (New York, 1911) 230, qtd. in Hankey 445.

18. William Richardson, *Essays on Shakespeare's Dramatic Character of Sir John Falstaff, and On His Imitation of Female Characters* (London, 1788) 57, qtd. in Hankey 426.

19. In her fascinating study, *Shakespeare and Victorian Women*, Marshall analyzes Victorian "women variously negotiating their Shakespearean legacy and attempting to plot its meaning for themselves. . . ." Specifically citing Jameson's work, Marshall notes, "an historicist attentiveness to the cultural situation of the playwright and his women generally signals a recognition of Shakespeare as fundamentally, and often liberatingly, non-Victorian" (6).

20. Charles Cowden Clarke, *Shakespeare-Characters; Chiefly Those Subordinate* (London, 1863) 401, qtd. in Hankey 432.

21. In Clarke's sketch, Portia's father is so heartsick after the loss of his wife that he leaves, directing Bellario to oversee the rearing of his daughter. Portia and her father are reunited when she is seventeen, but he dies a few years later, leaving behind the infamous will that promises his daughter to the suitor who chooses the correct casket (gold, silver, or lead). Clarke mentions that while Bellario is Portia's uncle, she calls him "cousin" (42); this most likely is in explanation of Portia's line in *The Merchant of Venice*, "See thou render this / Into my cousin's hands, Doctor Bellario" (3.4.49–50).

22. In a letter to Helen Faucit, Jewsbury wrote, "Many thanks for writing and sending me *Ophelia* . . . please do another. Portia is one of my great heroines. . . ." See Sir Theodore Martin, *Helena Faucit (Lady Martin)* (Edinburgh, 1900) 369, qtd. in Foulkes 28. This letter prompted Faucit to write her "Letter on Portia" (Foulkes 28).

23. "Our Prize Competition. Essay Writing on a Great English Author—My Favourite Heroine from Shakespeare," *The Girls' Own Paper*, March 10, 1888, 380–81, qtd. in Marshall 41.

24. One of the rebuked essays read, "My favourite heroine from Shakespeare is the 'Lady Lawyer, Portia.' . . . She is evidently Shakespeare's pet creation, and can

we not deduct [*sic*] from this, that the great writer would give to women a more important position that they hitherto occupied?" ("Our Prize Competition" 380–81, qtd. in Marshall 41).

25. Hankey also argues that women writers had to "tread carefully," explaining that "they had internalized the feminine ideal, at least in part, and needed some subterfuge to do justice, as they saw it, to Portia without disturbing that ideal" (433–34). Hankey explains that her study of the history of women's interest in Portia has revealed more of "a private sense of identification with the character, a feeling almost of consanguinity" than "a campaign to widen the definition of Womanliness to include, say, intellect and independent-mindedness" (434).

26. Women's efforts to be admitted into the legal profession in England are detailed in chapter 4. Ms. Thompson was one of the four plaintiffs in the 1913 case, *Bebb v. the Law Society*, discussed in that chapter.

27. In "Feminist Legal Methods," Katharine Bartlett sets out various feminist methods to be applied to law. As she explains, these methods seek to make women's experiences and voices relevant: "All of these methods reflect the status of women as 'outsiders,' who need ways of challenging and undermining dominant legal conventions and of developing alternative conventions which take better account of women's experiences and needs" (831). Methodologies that she discusses in detail include (i) "identifying and challenging those elements of existing legal doctrine that leave out or disadvantage women and members of other excluded groups" and (ii) "seeking insights and enhanced perspectives through collaborative or interactive engagements with others based upon personal experience and narrative" (831).

28. Works such as George Eliot's *Adam Bede* and Thomas Hardy's *Jude the Obscure* have received serious attention in law and literature studies. For insightful examinations of legal and literary connections in these novels, for example, see Rodensky 100–21 and McDonagh 145–52 (*Adam Bede*), and Marsh 269–327 and McDonagh 181–83 (*Jude the Obscure*). *In Contempt* presents these more canonical texts in relationship to "outlaw texts": moreover, it approaches them differently, through the lens of feminist jurisprudence.

29. In her *Introduction to Feminist Legal Theory*, Martha Chamallas explains, "Feminist legal theory responds to a basic insight about life and law. It proceeds from the assumption that gender is important in our everyday lives and recognizes that being a man or a woman is a central feature of our lives, whether we are pleased or distressed by the thought of gender difference. Feminist legal theory takes this approach into the study of law by examining how gender has mattered to the development of the law and how men and women are differently affected by the power of law" (xix).

Chapter 1

1. Wollstonecraft died in childbirth before completing *Maria*. Godwin edited the manuscript, which was published four months after her death. He wrote his own preface to the novel and provided bracketed editorial information throughout the text.

2. Kelly argues that Godwin's novel *Things As They Are; or, The Adventures of Caleb Williams* (1794), as well as other English Jacobin political novels, were models for Wollstonecraft's work (xv–xvii). Krueger, noting Godwin's belief with respect to

his own writing that a novel would have a wider audience, argues that Wollstonecraft's choice of this genre can be viewed as an effort "to assert a more capacious understanding of rationality and to engage male as well as female readers in an experience of intersubjective communication that would undermine efforts to exclude evidence of 'unrecorded despotism' from rational thought" (*Reading for the Law* 113).

3. In her analysis of Gothic theory after 1760, Harriet Guest characterizes *Maria* as a Gothic novel. Her brief discussion of the novel focuses on its presentation of "the Gothic 'spirit of liberty'" (137), which Guest suggests, "in its privacy and specificity, articulates a gender-specific utopian politics" (137). Tilottama Rajan calls *Maria* "a form of political Gothic" (233). While I agree with Rajan's assessment that the novel "retains the Gothic setting as a socially imposed metaphor," I read Wollstonecraft's use of the Gothic as more radical than Rajan, who emphasizes the form's "complicity in attitudes of patriarchy" (237).

4. Laurie Langbauer offers a different interpretation of *Maria*'s "breakdown of language and shattering of meaning," suggesting associations with the maternal and semiotic forces (102).

5. A legal fiction is an assumption that certain facts exist, whether or not they really do. Thus, under the law, the husband and wife are one person even though, in reality, this is an impossibility. While coverture applied only to married women, its role in shaping cultural representations of and ideas about women made it a legal concept that significantly affected the everyday lives of all women.

6. Other of Sedgwick's categories that could be discussed in connection with coverture and *Maria* include "sleeplike and deathlike states," "the poisonous effects of guilt and shame," "nocturnal landscapes and dreams," and "the madhouse" (9–10).

7. Actually, four categories of persons were excluded from many civil and all political rights in England: criminals, idiots, women, and minors (Cobbe 110). Cobbe's essay interrogates the inappropriateness of these associations.

8. For a detailed analysis of a wife's legal disabilities (including exceptions to the general rules), see Doggett 34–61. For a most thorough discussion of women's property rights in the eighteenth century, see Staves.

9. Holcombe reports that while, "[s]ince the late seventeenth century, courts had held that chastisement did not extend to physical punishment but meant only admonition of the wife and her confinement to the house . . . older interpretations lingered on, and it was generally believed that a man could beat his wife, although not in a violent and cruel manner—not with a stick thicker than his thumb" (30). Holcombe also describes two legal actions a wife could take against an abusive husband: she could prosecute him for attempting, threatening, or actually causing her grievous bodily harm, or she could apply to the court for an order binding her husband to keep the peace (30). If he was imprisoned, however, she might lose her means of support. And, then, as now, he might prove more of a danger to her after she had publicly accused him of abuse (in the nineteenth century, the wife would have been required to return home with her husband [Doggett 14–15]). For a discussion of the sources and extent of, and the challenges to, a husband's right to beat his wife, see Doggett 4–15.

10. For a fascinating discussion of the details of various petitions for divorce, including those of the four successful women's petitions in the early part of the nineteenth century, see Horstman 20–45.

11. See chapter 5 for specific discussion of the 1891 legal case *Queen v. Jackson*,

which set forth the "new" rule that a husband could not lawfully keep his wife confined.

12. Coverture literally took the voice of married women (they had no legal identity); the ideology that coverture represented and the overwhelming influence that it exerted in naturalizing the subordination of women also effectively silenced unmarried women.

13. This was a suit that could be brought by a husband against his wife's lover. The wife was not a party to the suit; rather she was the "property" that had been damaged. These suits were called actions for criminal conversation and they "came to look uncomfortably near to setting a price on the wife's virtue" (Horstman 4).

14. In "Word, Dialogue and Novel," Kristeva discusses two other types of "ambivalent" words: those that are "characterized by the writer's exploitation of another's speech—without running counter to its thought—for his own purposes" and those "characterized by the active (modifying) influence of another's word on the writer's word. It is the writer who 'speaks,' but a foreign discourse is constantly present in the speech that it distorts" (44).

15. Sunstein argues that Darnford's character is based on Gilbert Imlay, an American author who abandoned Wollstonecraft and their child Fanny (236, 239–43, 253, 275, 279, 299, 305–7). Wollstonecraft attempted to commit suicide twice in connection with this relationship.

16. For a discussion of the interrelationship between economics and power in *Maria*, see Frost 259–60.

17. In his 1957 *The Rise of the Novel*, Watt elaborates on these connections: "The novel's mode of imitating reality may . . . be equally well summarized in terms of the procedures of another group of specialists in epistemology, the jury in a court of law. Their expectations, and those of the novel reader coincide in many ways: both want to know 'all the particulars' of a given case . . . and they also expect the witnesses to tell the story 'in his own words.' The jury in fact takes the 'circumstantial view of life,' which T. H. Green found to be the characteristic outlook of the novel" (31).

18. Linking changes in law to literary practices, Welsh notes, "Precisely in the decades when the 'probative force' of circumstantial evidence was most seriously sought after by theorists and practitioners of the law, the attitude of English novelists toward fictionality underwent a change. . . . [I]ncreasingly, through the conscious practice of Fielding and others, the claim to represent reality in novels was expressed by their internal connectedness of circumstances, their deliberate response to the challenge of making representations, until by the time of James novelists scorned either to pretend truth or to concede falsehood in their work" (42).

19. Schramm's study also identifies two specific issues with Welsh's analysis, relating to the distinction he draws between testimony and circumstantial evidence. First, she explains that circumstantial evidence was presented, for the most part, to the court as a form of testimony, thus also requiring "inference and interpretation to attest . . . probative value" (20). Second, she complicates the distinction by taking into account professional representations made by lawyers, arguing that "the rise of the third-person realist novel is simultaneously in imitation of, and in reaction against, the increasing prominence of the activities of defence counsel" (23). Schramm's study focuses on first-person testimonial speeches in fictional trials. But see Lisa Rodensky's study, which, in analyzing the novel's "license to represent interiority not by inference but directly" (21), complicates analogies between real-

life advocates and narrators: "While both lawyers and third person narrators may present details about the thoughts of the accused, it is worth considering the difference it makes that the details presented by the third person narrator exist in an imaginative context in which the narrator may have unique and unchallenged access to those thoughts—the kind of access that no person (whether or not a lawyer) could ever hope to have" (24).

20. Focusing on crime fiction, Grossman argues more generally that the novel "defined itself against and through the cultural and material presence of the law court—a symbolic and real *place* where stories are reconstructed" (6).

21. Miller primarily discusses the works of Dickens, Anthony Trollope, and Wilkie Collins. In discussing the law, Said focuses on Dickens; however, he also cites Jane Austen and George Eliot as authors in whose works "consolidation of authority includes, indeed is built into the very fabric of, both private property and marriage, institutions that are only rarely challenged" (77).

22. In *Fiction and the Law: Legal Discourse in Victorian and Modernist Literature*, Kieran Dolin, although from a different perspective than this study, also identifies the novel as a site for the critique of the law. Analyzing literary representations of legal trials to illustrate the novel's role in social reform, he explains that "the framing of a legal trial within a larger narrative operates to highlight the special interpretive assumptions and processes of law" that reveal "the possibility of variation between legal and other interpretations" (19). Dolin's study, like Miller's and Said's, also focuses on well-known texts, specifically *The Heart of Midlothian; Bleak House; Orley Farm; Billy Budd, Sailor; Lord Jim;* and *A Passage to India*. Emphasizing the connections between nineteenth-century literature and legal insiders, Dolin discusses the "juridical connections" of many of the writers he includes (4).

23. For explorations of the connections between societal attitudes toward women and madness, see Showalter, who writes:

> The advent of the Victorian era coincided with a series of significant changes in society's response to insanity and its definition of femininity. New legislation made the public asylum the primary institution for the treatment of the insane. . . . As the inmate population of public asylums increased during the century, so too did the percentage of women; by the 1850s women were the majority of the inmate population, and the asylum rather than the attic was identified as the madwoman's appropriate space. . . . They designed their asylums not only to house feminine irrationality but also to cure it through paternalistic therapeutic and administrative techniques. (17–18)

Also, see chapter 5 of this book for more information on nineteenth-century laws relating to mental illness and asylums.

24. See Surridge for an excellent study of a wide variety of Victorian novels that shed light upon "Victorian novelists' intense engagement with the issue of marital violence" (12).

25. While judges had no specific authority to exclude women spectators from the courts, as Beaumont explains in his pamphlet "Women and the Law Courts," it was a fairly common informal practice:

> The right of the public to witness legal proceedings is unquestionable,

but, unfortunately for women, judges usually act in this matter as though the public must be interpreted to mean the male sex only. When cases are to be tried in which questions will arise affecting the relations between the sexes, questions in which women may well be considered to have a special interest and a special responsibility in seeing fair play, the first sign of impartiality on the part of the court, is the exclusion of female spectators. (1)

Emphasizing that law courts were almost exclusively a male space, he comments, "With the exception of a very few heroic women, who in recent years have risen superior to the enervating conditions of their sex and braved the terrors of conventionality, the cause of womanhood in our law courts is left entirely to male judges, male advocates, and male juries, under the supervision of male spectators, reporters, and editors" (2).

26. In this excellent study, Heinzelman makes a persuasive case for the influence of the French romance on the development of the novel form. As her analysis illustrates, a combination of critical bias against gender (women) and nationality (French) led to the English novel being defined in a way to exclude the influences of the romance altogether.

27. In her study of New Woman novels, for example, Ardis discusses how the overtly political aspects of these works have been taken as signs of "aesthetic deficiency" (3); thus, they have been disqualified from much "literary" study. Specifically with respect to literary and legal discourse on issues of domestic violence, see Tromp for a compelling analysis of the ways in which sensation novels, which "have only recently come under serious consideration in Victorian studies" (3), served as "the pivot on which a cultural shift occurred, generating a kind of chaos in understanding and necessitating new dialogues about violence and married life" (5).

Chapter 2

1. Act to Prevent the Destroying and Murthering of Bastard Children 1623 (21 James 1, c. 27). The text is from Pickering, *Statutes at Large* 298. I refer to this statute as the 1623 statute because that is the date cited in this source. In the *Statutes of the Realm*, the date is cited as 1623–4.

2. The 1623 statute was enacted out of concern that "lewd women" were escaping the strictures of the bastardy clauses of the "poor law" of 1576 (18 Eliz. 1, ch. 3), which mandated that an unmarried pregnant woman declare the name of the father of her unborn child so that the parish could collect support from him and provided for corporal punishment and gaol time for both parents. Women, however, bore the brunt of this social control, with fathers either fleeing or disputing accusations of paternity (Hoffer and Hull 13–17). With the high rate of infant mortality, the bastardy laws provided much incentive for an unwed mother to conceal her pregnancy. In the not unlikely event that her child was stillborn or died from other natural causes, she might, through concealment, be able to escape certain punishment under the bastardy laws, as well as the social judgment that the law abetted and legitimized. The 1623 statute greatly raised the stakes of concealment— if discovered, the woman was presumed guilty of a capital offense (the statute also solved the difficult evidentiary problem of proving premeditation in concealment

cases). Hoffer and Hull report a fourfold increase in the prosecution of infanticide cases after passage of the statute (27), as well as a growing association between guilty verdicts and the illegitimacy of the victims (23).

3. The evidence given by the doctor, which we only know is "heavy on her" (474), also most likely goes to proving that Hetty has borne a child.

4. A well-known literary precedent of a fallen woman returning to the presumed burial spot of her infant is William Wordsworth's "The Thorn" (1798). In this lyrical ballad, Martha Ray has returned for twenty-two years to a mountaintop area where many believe an infant she may have hanged or drowned is buried. The sea-captain whom the narrator of the poem cross-examines, however, defends Martha, saying, "But kill a new-born infant thus! / I do not think she could" (223–24). Martha is never prosecuted, and the question of whether she repeats her refrain "Oh misery! Oh misery!" (65) because of her murder of the child, the natural death of the child, or some other combination of reasons is left open.

5. Krueger emphasizes that Hetty is "the farm girl seduced by the aristocrat Arthur Donnithorne," who thinks "that her role in a fairy-tale romance will bring her new freedom" (*Reader's Repentence* 253). She sees Hetty as typifying the "tragic vulnerability of both women and children in a society ruled by Donnithorne's law" (254). McDonagh explains jostling interpretations of Hetty in terms of two competing child-murder narratives in *Adam Bede*, one that emphasizes Hetty's own childishness in a way that draws mother and child together as "equal victims of other crimes—lechery and seduction" and another more disciplinary narrative that represents Hetty as "an outré form of femininity for which there is no place in a social body made up of families" (248).

6. For less sympathetic readings of Hetty, see, for example, Catherine Hancock, who explores the ways in which Arthur and Adam both "fall prey to the assumption that Hetty's remarkable good looks reflect an inner beauty and perfection of womanliness," while lurking behind this façade is "Hetty's true nature: her narcissism, insensitivity to the needs of others, and above all else, what Eliot calls 'hardness'" (304). Also, Aeron Hunt describes Hetty as "economic and competitive" and resembling "another grotesque economic woman, the consumer" in the ways in which she misapprehends "true value as merely the market value" (85). Hunt argues that Hetty's portrayal is linked to the inflammatory infanticide discourse of the mid-nineteenth century through Hetty's acquiescence "to the belief that the law of the market determines all social relations" and "subscribes to a model that represents human value as exchangeable and reducible to money" (85).

7. For a detailed analysis of social cognition theory and its applicability to law, see Krieger.

8. Krueger argues that literary treatments of infanticide may have "contributed to this effort to protect women from the state by elaborating a representation of infanticide that insisted on its private character" ("Literary Defenses" 271).

9. Miriam Jones argues that Eliot portrays Hetty in stark contrast to the sympathetic women accused of infanticides in the mid-century broadsides: "[W]ith her disdainful descriptions she attacks the cliché of the helpless woman and firmly directs her readers away from the paternalistic, infantilizing sympathy provoked by stock representations" (310). Jones takes the position that "Eliot allocates blame disproportionately: that Hetty is punished, Arthur is excused, and Adam is figured as the true sufferer because the male characters, unlike Hetty, are represented as having the ability to learn from mistakes" (311).

10. Jones agrees that the narrative voice, which she characterizes as "a punitive courtroom spectator," complicates interpretations of Hetty as sympathetic in the trial scene (312).

11. The complex relationship between law, religion, and truth explored in the confession scene in *Adam Bede* similarly is of concern in Sir Walter Scott's *The Heart of Midlothian*, an 1819 novel also involving a woman accused of infanticide. Technically, Effie Deans is accused of concealing her pregnancy, which was a capital offense in Scotland if the child was missing or subsequently found dead. Much in the same way that Hetty's story becomes the story of Adam Bede, Effie's trials serve as a vehicle to highlight her sister's heroic efforts on her behalf. Jeannie Deans is the heroine of the novel, and she is a heroine of truth. Even knowing that her sister did not kill her child, Jeannie refuses to commit perjury and save her sister by testifying that they had discussed her pregnancy, thus proving that there had been no concealment. Following the law of her religion, Jeannie follows the law of the land; these laws to Jeannie are knowledge and truth: "He has given us a law . . . for the lamp of our path; if we stray from it we err against knowledge—I may not do evil, even that good may come out of it" (164). For Jeannie Deans, law is truth.

12. Hancock argues that the resolution at the end of the novel is possible only because "Hetty—along with her dangerous sexuality and destructive maternity" (308) have been banished. McDonagh concludes that the infanticide "paradoxically facilitates the constitution of the new society at the end of the novel, symbolized by the marriage of Dinah and Adam" (248). Hetty's murder of her child "takes on the role of a sacrifice that will enable the eventual reconstitution of the social order" (248).

13. But see, for example, Marck, who argues that because the moral of the novel depends "on the conscious memory of Hetty and the recollection/retelling of her fall," she "continues to disrupt the narrator's claim to a true reading of events" and has the "power to disturb the narrator's moral" (467). Logan also analyzes "the enigma of Hetty Sorrel's character" (21), arguing that the issues raised by this complex character "remain unresolved by the novel's conclusion" (18).

14. Welsh traces this shift from the lawyer Henry Fielding's 1749 novel *The History of Tom Jones*. He argues that strong representations were central to the British novel throughout the nineteenth century until modernism "challenged the conclusive aspect of literary realism" (255).

15. In her analysis of class in *Adam Bede*, Miriam Jones describes Hetty as "representative of her class in her limited character and her dangerous sexuality" but deviant in her act of infanticide, querying, "[j]ust what is the reader being told in *Adam Bede* about the infanticidal woman?" Her response suggests the power of the prosecutorial narrative voice in making a strong case against Hetty: "She is limited, vain, unintelligent, venal, narcissistic, manipulative, lacking in spirituality, and exceptionally attractive physically"; moreover, "she was clearly born that way" (322).

16. Hancock describes Eliot as presenting a troubling norm for infanticide in *Adam Bede:* "As an unmarried woman whose fertility has not been sanctioned by the institution of matrimony, Hetty's story epitomizes one of the most dreaded fears of Victorian society. Her loss of sexual purity and lack of maternal feeling threatened the very foundations of Victorian culture" (308).

17. See Hancock for an analysis of two other late Victorian novels, Lucy Clifford's *Mrs. Keith's Choice* (1885) and Margaret Harkness's *A Manchester Shirtmaker* (1890), which "offer a radically different version of murderous maternity than that depicted in *Adam Bede*" (299). Hancock argues that while "the unmarried

Hetty murders her child . . . to efface all traces of her motherhood and thus avoid the censure of her family and community, the young widows in *A Manchester Shirt-maker* and *Mrs. Keith's Choice* . . . interpret their violence against children as the fullest expression of their maternal devotion" (299).

18. A popular novel, *The Broad Arrow*, published under the pseudonym Oliné Keese, was reprinted in at least eight editions by 1918. See Hergenhan 142–43.

19. While criticism of the 1960s and 1970s accused the novel of being too didactic in nature, with the author falling "more readily than Harriet Beecher Stowe into melodrama and sentimentality" (Poole 120) and more "at home as a writer of religious tracts" (Hergenhan 141), more recently the novel has been acknowledged as having "not yet received the critical attention it deserves" (Scheckter 89), and its heroine praised as "undoubtedly the most powerful female creation in Australian colonial literature" (Walker 88). Emphasizing the novel's literary merit, Walker states that "to come for the first time to *The Broad Arrow* is, because of the experience it deals with, and because of the power of the writing, a stunning experience" (88). I believe this novel, through the complex representation of Maida, unsettles institutions such as the law and religion more than has heretofore been suggested.

20. Leakey did more than write on behalf of fallen women; she helped to establish a home for them, the Exeter Home (Walker 87). In *Tainted Souls and Painted Faces*, Amanda Anderson identifies "a pervasive rhetoric of fallenness in mid-Victorian culture, one that constitutes sexually compromised women as lacking the autonomy and coherence of the normative masculine subject" (1). She describes how fallen women often are presented in realist fiction as "hyperdetermined and disturbingly 'false'" in order to make the other characters seem less "textually determined," more real, and more in control of their own stories (10). While the law sets the scene and helps script the plot of Maida's story, she is presented as a complex and independent woman who thinks and acts (to the extent possible) for herself. Like Elizabeth Barrett Browning with her presentation of the fallen woman Marian Erle in *Aurora Leigh*, Leakey "insists on particularizing the fallen woman, on rescuing her from a set of conventions that obscure the perception of her as an individual" (Anderson 177).

21. In her study of social-problem novels, Josephine Guy notes that a distinguishing feature of such novels was "their attempt to comment on, and stimulate debate about, matters of public and political concern" (4). She goes on: "social-problem novelists are commonly credited with the intention of trying to educate, and therefore by implication to change, the opinions and prejudices of their readers. In so doing, they are seen to be implying that the novel can, and should, have an important role to play in social and political life" (4). While Guy doesn't discuss any of Trollope's novels in her study, *Jessie Phillips* fits within this tradition. See Guy 3–12 for a general discussion of the social-problem novel.

22. Dickens's competitiveness with Frances Trollope early in his career led to such comments as "I will express no fuller opinion of Mrs. Trollope, than that I think Mr. Trollope must have been an old dog and chosen his wife from the same species" (letter to S. Laman Blanchard 506–7, qtd. in Kissel 116). For a discussion of Dickens's literary debt to Trollope, see Kissel 115–22.

23. All quotations from *Jessie Phillips* are from the three-volume Colburn edition. The parenthetical references list the volume first, followed by the page number.

24. The first known fictional woman detective appeared in 1864 in Andrew For-

rester's *The Female Detective*. See Klein 18. The first woman to practice law in Britain was admitted to the profession in 1922. See Abel-Smith and Stevens 194.

25. While sometimes referred to as "the bastardy clause," the Poor Law Amendment Act actually included several bastardy clauses.

26. By 1834, the 1623 statute had been repealed and infanticide was treated like any other case of murder, with even the mother being innocent until proven guilty. This change in the law, however, did not reflect a change in attitudes toward unmarried mothers. Rather, there was concern that the flagrant disregard of the statute's provisions was emasculating the law. Throughout the eighteenth century, there had been a sharp decline in the number of infanticide convictions, with both judges and juries showing an increasing leniency toward defendants. Judges, for example, were less likely to rule that the floating of the infant's lungs was conclusive evidence that it had been born alive, and juries were accepting a wide array of defenses. Defendants were acquitted who claimed an inability to keep the infant from falling onto a rough floor, into a bucket, or into a privy. Others argued that they had been unable to tie off umbilical cords or had missed when doing so and inflicted mortal wounds. See Hoffer and Hull 65–91. Upon a failed murder prosecution, however, the mother was again singled out for special treatment and could be charged with a new offense, concealment of birth, which carried a sentence of up to two years' imprisonment. A separate prosecution for concealment alone became possible in 1829 (Madhouses (Scotland) Act, 9 Geo. 4, c. 34).

27. See Ledwon 54–67 for an analysis of the Commissioners' Report in terms of melodrama. Ledwon argues that the Report deviates from conventional melodramatic conventions by figuring the persecuted innocent as male, in need of protection from predatory females.

28. The Commissioners' Report, published in March of 1834, was composed of selected materials taken from (i) questionnaires, known as Rural and Town Queries, that were mailed to parishes in 1832 and (ii) reports completed in 1833 by 26 assistant commissioners who had visited parishes throughout England and Wales. The answers to the questionnaires and the assistant commissioners' reports were published later in 1834. The Commissioners' Report, because of "the massive amount of evidence used to support its arguments, and its air of self-confidence," has been characterized as "by far the most influential work ever written on the economic effects of the Old Poor Law" (Boyer 64–65). This report, however, also selectively ignored much of the information contained in the questionnaires and assistant commissioners' reports (Boyer 62).

29. For an in-depth discussion of laws governing marriage up to and including Lord Hardwicke's Marriage Act, see Stone 30–37.

30. Sally Mitchell suggests that Jessie knows the sexual facts of life (*Fallen Angel* 23); however, I read her reactions to her pregnancy as suggesting sexual innocence.

31. In the Introduction to their collection *Narrating Mothers: Theorizing Maternal Subjectivities*, Brenda Daly and Maureen Reddy discuss the paucity of maternal voices in literature and theory and stress the importance to feminism of listening to mothers' stories (1–18).

32. See Mackay 157–72 for a discussion of the administration of the New Poor Law.

33. For information about women's petitions for relief under the Poor Law in the 1830s and 1840s, see Levine-Clark 62–67.

34. While Stallybrass focuses on sixteenth-century assumptions, Carol Smart

identifies similar ideas in the nineteenth century. See Smart, "Disruptive Bodies," for an analysis of the "complex ways in which discourses of law, medicine and social science interweave to bring into being the problematic feminine subject who is constantly in need of surveillance and regulation" and an exploration of the "dominant idea of disruption and unruliness which is seen to stem from the very biology of the body of Woman" (7).

35. For a discussion of several successful benefit-of-linen and want-of-help defenses, see Hoffer and Hull 68–71.

36. My discussion of Jessie's plea of "temporary insanity" is informed by Jill Matus's analysis of moral and maternal madness in the novel *Lady Audley's Secret*. See Matus 338–44.

37. Matus describes Lady Audley in *Lady Audley's Secret* as "not mad (insane) but mad (angry)" (344). I find this recharacterization particularly useful in examining the pervasive rhetoric of madness in specific confrontational scenes in *Jessie Phillips*.

38. See Shanley 82–93 for interesting comparisons between CALPIW's critique of the Infant Life Protection Act and the protests of the Ladies' National Association (LNA) against the Contagious Diseases Acts. Wolstenholme, Butler, and Becker were also members of the LNA.

39. In suggesting that Jessie Phillips has been erased, I do not want to discount the work that Helen Heineman, Sally Mitchell, and Lenora Ledwon have done on *Jessie Phillips*. Specifically in the context of infanticide, however, relative to a character such as Hetty Sorrel (*the* nineteenth-century literary character associated with infanticide), I think it is fair to characterize Jessie as lost.

40. This quotation appears in Sadleir 112 with no citation.

41. At the age of thirty, Trollope married a lawyer and became the mother of seven children over the next eight years. The Trollopes were plagued by financial difficulties, and Frances engaged in several business ventures in America before turning to writing at the age of 53 to support the family. (Her husband had grown increasingly unable to accept, let alone alleviate, the family's economic hardships.) Her first book, *Domestic Manners of the Americans* (1832), was an immediate success and marked the beginning of her twenty-five-year writing career.

42. Helen Heineman's extensive and important reclamation work on Trollope must be acknowledged. Her research in the 1970s and 1980s rescued Trollope from almost complete oblivion as an author. See *Triumphant* and *Frances Trollope*. The 1990s saw an increase in interest in Trollope's writing and life. See Kissel, Ransom, and Neville-Sington.

43. For analyses of her social reform novels—*Jonathan Jefferson Whitlaw; The Vicar of Wrexhill;* and *The Life and Adventures of Michael Armstrong, The Factory Boy*—see Heineman, *Frances Trollope* 58–76.

44. For two quite different approaches to Anthony Trollope and the law, see Coral Lansbury's *The Reasonable Man: Trollope's Legal Fiction*, which discusses the structure of his novels in terms of legal pleading, and R. D. McMaster's *Trollope and the Law*, which explores the novels within the contexts of nineteenth-century legal history and legal philosophy.

Chapter 3

1. While I use the term "birth control," it should be noted that Margaret Sanger

coined this term in 1914. The word "contraception" was coined in 1886 by an American physician; however, it was rarely used in Britain until after World War I. The most commonly used terms in the nineteenth century were "preventive checks," "artificial checks," "artificial limitation," and "Malthusian appliances." "Family limitation" was a broader term that also included "non-artificial" methods of birth control such as abstinence and the use of the "safe period." See Bland 190–91.

2. As Gail Cunningham has examined in her study, *The New Woman and the Victorian Novel, Jude* was widely received as an addition to the New Woman fiction (103), and Sue shares much in common with the New Woman heroines of 1890s popular fiction. Her objections to marriage, including her desire not to be anyone's sexual property, as well as her reading habits, her anti-religious feelings, and her "somewhat callous experimenting with emotions," ally her with heroines such as Hadria in Mona Caird's *The Daughters of Danaus*, Evadne in Sarah Grand's *The Heavenly Twins*, Gwen Waring in Iota's *A Yellow Aster*, and the heroines in George Egerton's *Keynotes* (110–11).

3. See Boumelha 11–25 for a discussion of the cultural debates surrounding sexual ideology and the "nature" of women in the 1880s and 1890s, including ideas about birth control. In introducing her analysis of women in the novels of Hardy, she explains that "the very fact that female sexuality was so much a matter for discussion, speculation and research, and the accompanying questioning of marriage, would have been enough to make unselfconscious writing involving these subjects almost impossible" (25). Interestingly, the novel does specify that Physician Vilbert sells "female pills," a common euphemism for abortifacients. Vilbert is closely associated with Arabella, who, despite her sexual appetites, has only one child. See Boumelha 152.

4. See Morgan for an insightful discussion of "alternative sightings" in the novel in which Sue is portrayed (through the eyes of the narrator and Arabella) as a sensual, corporeal, and sexual being. Morgan argues that it is Jude's perceptions and descriptions of Sue that perpetuate the idea of her sexlessness (143).

5. See Bland 196–97 for a discussion of feminist opposition to artificial birth control. Bland discusses concerns that contraception would encourage excessive indulgence, have brutalizing effects, and make sex "devoid of the higher feelings of love and monogamous emotional commitment" (197).

6. In discussing family limitation in an 1895 article in *The Saturday Review* entitled "The Maternal Instinct," the author ("A Woman of the Day") used similar language, commenting that New Women were "acquiring more or less the courage of their convictions" and that "those who were never destined by Nature for maternity will have none of it" (753).

7. See Gordon 299 (who argues that Little Father Time is a thinly veiled persona for Hardy, a time spirit who sees and fashions Jude's future); Gregor 221 (who sees Little Father Time as playing a choric role, a symbolic character who "introduces the processes of history into the lives of Jude and Sue"); and Edwards 32 (who sees him as symbolizing the mistakes his father has made in the past). Gordon also argues that the word "menny" is a macabre pun meaning "like men," and that the misspelling recalls the biblical verse, "Mene, mene, tekel, upharsin," meaning "God has numbered the days of your kingdom and brought it to an end" (299). In discussing the key role of class in Hardy's wordplay, Joss Marsh suggests that "menny" may be a pun on the word "mean" (288).

8. Gregor comments that Little Father Time's "sorrowful contemplative eyes

become ours as we watch them [Sue and Jude] desperately attempting to cheat time, repudiating the past, evading the social commitments of the present, indifferent with their ever increasing family to the demands of the future. With Father Time their 'dreamless paradise' fades into the light of common day" (221).

9. See J. A. and Olive Banks, *Feminism and Family Planning in Victorian England* (New York: Schocken, 1964) 84, qtd. in McLaren 94.

10. For a discussion of the influences of Anna Wheeler on William Thompson, Eliza Sharples on Richard Carlile, Frances Wright on Robert Dale Owen, and Harriet Taylor on John Stuart Mill, see McLaren 95–98. McLaren suggests that women were using men as mouthpieces.

11. References to the trial are taken from the published trial transcript. See Freethought.

12. The full indictment is reprinted in Freethought 322–23.

13. See Malthus, *Essay on the Principle of Population*, 6th ed. (London, 1826) 543, qtd. in Chandrasekhar 11.

14. For a detailed analysis of Malthusianism and its progeny, see McLaren 43–58.

15. This language from the handbill is set forth in Fryer 47. A copy of this handbill is located in The Place Museum in the British Museum.

16. For a discussion of the vicious attacks on Place and Carlile in such radical journals as *Black Dwarf* and *Cobbett's Weekly Register*, see Fryer 79–86.

17. Owen's earlier American editions included discussions of the sponge and the condom; however, he later rejected both of these methods.

18. *Fruits of Philosophy* describes very specific chemical solutions, the use of which Knowlton prefers to the withdrawal method and the sponge, both of which he believes are unreliable. He also dismisses the condom, morally tainted as the known method for protection against syphillis, as "by no means calculated to come into general use" (137).

19. Bradlaugh was wary of taking on the cause because there was disagreement amongst his fellow freethinkers on the issue of Neo-Malthusianism, a theory that accepts Malthusian fears about overpopulation but advocates birth control rather than moral restraint. Also, personally, Bradlaugh did not like Knowlton's book. While Bradlaugh's name will be forever associated with the famous trial, and he certainly played a major role in the proceedings, it was truly Besant's cause. Her biographer, Anne Taylor, describes Besant's pivotal role as follows:

> She insisted that the book was defensible, that it must be defended, and that the free-thought party would respond to an appeal. . . . Bradlaugh argued with her for some hours. . . . Watts's plea of guilty to an offence Annie felt to be disgraceful was a violation of her integrity; her fiery sense of honour was aroused. She told Bradlaugh she would never allow her work to appear over the imprint of a man who pleaded guilty to publishing obscene literature. Bradlaugh had rarely encountered a stronger will; he bent before its force. (104–5)

For more information on Bradlaugh, the famed freethinker, orator, secularist, and publisher of the *National Reformer*, see Fryer 141–50.

20. Annie Besant's determination to champion widespread dissemination of birth-control information was very much in keeping with the strong-minded nature

she exhibited throughout her life. Born Annie Wood in 1847, the only daughter of Emily Roche Morris and William Wood, Annie was five when her father died, leaving the family destitute. At the age of eight, she went to live with a wealthy, unmarried woman, Ellen Marryat, who provided her with an extensive private education over the course of eight years. Trained in Latin, German, French, history, and geography, among other things, she also was very much influenced by Marryat's strong Evangelical beliefs. At the age of twenty, she married the Reverend Frank Besant. Writing years later in her *Autobiography*, she comments that she feels "a profound pity for the girl standing at that critical point of life, so utterly, hopelessly ignorant of all that marriage meant, so filled with impossible dreams, so unfitted for the *rôle* of wife" (65). She also reflects on the devastating effects of her complete sexual ignorance: "My dreamy life, into which no knowledge of evil had been allowed to penetrate, in which I had been guarded from all pain, shielded from all anxiety, kept innocent on all questions of sex, was no preparation for married existence, and left me defenseless to face a rude awakening . . ." (71). She sees it as a mother's duty to educate her daughters about the facts of married life: "Many an unhappy marriage dates from its very beginning, from the terrible shock to a young girl's sensitive modesty and pride, her helpless bewilderment and fear. . . . [N]o mother should let her daughter, blindfold, slip her neck under the marriage yoke" (71). Her own marriage turned out to be disastrous, the yoke too much to bear, and after great suffering and a complete loss of her religious faith, she separated from Besant in 1873. Under the terms of a separation agreement, her husband obtained custody of their son Digby and she obtained custody of their daughter Mabel. This type of custody arrangement had become possible only six months earlier with passage of the Custody of Infants Act (36 & 37 Victoria, c. 12) (A. Taylor 60). See Besant, *Autobiography* 11–119 and A. Taylor 1–60 for additional information about Besant's childhood and her unhappy marriage.

21. In this article, Besant advocates the repeal of the Contagious Diseases Acts, which attempted to curb the spread of venereal disease by registering and sometimes incarcerating prostitutes. In the article, which was reprinted in 1885 as a pamphlet, she is defiant in her denunciation of patriarchal law: "In the name, then, of Liberty outraged, in the name of Equality disregarded, we claim the repeal of these one-sided Acts, even if the bond of Fraternity prove too weak to hold men back from this cruelty inflicted on their sisters" (6). The page references are to the 1885 pamphlet. See chapter 5 for a discussion of the movement to repeal the Contagious Diseases Acts.

22. In *Child Murder and British Culture 1720–1900*, McDonagh focuses on Besant and Bradlaugh's use of the trope of child murder to advance their "civilizing project" of birth control (177). See McDonagh 174–78 for her analysis of their defense at trial.

23. This description is quoted in Dinnage 31; no original citation is provided. The speaker most likely is referring to Besant's position as the "heroine of free-thought" (the title her biographer Anne Taylor gives to the chapter covering these years in Besant's life).

24. This is especially apparent in her references to prostitutes. While at times sympathizing with them as victims of a system that promoted vice (Freethought 103), she made a clear distinction between "depraved and dissolute women" (241)

(with whom birth control commonly was associated) and the wives and mothers for whom she was pleading.

25. This excerpt is from Hypatia Bradlaugh Bonner and J. M. Robertson, *Charles Bradlaugh, A Record of His Life and Work By His Daughter* (London: Fisher, 1894) n. pag., qtd. in Manvell 153.

26. See Banks and Banks for a detailed discussion of the newspaper coverage of the trial.

27. Hemming, *Law Reports; National Reformer* (June 2, 1878), qtd. in A. Taylor 131–32.

28. The Social Democratic Federation ("SDF"), under the leadership of H. M. Hyndman, opposed birth control. McLaren states that "[t]here was always a strong misogynist current evident in the writings of the SDF and it followed that birth control, which was already suspect because of its Malthusian connotations, would be open to further attacks when viewed as a means by which women sought to escape their natural duties" (162). McLaren also identifies, however, several social-ists or "men and women on the English left," who, like Besant, argued for family limitation (174). See McLaren for a discussion of birth-control advocates, including Daniel Chatterton, Stewart Headlam, John M. Robertson, Sidney and Beatrice Webb, George Bernard Shaw, and H. G. Wells.

29. Besant, *Is Socialism Sound?* (London, 1893) 23, qtd. in McLaren 179. For a discussion of the relationship between feminism and socialism in the late nineteenth century, see Ledger 36–39.

30. Besant explains in her *Autobiography* that she renounced Neo-Malthu-sianism after two years' instruction from Madame H. P. Blavatsky, "who showed me that however justifiable Neo-Malthusianism might be while man was regarded only as the most perfect outcome of physical evolution, it was wholly incompatible with the view of man as a spiritual being, whose material form and environment were the results of his own mental activity" (237).

31. Lewes cites Lyman Tower Sargent's 1988 bibliography as listing 593 British and American utopian texts written between 1889 and 1920 (12). See Sargent.

32. See Lewes 10–19 for an in-depth analysis of why nineteenth-century women were so drawn to the utopian genre. After noting the attractions to women of writing novels generally, Lewes specifically comments that utopian novels were accessible to the amateur because there were few daunting "monumental supertexts" (11). Lewes also argues that utopian novels served consolatory and cathartic functions (10–11).

33. In the "Apology" introducing his 1922 volume of poetry, *Late Lyrics and Earlier*, Hardy identifies his own philosophy as, not pessimism, but evolutionary meliorism. Quoting the following line from his earlier poem "In Tenebris," "If way to the Better there be, it exacts a full look at the Worst," Hardy clarifies this phi-losophy as "the exploration of reality, and its frank recognition stage by stage along the survey, with an eye to the best consummation possible: briefly, evolutionary meliorism" (viii). It may be that *Jude* is a "full look at the Worst," but arguably for the purpose of questioning whether or not there may be a "way to the Better." While I am unaware of any direct associations between Hardy and Clapperton, they both were influenced by George Eliot, who originally coined the term "meliorism." See Adams, Bailey, and Boris for discussions of evolutionary meliorism in connection with Hardy's novels and poems.

34. Clapperton analyzes and critiques State Socialism, the Democratic Federation, and Christian Socialism in her chapter of *Scientific Meliorism* entitled "Socialism versus Individualism" (389–408). She believes that "crude socialism in method has gone astray, and real socialism is yet in an early stage" (396). For Clapperton, "the only definition [of socialism] wide enough to be scientifically correct is this—*concerted action for social ends*" (396).

35. In an 1889 interview, Clapperton identified Wollstonecraft as one of the writers who had most influenced her ("Jane Hume Clapperton: Authoress" 1).

36. Wollstonecraft argued that the government should set up schools that educated boys and girls together. Specifically, "[t]he school for the younger children, from five to nine years of age, ought to be absolutely free and open to all" ("Vindication" 167). While class distinctions entered into her proposals for older children, she still maintained the need for the sexes being educated together at these older ages (168).

37. Clapperton, like Mona Caird, Sarah Grand, and other feminist writers of the late nineteenth century, was fascinated by the new field of eugenics. Unlike Sir Frances Galton, however, she did not espouse celibacy for those "unfit" to have children. Instead, she advocated the use of artificial checks. Parentage should be avoided, not marriage or sex. Also, Clapperton did not see population control as an issue for only the working classes. Many of her arguments are framed in terms of the ruin to women's health and the foreclosure of women's happiness from having too many children. While Clapperton was a proponent of eugenics, she was also interested in birth control for reasons wholly unrelated to eugenic practices. Specifically, she saw voluntary motherhood as key to women's emancipation.

38. It is the close relationship based on mutual interests between Margaret and Frank (who is married to Rose), and Rose's reaction to it, that *The Saturday Review* found particularly objectionable.

39. Hardy also advocates socialized child care in *Jude the Obscure*. Upon first learning of Little Father Time's existence, Jude comments, "The beggarly question of parentage—what is it, after all? What does it matter, when you come to think of it, whether the child is yours by blood or not? All the little ones of our time are collectively the children of us adults of the time, and entitled to our general care" (340–41). Collective childcare was a standard feature of the co-operative communities planned by Robert Owen and his followers (B. Taylor 51). Owenite and feminist William Thompson specifically called for men to share in childcare responsibilities (52).

40. These were the charges brought against Besant and Bradlaugh. Clapperton also followed Besant's lead in challenging the idea that birth control and socialism were incompatible.

41. See Davies for a collection of letters written by working-class women in 1913 and 1914 that present various views on aspects of mothering, including birth control.

42. That the Prime Minister suggested this meeting is set forth in the biography of Stopes's life written by Maude in 1933 (147), as well as in the biography written by Briant in 1962 (143). Hall emphasizes that Stopes "always claimed" that the meeting was Lloyd George's idea (191). See Hall's 1977 biography for what she professes is a more critical and objective view of Stopes's life. Hall comments that much of Maude's biography was dictated by Stopes herself and that Briant, although more

objective, also was too influenced by his close personal acquaintanceship with Stopes (Hall 11). Rose's 1992 biography also notes that "Marie always claimed that Lloyd George had advised her to 'make birth control respectable' and helped behind the scenes to make her great Queen's Hall meeting a success" (192). For more information on Stopes's relationship with Lloyd George and his mistress (and later wife) Frances Stevenson, see Rose 181, 190–92.

43. The attorney for Sutherland, for example, after making the rather odd and seemingly gratuitous comment that Bradlaugh "had a co-defendant, Mrs. Annie Besant—as clever a woman, perhaps, as Mrs. Stopes," offered the following examples of the ways in which Knowlton's book came nowhere near the obscenity of Stopes's:

> [Knowlton] specifically says that in the interests of decency, he does give no full description of the man's organ of generation or its action. . . . [Dr. Stopes] has no such reticence at all that Dr. Knowlton had, and she sets out in full with the most horrible detail, exactly how that organ acts under certain circumstances. Now, it is not a physiological treatise only, there are pages and pages of erotic stuff, so I suggest to you, what if this matter is directed to the goal to which she says her energies are directed? Why do you want pages of intimate, stimulating, exciting descriptions of the act of copulation, and how it takes place? (qtd. in Box 204)

44. *Daily News*, March 3, 1923, qtd. in Hall 237.

45. *Westminster Gazette*, March 3, 1923, qtd. in Hall 237.

46. March 5, 1923, MCS, duplicated letter. BL-S, qtd. in Hall 238.

47. This is a landmark case in the law of libel for differentiating between a plea of justification (which requires that all facts and comments be true) and a plea of fair comment (which requires that facts be true and expressions of opinion be fair). See Hyde 277 and Gatley 492–95.

48. "Stopery" was a term frequently used when referring to Dr. Stopes's activities or the advocacy of birth control in general (Maude 187).

49. Although she is briefly mentioned in a few books dealing with birth control (Bland, McLaren, and Porter and Hall) and the New Woman (Ardis, Boumelha, Ledger, and Waters), I was unable to locate Clapperton in any biographical dictionaries or similar sources. An 1889 interview with her that appeared on the front page of the *Women's Penny Paper* provides some facts about and insights into the life and beliefs of this forward-thinking writer. Born in Scotland in 1832, she remained at home to care for her ailing mother, "daily and hourly suffering from isolation" ("Jane Hume Clapperton: Authoress" 1). When her mother died in 1872, Clapperton devoted her leisure time to the study of social questions and, in 1881, began to write *Scientific Meliorism*. She brought the ideal home she described in that treatise into fictional reality in *Margaret Dunmore* in response to requests from her readers. Clapperton explained that she was "in entire sympathy with the movement for women's advance all along the line from rational education in every branch to professional activities and sharing with men public duties and responsibilities, as they fit themselves for these" (1). In addition to Wollstonecraft's works, the women's books that had most influenced her were those of Harriet Martineau and George Eliot (2). In an 1897 pamphlet entitled *Some Supporters of the Women's Suffrage Movement*, "Miss Clapperton" is listed under "Women in Literature" (Blackburn 38). She also

joined several other feminist activists such as Elizabeth C. Wolstenholme Elmy and Mona Caird in protesting a call from The Edinburgh National Society for Women's Suffrage to use the lash as punishment for men guilty of violent offenses against women. In a pamphlet entitled *Woman Suffragists and the Lash*, she responded to a "Sir" who had inquired about her position on this issue by explaining that it was "the outcome of confusion of thought and outraged feeling arising from the action of your sex in blocking the true path of progress. No real advance on the right lines," she wrote, "can take place so long as women are denied the Parliamentary Franchise and the same rights of citizenship as men" (2–3). In 1904, Clapperton published a third major work, *A Vision of the Future*. This treatise updates the ideas set forth in *Scientific Meliorism*.

50. Himes estimates that millions of people learned about more effective methods of birth control after the Besant trial. He judges this from two circumstances: (i) the tremendous increases in the circulation of works providing instruction on birth control; and (ii) the halving of the English birth rate since 1876 (243).

51. The Malthusian League had two objectives: "To agitate for the abolition of all penalties in the public discussion of the Population Question" and "To spread among the people, by all practicable means, a knowledge of the law of population, and of the consequences, and of its bearing upon human conduct and morals" (*The Malthusian*, May 15, 1909, p. 37, qtd. in Bland 202). Neo-Malthusian feminist members of this League, such as Alice Vickery, also worked to provide practical birth-control advice to working-class women (Bland 207–9).

52. Stopes resigned from the Malthusian League in 1921 and severed all ties by charging that the atheism of Besant and Bradlaugh had actually hindered efforts to advance family limitation. The Malthusian League remained in existence until 1927. See McLaren 107–115 for a history of the Malthusian League.

53. See chapter 5 for discussions of George Paston's *A Writer of Books* and Florence Dixie's *Gloriana*, novels that mention family limitation and population control in the contexts of discussions of greater rights for women.

54. In *Women and Sexuality in the Novels of Thomas Hardy*, Morgan provides a "revisionary study of Hardy's treatment of female sexuality" by analyzing the ways in which he hid or disguised some of his more disruptive and controversial views (xvi). Marsh argues that Sue's self-reproach concerning her unclear explanation to Little Father Time about the facts of life, "for with a false delicacy I told him too obscurely" (*Jude* 412), serves as a severe indictment of the "Victorian compulsion to euphemism" (Marsh 293). Marsh further comments, in this context, that Sue might have benefited from efforts to remove the "heavy constraining hand" on the publication of birth-control information (293).

55. The fact that contemporary reviews of *Jude* did not mention the Neo-Malthusian aspects of Little Father Time's note may have been only another method of silencing discussion of this most controversial topic. No mention is made of Neo-Malthusianism in the reviews of *Margaret Dunmore*.

Chapter 4

1. St. John-Stevas summarizes these arguments as follows: "Women didn't want the vote: women did want it and would dominate the country: women wouldn't use

the vote if it were given to them: the amendment gave them too much: the amendment gave them too little: the country would be at the mercy of feminine caprice, etc." (263).

2. Mary Abbott claimed that she was qualified and entitled to be placed on the list of voters. When the Revising Barrister for the borough of Manchester held that she was not so entitled, she appealed the decision to the Court of Common Pleas. The appeals of 5,346 other women were consolidated (*Chorlton* 374–75).

3. School boards were created in 1870 by Forster's Education Act (33 & 34 Vict., c. 75), and women were entitled to vote for and serve as members pursuant to this Act. Elizabeth Garrett was the first woman elected to a school board. In 1871, Mrs. Nassau was the first woman appointed as a poor-law inspector. See St. John-Stevas 273.

4. Women were not able to be elected as county or borough councillors until 1907, with passage of the Qualification of Women Act (7. Edw. 7, c. 33). See St. John-Stevas 274.

5. The key role of Coke is made clear in the opinion of one of the other judges who affirms that "the opinion of Lord Coke [in 4 *Institutes* 5], who clearly considered the law to be that women were disqualified at common law, would under any circumstances be of great authority: but, when it is supported by centuries of usage quite in accordance with his statement, the authority becomes such as it would be impossible for this Court to disregard" (*Chorlton*, Keating opinion 396).

6. Lawyers in England were (and still are) either solicitors or barristers. In the nineteenth century, a solicitor was literally, as Birks describes him in his aptly titled history *Gentlemen of the Law*, "the practical man of affairs who looks after the day-to-day management of legal business, the man to whom the layman takes his troubles" (3). Barristers were primarily advocates, with the exclusive right to plead cases in the superior courts. Generally speaking, the services of a barrister were retained by a solicitor rather than by the client directly. To train as a solicitor, one had to be articled to a practicing solicitor, serve an apprenticeship (typically of five years), and pass examinations administered by the Law Society (2–3). While dated, Birks's book provides a thorough and fascinating history of the "character" of the solicitor.

7. Barristers (as opposed to solicitors) are "called to the Bar." After being admitted to one of the four Inns of Court (Gray's Inn, Lincoln's Inn, the Inner Temple, or the Middle Temple), a law student had to "keep terms," evidenced by his dining in the hall of his Inn a specified number of times. For three years, graduates of English universities were required to dine twelve times each year and all other would-be barristers were required to dine twenty-four times each year. This represented a significant expense, especially for those who had to travel to London (Abel 38). Since 1872, students have also been required to pass a Bar examination. Law lectures were given by the Council of Legal Education (established by the four Inns in 1852), although many students engaged the services of private "crammers" (Abel 50). Judges were called from the ranks of barristers (Birks 2).

8. The novel *She* sold a nearly record-breaking 30,000 copies within a few months (Gilbert 124). Gilbert contends that the terse title suggests that the book might be "an abstract treatise on the female gender or a fictive exploration of the nature of womanhood" (124).

9. Gilbert describes the men's penetration of Africa as follows: "Lifted into lit-

ters, the explorers yield to a 'pleasant swaying motion' and, in a symbolic return to the womb, they are carried up ancient swampy birth-canals into 'a vast cup of earth' that is ruled by She-Who-Must-Be-Obeyed and inhabited by a people called the Amahaggar" (125).

10. All quotations from *She* are from the Oxford edition.

11. The first lectures at Cambridge given specifically for women were in 1870, and soon thereafter women began to be admitted to some of the "men's" lectures. Women were not granted degrees from Cambridge until 1948. See St. John-Stevas 269–70.

12. That it was no trouble for a mediocre male scholar (like Leo) or one with little real interest in the profession (like Haggard) to be called to the Bar accentuates the injustice of the barriers that kept even the most zealous women from making it into the club. Encouraged by his friend Justice Kotzé, who asked him, "Why not read for the Bar?" (Haggard, *Days* 173), Haggard embarked on such a course in 1881 as a member of Lincoln's Inn. He was admitted to the Bar in 1885, but by 1888 he had given up the practice of law. See Etherington 7–9. His biographer Morton Cohen explains, "Rider Haggard was not destined to serve the law long. His whimsical strain made him unsuited for chambers and the routine of legal affairs" (85).

13. Laura Chrisman argues that this matrilineal society, which emphasizes a woman's reproductive role and excludes her from the processes of production (women are exempt from manual labor), limits her to a domestic function (43).

14. In *Cassandra*, Florence Nightingale laments the mental and physical suffering that women endure as a result of their confinement within the domestic sphere. Far from celebrating women's role as angel in the house, Nightingale describes the plight of upper- and middle-class women as "like the Archangel Michael as he stands upon Saint Angelo in Rome. She has an immense provision of wings, which seem as if they would bear her over heaven and earth; but when she tries to use them, she is petrified into stone, her feet are grown into the earth, chained to the bronze pedestal" (228).

15. Neil Parsons explains that the "term 'Great White Queen' as applied to Queen Victoria (ruled 1837–1901) was put into the mouths of 'native' applicants by British settler records around the world and came to be accepted in metropolitan Britain as correct 'Sambo' pidgin" (xvii).

16. In fact, Queen Victoria expressed anti-feminist sentiments such as "[w]e women are not *made* for governing—and if we are good women, we must *dislike* these masculine occupations" (Mullen and Munson 60). Regardless of what she said, however, she was very active in government. Sir Charles Dilke, a republican detractor of Queen Victoria, complained in 1879, "The Queen *does* interfere . . . constantly" (D. Thompson 121). Thompson explains the Queen's political role as follows: "To the end of her life she took an active interest in all matters of state, demanded to be consulted and undoubtedly influenced many decisions" (122).

17. Mullen and Munson do not cite the original source of this comment by Helene Vacaresco.

18. Thompson comments that "the presence of a female in the highest political position in the country had at times given strength, if only by implication, to the arguments of her female subjects who were seeking greater educational and political opportunities" (120).

19. A few days after the travelers had arrived in the land of the Amahaggars, Holly, in trying to save his servant Mahomed from having the red-hot pot placed on his head and then being cooked and eaten, had shot the Amahaggar woman who was holding Mahomed and accidentally killed Mahomed at the same time. A deadly fight had ensued, and the Englishmen were saved only when the Amahaggar Father Billali intervened. Ayesha had sent orders that the Englishmen (the white men) were to be kept alive, and the men who had disobeyed her orders and tried to kill Holly, Leo, and Job were on trial.

20. The associations in the novel between savagery and dark skin are emphasized in that Holly no longer refers to Ayesha as savage once he realizes that she is not dusky.

21. The term "fortune" emphasizes the imperial nature of Leo and Holly's quest; they have come to Africa in search of whatever of value they might acquire (power, knowledge, eternal youth).

22. To support this argument, Brantlinger cites Benjamin Kidd's 1894 *Social Evolution*: "The Anglo-Saxon has exterminated the less developed peoples with which he has come into competition . . . through the operations of laws not less deadly [than war] and even more certain in their result. The weaker races disappear before the stronger through the effects of mere contact." See Kidd, *Social Evolution* (New York, 1894) 46, qtd. in Brantlinger 205. Brantlinger also analyzes Darwin's 1874 *The Descent of Man*, concluding that "Darwinism lent scientific status to the view that there were higher and lower races, progressive and nonprogressive ones, and that the lower races ought to be governed by—or even completely supplanted by—civilized, progressive races like the British" (206).

23. For a discussion of the racism in *She* and other imperial fiction by Haggard, see Katz 131–54.

24. In 1902, Slessor moved further inland to Enyong Creek. She accepted an appointment in 1905 as a Member of the Itu Native Court with the status of permanent vice-president. She received forty-eight pounds per annum for her services. See Livingstone, *Mary Slessor of Calabar* 231.

25. Most of these tales are compiled in Livingstone's biography, *Mary Slessor of Calabar*. He includes information from her correspondence, from the correspondence of government officials and other missionaries, as well as articles published in the *Mission Record*. In 1915, Livingstone made a collection of her "voluminous correspondence," which unfortunately was destroyed in World War II (Buchan viii).

26. The biography does not cite a source for Maxwell's account, but it does set it out in full.

27. Buchan reports that the Africans called Slessor "Eka Kpukpro Owo— 'Mother of All The Peoples'" (xii). Livingstone also quotes a missionary as saying, "[h]er power is amazing; she is really Queen of the whole Okoyong district" (*Mary Slessor of Calabar* 180). Livingstone refers to Slessor as the White Queen of the Okoyong several times in his biography, and he actually uses that as the title of the children's biography he wrote about her, *The White Queen of the Okoyong: Mary Slessor: A Story of Adventure, Heroism, and Faith.*

28. Livingstone's biography is entitled *Mary Slessor of Calabar: Pioneer Missionary*. It was not until Caroline Oliver titled her chapter on Slessor in her 1982 book, *Western Women in Colonial Africa*, "Mary Slessor: Missionary and Magistrate," that Slessor's position as a magistrate was given any prominence at all.

29. While Kingsley crosses boundaries that enable her to represent a woman with power, her views are steeped in imperialist structures of attitude and reference.

30. Buchan provides more specific information on why the twins were killed. Specifically, the Efiks and other Cross River tribes "believed that one twin was the child of a devil which secretly mated the mother, and since it was impossible to tell which was the devil's baby both must die" (55).

31. Miss Cave told the press that she would proceed to seek admission to the rolls as a solicitor and would study for a law degree at the University of London (*The Law Times* 107). While the professional bodies allowed only men as members, women were able to earn degrees in law at universities (Abel-Smith and Stevens 192–93). The suffragette Christabel Pankhurst was another woman who had studied law but wasn't permitted to practice it. Sachs and Wilson suggest that she was more effective on the other side of the law:

> It is interesting to speculate what the result on the suffrage movement would have been had women been admitted to legal practice at that time; if many leading rebels and revolutionaries have been lawyers, few leading lawyers have been rebels, and it is highly likely that even the spirited Christabel Pankhurst would have been totally contained by the Bar. As it was, "the hot strife at the Bar," which allegedly was too much for women, appealed to her temperament, and in her capacity as a defendant she manifested such forensic brilliance that it was the male witnesses, magistrates and lawyers who found the combat too intense, not her. The courtroom became an arena in which she was far more effective as a feminist lawbreaker than she would have been as a female barrister, and the occasion when she humiliated Lloyd George in the witness box—a Government Minister, solicitor and orator of note—stands out as one of the notable pieces of cross-examination of her era. (173)

Pankhurst's study of the law, however, was no doubt useful to her as a leader of the suffrage movement.

32. See Susan Kingsley Kent's excellent study of the feminist movement in the late nineteenth and early twentieth centuries, *Sex and Suffrage in Britain, 1860–1914*. As Kent argues, "The ultimate source and embodiment of patriarchal power was seen to lie in political expression, or law, and the vote was perceived as a strategic tool for changing law. Thus, the demand for women's enfranchisement was a direct strike at the very seat and symbolic locus of patriarchal power" (13). Bebb's case was another such strike.

33. The attorney also noted that women were permitted to practice law in many of Britain's colonies, as well as in foreign countries (*Bebb* 289). While he did not offer specific information, it is true that women were lawyers elsewhere. In Canada, Clara Brett Martin was admitted as both a solicitor and a barrister in 1897. Women were allowed to be lawyers in Australia as early as 1903. Ellen Melville set up practice in New Zealand in 1909. See Corcos 323–26. In the United States, Arabella A. Mansfield was admitted to practice law in Iowa in 1869 (Sachs and Wilson 95). In France, legislation allowing women to enter the legal profession was passed in 1900 (Corcos 326–27). See Mossman for a book-length study of the first women lawyers in the United States, Canada, Britain, New Zealand, India, and Europe.

34. A bill relating specifically to barristers, the Barristers and Solicitors (Quali-

fication of Women) Bill, does not appear to have passed. However, the 1919 Sex Disqualification (Removal) Act accomplished the same end (Corcos 386). As Helena Kennedy comments, "It was not until the passage of the Sex Disqualification (Removal) Act of 1919 that the admission of women was forced upon the Inns by Parliament, and since that date the acceptance of women has continued to be slow and grudging" (148). For a discussion of women at the Bar today, see Kennedy 148–62.

35. No mention of this first admission was made in the legal papers, and *The Law Society Gazette* continued to list names of women under the heading "Gentlemen Applying for Admission" for some time (Kirk 111). See Abel 172–76 for a discussion of women's numbers and roles as solicitors from the 1920s to the present.

36. See Abel 80–85 for a discussion of women's numbers and roles within the Bar from the 1920s to the present.

37. See Burton 110–51 for a discussion of Sorabji's experience of studying law at Oxford. See Mossman 232–37 for additional information on Sorabji's legal work in India, both before and after she was officially admitted into the legal profession.

38. This legislation gave the vote to six million out of thirteen million adult women (Perkin, *Victorian Women* 243). Universal suffrage for women was not attained until 1928 with passage of the Representation of the People (Equal Franchise) Act (18 & 19 Geo. 5, c. 12).

39. Perkin suggests that the influence of women members of parliament, as well as millions of women voters, was responsible for the passage of sixteen Acts protecting women's interests in the early 1920s (*Victorian Women* 244).

40. For a history of the legal battle of women to gain access to the House of Lords, especially the key role played by Margaret Haig Thomas Mackworth, Viscountess Rhondda, see Eoff 81–88.

41. This meant she was also appointed a Bencher at her Inn of Court, making her the first woman to sit on the very prestigious governing body of an Inn (Lane 136–37).

42. For a probing and reflective analysis of the influence women have had on the law and the legal process in both the nineteenth and twentieth centuries, see the chapter "Women as Citizens" in Atkins and Hoggett 181–99.

Chapter 5

1. Weldon ran an orphanage for children. In 1877, she had moved the children from Tavistock House to Argueil, France. She trained these children in voice. Weldon was a well-known and talented vocalist, performing at such venues as Covent Garden in London and the Opéra Comique in Paris. She was also a spiritualist. For an analysis of this attempted abduction that focuses on Weldon as a spiritualist, see Walkowitz, *City* 172–80.

2. Louisa Lowe had been waging this campaign since at least 1845, when she founded the Alleged Lunatic's Friend Society. Also a writer, Lowe published *The Bastilles of England; or the Lunacy Laws at Work* in 1883. This book includes a rich collection of stories of unjust confinements, including a recounting of Weldon's escape. After describing Weldon's refusal to comply with Harry's wishes that she move from Tavistock House, Lowe poses a significant question, one whose all too

dangerous implications signify beneath her irony, "Who but a lunatic would thus oppose a husband's will?" (41).

3. Trial testimony indicates that 30,000 tickets were printed for one of her lectures at St. James Hall ("Weldon v. Winslow," 15 Mar. 1884, 4).

4. Weldon acknowledged that she was fortunate to have sufficient funds and friends to protect her. In *How I Escaped the Mad Doctors*, she emphasizes this point by concluding with the line, "Had I been quite a poor woman, unable to pay printers; in spite of all my courage and energy, I should have been quite ruined long ago" (22).

5. Created in 1845, the Lunacy Commission was a central regulatory body that administered the lunacy laws (Forsythe, Melling, and Adair 69).

6. Lord Ashley, the seventh Earl of Shaftesbury, became a Lunacy Commissioner in 1828. He was Chairman of the Commissioners from 1845 until his death in 1885. See K. Jones 133, 197; Forsythe, Melling, and Adair 71.

7. Weldon primarily worked on her own cases, but many sought her legal advice. Treherne comments that "[l]etters would reach her from all corners of the globe; some came to Red Lion Court with the simple address, '*The* Mrs. Weldon, London'; letters asking advice on all possible points of law . . ." (96). On Weldon's death, the headlines read, "A Noted Portia Dead"; "Famous Lady of the Law Courts Dead"; "Death of a Noted Litigant" (Treherne 238).

8. Manisty also stated that "it was revolting to one's sense of right that merely because the person has some strange or eccentric ideas therefore she is to be shut up for life" ("Weldon v. Winslow," 9 Apr. 1884, 4).

9. A writer in the newspaper *Truth* commented after her death, "Remembering Mrs. Weldon, I can quite understand the objections of the Bar to lady barristers. There was a remarkable choice of able men at the Bar in Mrs. Weldon's time, but if she had brought an action against me I should not have felt safe with the best of them . . ." (qtd. in Treherne vi).

10. This is the comment of an unidentified barrister who knew Weldon in the 1880s and was familiar with her law "practice."

11. It is only at the end of the *Life* article that it is clarified that the picture shows Weldon dressed as Serjeant Buzfuz (163).

12. Kathleen Jones credits Weldon with being very influential in the legislative reform of the lunacy laws. She specifically cites the importance of the case *Weldon v. Winslow* (198).

13. Indeed, it was the judge of the divorce court who had to grant the order for attachment against Harry Weldon who appealed to the House of Lords for legislative action.

14. While this quotation suggests that Weldon's motivations may have been misunderstood, it is not at all incorrect to name her a champion of women's rights. One of her concerns was that this law would make it too easy for men to abandon their wives. As desertion happened anyway, however, this amendment offered much needed protection to heretofore unrepresented (by themselves or anyone else) women.

15. This was the heading the *London Times* used in reporting this case. Its first story on March 10, 1891, was titled "Remarkable Abduction Case" (8).

16. Glaspell turned her 1916 one-act dramatic production *Trifles* into the 1917 short story "A Jury of Her Peers."

17. Haughton's actions and testimony fit the profile of a batterer. A batterer

wants sole possession of his wife, often driving away her friends and family. Batterers also are masters of justification (Waits 193–95).

18. Waits explains that "[e]ven when confronted with undeniable evidence of his violence, he [the batterer] will minimize its severity" (194).

19. See Doggett 45–46 for a discussion of the marital immunity in British rape law until the decision in *R. v. R.*, 3 W.L.R. 767 (1991).

20. Elizabeth Wolstenholme Elmy to Harriet M'Ilquham, 21 March 1891, Elmy Collection, British Library, qtd. in Shanley 182.

21. Ann Ardis has identified more than one hundred New Woman novels written between 1883–1900 (4). For information on the popularity of these novels, their readership, and their detractors, see Flint 294–316.

22. For insightful analyses of many New Woman novels and discussions of the historical and social contexts of this genre, see Ardis and Cunningham.

23. When Grand was 15, she formed a club to perpetuate the principles of Josephine Butler. These activities resulted in her dismissal from school (Kersley 81).

24. The Acts included no definition of "common prostitute." Dr. William Acton, one of the leading proponents of the Acts, quoted the following working definition that had been given in testimony before Parliament: "[a prostitute is] any woman whom there is fair and reasonable ground to believe is, first of all going to places which are the resorts of prostitutes alone, and at times when immoral persons are usually out. It is more a question of mannerism than anything else" (qtd. in Murray 425). In other words, all women were vulnerable.

25. The Contagious Diseases Act of 1869 extended the reach of the Acts to non-military districts. For a detailed discussion of the specific provisions of the Contagious Diseases Acts, see Walkowitz, *Prostitution* 69–89.

26. Josephine Butler, *Personal Reminiscences of a Great Crusade* (London, 1898) 42, qtd. in Kent 66.

27. West sees the law and literature movement as a necessary and powerful check on the more established interdisciplinary arena of law and economics. West focuses on two distinct characteristics of the "economic man" of the field of law and economics. First, he is "perfectly rational" ("Economic Man" 869), always knowing and motivated to seek what is best for himself. Secondly, he has no empathetic understanding of others. West argues that these characteristics of "economic man" do not describe real people. "Literary woman," by contrast, understands that people are multimotivational and act in complex ways. She has the ability to empathize.

28. West explains that she uses the term "literary woman" for reasons of rough justice and accuracy: "In the interest of rough justice, I use the word 'woman' to include men as well as women, 'she' to include the male pronoun, and 'womankind' to include mankind. In the interest of accuracy, women's moral voice seems to be distinctively tied to the moral value of empathy I discuss in this paper, and the literary method of narrative" ("Economic Man" 867n2).

29. West clarifies that "[t]he knowledge we learn . . . through metaphor, allegory, narrative, literature, and culture—is a peculiar sort of knowledge, but it is absolutely essential to any meaningful quest for justice, legal or otherwise" ("Economic Man" 876–77). Contrasting these ideas to those of the proponents of law and economics, West claims, "Knowledge of the other's subjectivity is not rationally acquired, and it cannot be rationally calculated, quantified, aggravated, or compared. It is knowledge

that moves us rather than informs us. We 'make room' for this knowledge in our heart, not in our head" (877).

30. While Josephine Butler and her followers called for radical feminist reforms, not all women who advocated repeal of the Acts wanted to become or be associated with public women. Many reformers adhered to a separate-sphere ideology, stressing women's moral supremacy, purity, and domestic virtue. Yet even those women who fought the Acts on purely moral grounds were influenced by the powerful narratives of women's suffering (Walkowitz, *Prostitution* 110). See Walkowitz, *Prostitution*, for a complex study of the various and diverse ideas and motivations of the repealers.

31. J. J. Garth Wilkinson, *The Forcible Introspection of the Women for the Army and Navy by the Oligarchy Considered Physically* (London, 1870) 15, qtd. in Walkowitz, *Prostitution* 108.

32. Butler, *Personal Reminiscences* n. pag., qtd. in Murray 295–96.

33. For a detailed analysis of the "anxiety of authorship" and "struggle for artistic self-definition" typical of nineteenth-century women writers, see Gilbert and Gubar 45–92.

34. Beth's mother is a most complex character. She frequently beats Beth severely, and we despise her for this treatment; however, as this opening scene suggests, she is not presented as completely unsympathetic. Although Mrs. Caldwell's behavior is not excused, stories of her own experiences provide contexts that at least work to explain her complicated motivations.

35. Butler was described by a journalist as "a shrieking sister, frenzied, unsexed, and utterly without shame" (qtd. in Petrie 20). In 1888, Caird published an essay in the *Westminster Review* critiquing the institution of marriage. The article was taken up by the *Daily Telegraph*, which received 27,000 letters in response to its related inquiry, "Is Marriage A Failure?" (Hamilton 306). For a collection of essays elaborating on Caird's views on marriage, see Caird, *Morality of Marriage*. Caird also makes a fictional case against marriage in her New Woman novel *Daughters of Danaus* (1894).

36. This review that appears in the *Academy* is anonymous; however, Anita Miller identifies it as written by Arnold Bennett (262).

37. Dixie dedicates the novel as follows:

> To all women and such honorable upright, and courageous men as, regardless of Custom and Prejudice, Narrowmindedness and Long-Established Wrong, will bravely assert and uphold the Laws of Justice, of Nature, and of Right; I dedicate the following pages, with the hope that a straightforward inspection of the evils afflicting Society, will lead to their demolition in the only way possible—namely, by giving to Women equal rights with Men. Not till then will Society be purified, wrongdoing punished, or Man start forward along that road which shall lead to Perfection. (vii)

38. Eleanor Marx-Aveling was a socialist who was deeply concerned with women's place in society. See Marx-Aveling and Marx-Aveling for a discussion of her thoughts on such issues as marriage and prostitution. In contrast to Dixie, Marx-Aveling believed that establishing a socialist society was the necessary first step to women's equality (27).

39. In 1819, a peaceful working-class demonstration in Peterloo became a mas-

sacre as Hussars and a Yeomanry Cavalry charged through the crowd on horseback. E. P. Thompson reports that eleven people died and 421 were injured. Saber wounds accounted for 161 of the injuries (687). See E. P. Thompson 669–700 for an analysis of Peterloo.

40. In 1795, an act was passed making it illegal to hold meetings of over fifty people without the consent of a magistrate (E. P. Thompson 145). In 1819, reformers were claiming rights to "political organisation, the freedom of the press, and the freedom of public meeting; beyond these three, there was the right to vote" (E. P. Thompson 672).

Afterword

1. Dixie does not address inequalities based on race in *Gloriana*. While her utopian vision includes "England, Ireland, Scotland, and Wales peacefully attending to their private affairs in their Local Parliaments" (284), they send delegates, along with "representative men and women from all parts of our glorious Empire" (284), to an Imperial Assembly. See chapter 4 of this book for a discussion of issues of race and Empire in the nineteenth century. Prejudices based on sexual orientation became Victorian spectacle five years after *Gloriana* was published with the 1895 Oscar Wilde trials. Wilde was sentenced to two years' hard labor when he was convicted under the Criminal Law Amendment Act of 1885 of committing an "act of gross indecency with another male person." See Showalter 14.

2. See Kalsem for analysis of the way that studying historical narrative advocacy by women "can enrich our understanding and critical consideration of legal history, the meaning of law, and law's meanings" (280).

3. I use the term "official" legal texts in the positive law sense of "the written law of a centralized government that has assumed authority over law." See Constable 111.

4. Baron describes the law and literature movement as fractured into primarily three disparate strands: humanist ("law *in* literature"); hermeneutic ("law *as* literature"); and narrative jurisprudence. For an understanding of some of the basic premises from which the current movement has evolved (including defining disagreements), see White, *The Legal Imagination* and *Heracles' Bow;* Posner, *Law and Literature* (1988); R. Weisberg; and West, *Narrative, Authority, and Law.* Other key books and collections in this field include Fish; White, *Acts of Hope;* Heinzelman and Wiseman; I. Ward; Brooks and Gewirtz; Posner, *Law and Literature* (1998; 2009); Freeman and Lewis; Kahn; Aristodemou; Binder and Weisberg; Heinzelman; and Krueger, *Reading for the Law.*

5. Far from considering itself represented by West's figure of "literary woman," the history of the field of law and literature reveals a tradition of the exclusion of women. In 1992, one of the leading scholars in this area, Richard Weisberg, proposed a "Great Books" syllabus that spans a 500-year period and includes only one novel by a woman (117). In response to Carolyn Heilbrun and Judith Resnick's critique that the law and literature movement was ignoring women's writing, Weisberg argued that books should not be chosen to satisfy some "social litmus test," and then asserted that "the field of Law and Literature fully accepts responsibility for hewing to the Great Books" because it defines "'best' quite differently from the current myopic fashion" (120). See Heilburn and Resnick. A 1994 nation-

wide survey revealed that of the 68 literary texts most often assigned in law and literature courses, only six were by women (Gemmette, "Joining the Class Action" 686–87). Only one work by a woman was included in the list of top twenty secondary sources assigned (671). But see Heinzelman and Wiseman for an excellent collection of essays that worked to change the nature of this terrain with its exploration of the connections between law, literature, and feminism. Also, Elizabeth Gemmette has published a four-volume collection of literary works with legal themes (actual short stories, drama, and novellas, and a bibliography including summaries of novels), which includes many works by women. See Gemmette, *Law and Literature*. Significantly, in two recent book-length studies, Heinzelman, *Riding the Black Ram*, and Krueger, *Reading for the Law*, gender is central to the analysis.

BIBLIOGRAPHY

Abel, Richard L. *The Legal Profession in England and Wales.* Oxford: Basil, 1988.

Abel-Smith, Brian, and Robert Stevens. *Lawyers and the Courts: A Sociological Study of the English Legal System 1750–1965.* Cambridge: Harvard University Press, 1967.

Abrams, Kathryn. "Hearing the Call of Stories." *California Law Review* 79 (1991): 971–1052.

Rev. of *Adam Bede. Athenaeum* 26 Feb. 1859: 284.

Adams, Sandra Sleeth. "'A Full Look at the Worst': The Failure of Evolutionary Meliorism in *Tess of the d'Urbervilles* and *Jude the Obscure.*" PhD diss. Kent State University, 1981.

Anderson, Amanda. *Tainted Souls and Painted Faces: The Rhetoric of Fallenness in Victorian Culture.* Ithaca: Cornell University Press, 1993.

"Appeal." *The Oxford English Dictionary.* 2nd ed. 1989.

Ardis, Ann L. *New Women, New Novels: Feminism and Early Modernism.* New Brunswick: Rutgers University Press, 1990.

Aristodemou, Maria. *Law and Literature: Journeys from Her to Eternity.* Oxford: Oxford University Press, 2000.

Atkins, Susan, and Brenda Hoggett. *Women and the Law.* Oxford: Basil, 1984.

Bailey, J. O. "Evolutionary Meliorism in the Poetry of Thomas Hardy." *Studies in Philology* 60 (1963): 569–87.

Bakhtin, M. M. "Epic and Novel." *The Dialogic Imagination: Four Essays by M. M. Bakhtin.* Trans. Caryl Emerson and Michael Holquist. Ed. Michael Holquist. Austin: University of Texas Press, 1981. 3–40.

———. "From the Prehistory of Novelistic Discourse." *The Dialogic Imagination: Four Essays by M. M. Bakhtin.* Trans. Caryl Emerson and Michael Holquist. Ed. Michael Holquist. Austin: University of Texas Press, 1981. 41–83.

Banks, J. A., and Olive Banks. "The Bradlaugh-Besant Trial and the English Newspapers." *Population Studies* 8 (1954): 22–34.

Barnett, Hilaire, ed. *Sourcebook on Feminist Jurisprudence.* London: Cavendish, 1997.

Baron, Jane B. "Law, Literature, and the Problems of Interdisciplinarity." *Yale Law Journal* 108 (1999): 1059–85.

———. "Resistance to Stories." *Southern California Law Review* 67 (1994): 255–85.

Bartlett, Katharine T. "Feminist Legal Methods." *Harvard Law Review* 103 (1990): 829–88.

———. "Perspectives in Feminist Jurisprudence." *Feminist Jurisprudence, Women and the Law: Critical Essays, Research Agenda, and Bibliography.* Ed. Betty Taylor, Sharon Rush, and Robert J. Munro. Littleton: Rothman, 1999. 3–21.

Bartlett, Katharine T., and Rosanne Kennedy. *Feminist Legal Theory: Readings in Law and Gender.* Boulder: Westview, 1991.

Battiscombe, Georgina. *Shaftesbury: The Great Reformer 1801–1885.* Boston: Houghton, 1975.

Beaumont, Charles M. *Women and the Law Courts.* N.p.: Women's Emancipation Union, [c. 1892].

Bebb v. Law Society. 1 Ch. 286. C.A. 1914.

Bender, Leslie. "A Lawyer's Primer on Feminist Theory and Tort." *Journal of Legal Education* 38 (1988): 3–37.

Bentley, David. "She-Butchers: Baby-Droppers, Baby-Sweaters, and Baby Farmers." *Criminal Conversations: Victorian Crimes, Social Panic, and Moral Outrage.* Ed. Judith Rowbotham and Kim Stevenson. Columbus: The Ohio State University Press, 2005. 198–214.

Beresford-Hope v. Sandhurst. 23 Q.B.D. 79. 1884.

Besant, Annie. *Annie Besant: An Autobiography.* London: Fisher, 1893.

———. *The Legislation of Female Slavery in England.* London: Besant, 1885.

Binder, Guyora, and Robert Weisberg. *Literary Criticisms of Law.* Princeton: Princeton University Press, 2000.

Birks, Michael. *Gentlemen of the Law.* London: Stevens, 1960.

Blackburn, Helen, ed. *Some Supporters of the Women's Suffrage Movement.* London: Central Committee of the National Society for Women's Suffrage, 1897.

Blackstone, William. *Commentaries on the Laws of England.* Vol. 1. Oxford: Clarendon, 1765.

Bland, Lucy. *Banishing the Beast: Sexuality and the Early Feminists.* New York: New Press, 1995.

Boris, Sarah A. *"Till [They] Fashion All Things Fair": Evolutionary Meliorism and Generic Practice in the Works of George Eliot and Thomas Hardy.* PhD diss. Brandeis University, 1992. Ann Arbor: UMI, 1993. 9317072.

Boumelha, Penny. *Thomas Hardy and Women: Sexual Ideology and Narrative Form.* Sussex: Hanover, 1982.

Box, Muriel, ed. *The Trial of Marie Stopes.* London: Femina, 1967.

Boyer, George R. *An Economic History of the English Poor Law 1750–1850.* Cambridge: Cambridge University Press, 1990.

Brantlinger, Patrick. "Victorians and Africans: The Genealogy of the Myth of the Dark Continent." *"Race," Writing, and Difference.* Ed. Henry Louis Gates. Chicago: University of Chicago Press, 1986. 185–222.

Briant, Keith. *Marie Stopes: A Biography.* London: Hogarth, 1962.

Brontë, Emily. *Wuthering Heights.* 1847. New York: Signet, 1993.

Brooks, Peter, and Paul Gewirtz, eds. *Law's Stories: Narrative and Rhetoric in the Law.* New Haven: Yale University Press, 1996.

Buchan, James. *The Expendable Mary Slessor.* New York: Seabury, 1981.

Bunn, David. "Embodying Africa: Woman and Romance in Colonial Fiction." *English in Africa* 15 (1988): 1–27.

Burton, Antoinette. *At the Heart of the Empire: Indians and the Colonial Encounter in Late-Victorian Britain.* Berkeley: University of California Press, 1998.

Cain, Patricia A. "Feminist Jurisprudence: Grounding the Theories." *Berkeley Women's Law Journal* 4 (1989–90): 191–214.

Caird, Mona. *The Morality of Marriage and Other Essays on the Status and Destiny of Woman.* London: Redway, 1897.

Carroll, Lewis. *Alice's Adventures in Wonderland.* 1865. London: Dent, 1993.

Chamallas, Martha. *Introduction to Feminist Legal Theory.* 2nd ed. New York: Aspen, 2003.

Chandrasekhar, Sripati. *"A Dirty, Filthy Book": The Writings of Charles Knowlton and Annie Besant on Reproductive Physiology and Birth Control and an Account of the Bradlaugh-Besant Trial.* Berkeley: University of California Press, 1981.

Chorlton v. Lings. 4 L.R.–C.P. 374. 1868.

Chrisman, Laura. "The imperial unconscious? Representations of imperial discourse." *Critical Quarterly* 32 (1990): 38–58.

Clapperton, J. H. *Margaret Dunmore; or, A Socialist Home.* London: Swan, 1888.

———. *Scientific Meliorism and the Evolution of Happiness.* London: Kegan, 1885.

———. *A Vision of the Future.* London: Swan, 1904.

Clarke, Mary Cowden. *The Girlhood of Shakespeare's Heroines; in A Series of Fifteen Tales.* London: Smith, 1850.

"Clitheroe Abduction." *London Times* 20 Mar. 1891: 9.

"Clitheroe Abduction Case." *London Times* 11 Mar. 1891: 8.

———. *London Times* 12 Mar. 1891: 12.

———. *London Times* 30 Mar. 1891: 4.

"Clitheroe Case." *London Times* 28 Mar. 1891: 5.

———. *London Times* 1 Apr. 1891: 5.

———. *London Times* 17 Apr. 1891: 6.

Cobbe, Frances Power. "'Criminals, Idiots, Women, and Minors.'" *"Criminals, Idiots, Women, and Minors": Victorian Writing by Women on Women.* Ed. Susan Hamilton. Peterborough: Broadview, 1995. 108–31.

Cohen, Morton N. *Rider Haggard: His Life and Works.* New York: Walker, 1960.

Commissioners' Report. London: Fellowes, 1834.

Committee For Amending the Law in Points Wherein It Is Injurious to Women. *Infant Mortality: Its Causes and Remedies.* Manchester: Ireland, 1871.

Constable, Marianne. *The Law of the Other: The Mixed Jury and Changing Conceptions of Citizenship, Law, and Knowledge.* Chicago: University of Chicago Press, 1994.

"Contempt." *The Oxford English Dictionary.* 2nd ed. 1989.

Coombe, Rosemary J. "New Direction: Critical Cultural Legal Studies." *Yale Journal of Law and the Humanities* 10 (1998): 463–86.

Corcos, Christine Alice. "Portia Goes to Parliament: Women and Their Admission to Membership in the English Legal Profession." *Denver U Law Review* 75 (1998): 307–417.

Creeger, George R. "An Interpretation of *Adam Bede.*" *ELH* 23 (1956): 218–38.

Cunningham, Gail. *The New Woman and the Victorian Novel.* New York: Barnes, 1978.

Daly, Brenda O., and Maureen T. Reddy. Introduction. *Narrating Mothers: Theorizing Maternal Subjectivities.* Ed. Daly and Reddy. Knoxville: University of Tennessee Press, 1991.

Davies, Margaret Llewelyn, ed. *Maternity: Letters from Working Women.* 1915. New York: Norton, 1978.

Day, William Patrick. *In the Circles of Fear and Desire: A Study of Gothic Fantasy.* Chicago: University of Chicago Press, 1985.

Delgado, Richard. "Storytelling for Oppositionists and Others: A Plea For Narrative." *Michigan Law Review* 87 (1989): 2411–41.

De Souza v. Cobden. 1 Q.B. 687. 1891.

Dickens, Charles. *David Copperfield.* 1850. Ed. Trevor Blount. London: Penguin, 1985.

———. *Oliver Twist.* 1837–39. Ed. Peter Fairclough. London: Penguin, 1966.

Dinnage, Rosemary. *Annie Besant.* New York: Penguin, 1986.

Dixie, Lady Florence. *Gloriana; or, The Revolution of 1900.* New York: Standard, 1892.

Doggett, Maeve E. *Marriage, Wife-Beating and the Law in Victorian England.* London: Weidenfeld, 1992.

Dolin, Kieran. *A Critical Introduction to Law and Literature.* Cambridge: Cambridge University Press, 2007.

———. *Fiction and the Law: Legal Discourse in Victorian and Modernist Literature.* Cambridge: Cambridge University Press, 1999.

Dowd, Nancy E., and Michelle S. Jacobs, eds. *Feminist Legal Theory: An Anti-Essentialist Reader.* New York: New York University Press, 2003.

Edwards, Suzanne. "A Shadow from the Past: Little Father Time in *Jude the Obscure.*" *Colby Library Quarterly* 23 (1987): 32–38.

Eliot, George [Mary Anne Evans]. *Adam Bede.* 1859. Ed. Stephen Gill. London: Penguin, 1980.

Elliott, M. L. *Shakespeare's Garden of Girls.* London: Remington, 1885.

Elmy, Elizabeth Wolstenholme. *The Decision in the Clitheroe Case and Its Consequences: A Series of Five Letters.* Manchester: Guardian, 1891.

Eoff, Shirley M. *Viscountess Rhondda, Equalitarian Feminist.* Columbus: The Ohio State University Press, 1991.

Etherington, Norman. *Rider Haggard.* Boston: Twayne, 1984.

Fenn, Henry Edwin. *Thirty-Five Years in the Divorce Court.* Boston: Little, 1911.

Fineman, Martha L. "Images of Mothers in Poverty Discourses." *Duke Law Journal* (1991): 274–95.

Finley, Lucinda. "Breaking Women's Silence in Law: The Dilemma of the Gendered Nature of Legal Reasoning." *Notre Dame Law Review* 64 (1989): 886–910.

Fish, Stanley. *Doing What Comes Naturally: Change, Rhetoric, and the Practice of Theory in Literary and Legal Studies.* Durham: Duke University Press, 1989.

Fitzpatrick, Peter. *Dangerous Supplements: Resistance and Renewal in Jurisprudence.* Durham: Duke University Press, 1991.

Flint, Kate. *The Woman Reader 1837–1914.* Oxford: Clarendon, 1993.

Forsythe, Bill, Joseph Melling, and Richard Adair. "Politics of Lunacy: Central State Regulation and the Devon Pauper Lunatic Asylum, 1845–1914." *Insanity, Institutions and Society, 1800–1914: A Social History of Madness in Comparative*

Perspective. Ed. Joseph Melling and Bill Forsythe. London: Routledge, 1999. 68–92.

Foulkes, Richard. "Helen Faucit and Ellen Terry as Portia." *Theatre Notebook: A Journal of the History and Technique of the British Theatre* 31 (1977): 27–37.

Freeman, Michael, and Andrew D. E. Lewis, eds. *Law and Literature: Current Legal Issues 1999.* Vol. 2. Oxford: Oxford University Press, 1999.

Freethought Publishing. *The Queen v. Charles Bradlaugh and Annie Besant.* London: Freethought, 1877.

Frost, Cy. "Autocracy and the Matrix of Power: Issues of Propriety and Economics in the Work of Mary Wollstonecraft." *Tulsa Studies in Women's Literature* 10 (1991): 253–71.

Fryer, Peter. *The Birth Controllers.* New York: Stein, 1966.

Gatley, Clement. *Gatley on Libel and Slander in a Civil Action.* Ed. Richard O'Sullivan. 4th ed. London: Sweet, 1953.

Gemmette, Elizabeth Villiers. *Law and Literature: An Annotated Bibliography of Law-Related Works.* Troy, New York: Whitston, 1998.

———. "Law and Literature: Joining the Class Action." *Valparaiso U Law Review* 29 (1995): 665–693.

———. *Law and Literature: Legal Themes in Drama.* Troy, NY: Whitston, 1995.

———. *Law and Literature: Legal Themes in Novellas.* Troy, NY: Whitston, 1996.

———. *Law and Literature: Legal Themes in Short Stories.* Troy, NY: Whitston, 1995.

"George Paston." *Academy* 24 Dec. 1898: 520.

Gilbert, Sandra M. "Rider Haggard's Heart of Darkness." *Coordinates: Placing Science Fiction and Fantasy.* Ed. George E. Slusser, Eric S. Rabin, and Robert Scholes. Carbondale: Southern Illinois University Press, 1983. 124–38.

Gilbert, Sandra M., and Susan Gubar. *The Madwoman in the Attic: The Woman Writer and the Nineteenth-Century Literary Imagination.* New Haven: Yale University Press, 1979.

Godwin, William. *Memoirs of Mary Wollstonecraft.* Ed. W. Clark Durant. London: Constable, 1927.

———. Preface. *The Wrongs of Woman; or, Maria. A Fragment.* By Mary Wollstonecraft. Ed. Gary Kelly. Oxford: Oxford University Press, 1976. 71–72.

Gordon, Walter K. "Father Time's Suicide Note in *Jude the Obscure.*" *Nineteenth-Century Fiction* 22 (1967): 298–300.

Gould, Rosemary. "The History of an Unnatural Act: Infanticide and *Adam Bede.*" *Victorian Literature and Culture* (1997): 263–77.

Grand, Sarah. *The Beth Book.* 1898. New York: Dial, 1980.

Gray, Maxwell [Mary Gleed Tuttiet]. *The Last Sentence.* New York: Tait, 1893.

Gregor, Ian. *The Great Web: The Form of Hardy's Major Fiction.* London: Faber, 1974.

Grierson, Edward. *Storm Bird: The Strange Life of Georgina Weldon.* London: Chatto, 1959.

Grossman, Jonathan H. *The Art of Alibi: English Courts and the Novel.* Baltimore: Johns Hopkins University Press, 2002.

Guest, Harriet. "The Wanton Muse: Politics and Gender in Gothic Theory after 1760." *Beyond Romanticism: New Approaches to Texts and Contexts 1780–1832.* Ed. Stephen Copley and John Whale. London: Routledge, 1992. 118–39.

Guy, Josephine M. *The Victorian Social-Problem Novel: The Market, the Individual and Communal Life.* New York: St. Martin's, 1996.

Haggard, H. Rider. *The Days of My Life.* Vol. 1. London: Longman, 1926.

———. *She.* 1887. Ed. Daniel Karlin. Oxford: Oxford University Press, 1991.

———. *She: A History of Adventure.* 1887. London: Longman, 1919.

Hall, Ruth. *Passionate Crusader: The Life of Marie Stopes.* New York: Harcourt, 1977.

Hamilton, Susan, ed. *"Criminals, Idiots, Women, and Minors": Victorian Writing by Women on Women.* Peterborough, ON: Broadview, 1995.

Hancock, Catherine R. "'It Was Bone of Her Bone, and Flesh of Her Flesh, and She Had Killed It': Three Versions of Destructive Maternity in Victorian Fiction." *Literature Interpretation Theory* 15 (2004): 299–320.

Hankey, Julie. "Victorian Portias: Shakespeare's Borderline Heroine." *Shakespeare Quarterly* 45 (1994): 426–48.

Hardy, Thomas. Apology. *Late Lyrics and Earlier.* London: Macmillan, 1922.

———. *Jude the Obscure.* 1895. Ed. C. H. Sisson. London: Penguin, 1985.

Heilbrun, Carolyn, and Judith Resnick. "Convergences: Law, Literature, and Feminism." *Yale Law Journal* 99 (1990): 1913–56.

Heineman, Helen. *Frances Trollope.* Boston: Twayne, 1984.

———. "Frances Trollope's Jessie Phillips: Sexual Politics and the New Poor Law." *International Journal of Women's Studies* 1 (1978): 60–80.

———. *Mrs. Trollope: The Triumphant Feminine in the Nineteenth Century.* Athens: Ohio University Press, 1979.

Heinzelman, Susan Sage. *Riding the Black Ram: Law, Literature, and Gender.* Stanford: Stanford University Press, 2010.

Heinzelman, Susan Sage, and Zipporah Batshaw Wiseman, eds. *Representing Women: Law, Literature, and Feminism.* Durham: Duke University Press, 1994.

Hergenhan, L. T. "*The Broad Arrow:* An Early Novel of the Convict System." *Southerly* 2 (1976): 141–59.

Higginbotham, Ann R. "'Sin of the Age': Infanticide and Illegitimacy in Victorian London." *Victorian Studies* 32 (1989): 319–37.

Himes, Norman E. *Medical History of Contraception.* New York: Schocken, 1970.

Hoffer, Peter C., and N. E. H. Hull. *Murdering Mothers: Infanticide in England and New England 1558–1803.* New York: New York University Press, 1981.

Holcombe, Lee. *Wives and Property: Reform of the Married Women's Property Law in Nineteenth-Century England.* Toronto: University of Toronto Press, 1983.

Holquist, Michael. Glossary. *The Dialogic Imagination: Four Essays by M. M. Bakhtin.* Trans. Caryl Emerson and Michael Holquist. Austin: University of Texas Press, 1981. 423–34.

Horstman, Allen. *Victorian Divorce.* London: Croom, 1985.

Hunt, Aeron. "Calculations and Concealments: Infanticide in Mid-Nineteenth Century Britain." *Victorian Literature and Culture* 34 (2006): 71–94.

"Husband and Wife." *Solicitors' Journal* 28 Mar. 1891: 357–59.

Huxley, Elspeth. Introduction. *Travels in West Africa.* By Mary Kingsley. London: Everyman, 1987.

Hyde, H. Montgomery. *Their Good Names: Twelve Cases of Libel and Slander with Some Introductory Reflections on the Law.* London: Hamish, 1970.

"In re Jackson." *Justice of the Peace* 18 Apr. 1891: 246–48.

Jackson, Edmund Haughton. *The True Story of the Clitheroe Abduction; or, Why I Ran Away With My Wife*. Manchester: Blackburn, 1891.

Jackson, Emily. "Clitheroe Abduction Case." *London Times* 18 Apr. 1891: 14.

———. "Clitheroe Abduction Case." *London Times* 20 Apr. 1891: 12.

———. "Clitheroe Case." *London Times* 21 Apr. 1891: 12.

———. "Clitheroe Case." *London Times* 22 Apr. 1891: 12.

———. "Clitheroe Case." *London Times* 23 Apr. 1891: 12.

Jameson, Anna. *Characteristics of Women, Moral, Poetical, and Historical*. Vol. 1. Philadelphia: Carey, 1833.

"Jane Hume Clapperton: Authoress." *Women's Penny Paper* June 1889: 1–2.

Rev. of *Jessie Phillips: A Tale of the Present Day*. *Athenaeum* 28 Oct. 1843: 956–57.

———. *John Bull* 18 Nov. 1843: 732.

Jex-Blake v. Senatus. 11 M. 747. 1873.

Jones, Kathleen. *Lunacy, Law, and Conscience 1744–1845: The Social History of the Care of the Insane*. London: Routledge, 1955.

Jones, Miriam. "'The Usual Sad Catastrophe': From the Street to the Parlor in *Adam Bede*." *Victorian Literature and Culture* (2004): 305–26.

"Judgement." *The Oxford English Dictionary*. 2nd ed. 1989.

"The Judges' Opinion Upon Child-Murder." *Spectator* 12 July 1890: 44.

Jump, Harriet Devine. *Mary Wollstonecraft: Writer*. New York: Harvester, 1994.

Kahn, Paul W. *The Cultural Study of Law: Reconstructing Legal Scholarship*. Chicago: University of Chicago Press, 1999.

Kalsem, Kristin Brandser. "Looking for Law in All the 'Wrong' Places: Outlaw Texts and Early Women's Advocacy." *Southern California Review of Law and Women's Studies* 13 (2004): 273–325.

Katz, Wendy R. *Rider Haggard and the Fiction of Empire*. Cambridge: Cambridge University Press, 1987.

Keese, Oliné [Caroline Leakey]. *The Broad Arrow: Being Passages from the History of Maida Gwynnham 'A Lifer.'* Hobart: Walch, 1900.

Kelly, Gary. Introduction. *The Wrongs of Woman; or, Maria. A Fragment*. By Mary Wollstonecraft. Ed. Gary Kelly. Oxford: Oxford University Press, 1976. vii–xxi.

Kemble, Frances Ann. *Record of a Girlhood*. Vol. 2. London: Bentley, 1878.

Kennedy, Helena. "Women at the Bar." *The Bar on Trial*. Ed. Robert Hazell. London: Quartet, 1978. 148–62.

Kent, Susan Kingsley. *Sex and Suffrage in Britain 1860–1914*. Princeton: Princeton University Press, 1987.

Kersley, Gillian. *Darling Madame: Sarah Grand and Devoted Friend*. London: Virago, 1983.

Kingsley, Mary. *Travels in West Africa*. Ed. Elspeth Huxley. London: Everyman, 1987.

Kirk, Harry. *Portrait of a Profession: A History of the Solicitor's Profession 1100 to the Present Day*. London: Oyez, 1976.

Kissel, Susan S. *In Common Cause: The "Conservative" Frances Trollope and the "Radical" Frances Wright*. Bowling Green: Bowling Green State University Press, 1993.

Klein, Kathleen Gregory. *The Woman Detective: Gender & Genre*. 2nd ed. Urbana: University of Illinois Press, 1995.

Knowlton, Charles. *Fruits of Philosophy: An Essay on the Population Question*. 1884. Rpt. in *"A Dirty, Filthy Book": The Writings of Charles Knowlton and*

Annie Besant on Reproductive Physiology and Birth Control and an Account of the Bradlaugh-Besant Trial. Ed. Sripati Chandrasekhar. Berkeley: University of California Press, 1981. 87–147.

Krieger, Linda Hamilton. "The Content of Our Categories: A Cognitive Bias Approach to Discrimination and Equal Opportunity." *Stanford Law Review* 47 (1994–95): 1161–1248.

Kristeva, Julia. *Revolution in Poetic Language.* Trans. Margaret Waller. 1984. Rpt. (in part) in *The Kristeva Reader.* Ed. Toril Moi. Oxford: Blackwell, 1986. 89–136.

———. "Word, Dialogue and Novel." (1966). Rpt. and trans. in *Desire in Language.* Trans. Alice Jardine, Thomas Gora and Leon S. Roudiez. 1980. Rpt. in *The Kristeva Reader.* Ed. Toril Moi. Oxford: Blackwell, 1986. 34–61.

Krueger, Christine L. "Literary Defenses and Medical Prosecutions: Representing Infanticide in Nineteenth-Century Britain." *Victorian Studies* 40 (1997): 272–94.

———. *The Reader's Repentence.* Chicago: University of Chicago Press, 1992.

———. *Reading for the Law: British Literary History and Gender Advocacy.* Charlottesville: University of Virginia Press, 2010.

———. "Victorian Narrative Jurisprudence." *Law and Literature.* Ed. Michael Freeman. Oxford, Oxford University Press, 1999. 437–61.

"Lady Lawyers." *Solicitors' Journal* 20 Dec. 1879: 139.

Lane, Dame Elizabeth. *Hear the Other Side: Audi alteram partem: The Autobiography of England's First Woman Judge.* London: Butterworths, 1985.

Lang, Elsie M. *British Women in the Twentieth Century.* London: T. Werner Laurie, 1929.

Langbauer, Laurie. *Women and Romance: The Consolations of Gender in the English Novel.* Ithaca: Cornell University Press, 1990.

Lansbury, Coral. *The Reasonable Man: Trollope's Legal Fiction.* Princeton: Princeton University Press, 1981.

"Law." *The Oxford English Dictionary.* 2nd ed. 1989.

"Law Report." *London Times* 17 Mar. 1891: 3.

The Law Times 5 Dec. 1903: 107.

Leakey, Caroline. *The Broad Arrow: Being Passages from the History of Maida Gwynnham 'A Lifer.'* Hobart: Walch, 1900.

Ledger, Sally. *The New Woman: Fiction and Feminism at the* fin de siècle. Manchester: Manchester University Press, 1997.

Ledwon, Lenora P. "Legal Fictions: Constructions of the Female Legal Subject in Nineteenth-Century Law and Literature." PhD diss. University of Notre Dame, 1992.

Lerner, Gerda. *The Creation of Patriarchy.* New York: Oxford University Press, 1986.

Levine-Clark, Marjorie. *Beyond the Reproductive Body: The Politics of Women's Health and Work in Early Victorian England.* Columbus: The Ohio State University Press, 2004.

Lewes, Darby. *Dream Revisionaries: Gender and Genre in Women's Utopian Fiction 1870–1920.* Tuscaloosa: University of Alabama Press, 1995.

Livingstone, W. P. *Mary Slessor of Calabar: Pioneer Missionary.* London: Hodder, 1916.

———. *The White Queen of Okoyong: Mary Slessor: A Story of Adventure, Heroism and Faith.* London: Hodder, 1919.

Logan, Deborah A. "Am I My Sister's Keeper? Sexual Deviance and the Social Community." *The Victorian Newsletter.* (Fall 1996): 18–27.

Lowe, Louisa. *The Bastilles of England; or, The Lunacy Laws at Work.* London, 1883.

"The Lunacy Laws." *London Times* 6 Nov. 1878: 9.

Mackay, Thomas. *A History of the English Poor Law.* Vol. III. New York: Putnam's, 1900.

Mangum, Teresa. *Married, Middlebrow, and Militant: Sarah Grand and the New Woman Novel.* Ann Arbor: University of Michigan Press, 1998.

Manvell, Roger. *The Trial of Annie Besant and Charles Bradlaugh.* New York: Horizon, 1976.

Marck, Nancy Anne. "Narrative Transference and Female Narcissism: The Social Message of *Adam Bede.*" *Studies in the Novel* 35 (2003): 447–70.

Rev. of *Margaret Dunmore: or, A Socialist Home. The Academy* 3 Mar. 1888: 147–48.

———. *The Athenaeum* 11 Feb. 1888: 177.

———. *The Saturday Review* 25 Feb. 1888: 235–36.

Marsh, Joss. *Word Crimes: Blasphemy, Culture, and Literature in Nineteenth-Century England.* Chicago: University of Chicago Press, 1998.

Marshall, Gail. *Shakespeare and Victorian Women.* Cambridge: Cambridge University Press, 2009.

Marx-Aveling, Edward, and Eleanor Marx-Aveling. "The Woman Question." 1886. *Thoughts on Women and Society.* Ed. Joachim Muller and Edith Schotte. New York: International, 1986.

"The Maternal Instinct." *The Saturday Review* 8 June 1895: 752–53.

Matus, Jill L. "Disclosure as 'Cover-up': The Discourse of Madness in *Lady Audley's Secret.*" *University of Toronto Quarterly* 62 (1993): 334–55.

Maude, Aylmer. *Marie Stopes: Her Work and Play.* New York: Putnam's, 1933.

Maurer, Shawn Lisa. "The Female (as) Reader: Sex, Sensibility, and the Maternal in Wollstonecraft's Fictions." *Essays in Literature* 19.1 (1992): 36–54.

McDonagh, Josephine. *Child Murder and British Culture 1720–1900.* Cambridge: Cambridge University Press, 2003.

McLaren, Angus. *Birth Control in Nineteenth-Century England.* New York: Holmes, 1978.

McMaster, R. D. *Trollope and the Law.* New York: St. Martin's, 1986.

Mezey, Naomi. "Law as Culture." *Yale Journal of Law and the Humanities.* 13 (2001): 35–67.

Miller, Anita. Afterword. *A Writer of Books.* By George Paston. Chicago: Academy, 1999.

Miller, D. A. *The Novel and the Police.* Berkeley: University of California Press, 1988.

Minow, Martha. "'Forming Underneath Everything That Grows:' Toward a History of Family Law." *Wisconsin Law Review* (1985): 819–98.

———. "Stories in Law." *Law's Stories: Narrative and Rhetoric in the Law.* Ed. Peter Brooks and Paul Gewirtz. New Haven: Yale University Press, 1996. 24–36.

Mitchell, Sally. *The Fallen Angel: Chastity, Class and Women's Reading, 1835–1880.* Bowling Green: Bowling Green University Popular Press, 1981.

———. *Frances Power Cobbe: Victorian Feminist, Journalist, Reformer.* Charlottesville: University of Virginia Press, 2004.

Moore, George. *Esther Waters.* 1894. Oxford: Oxford University Press, 1983.

Morgan, Rosemarie. *Women and Sexuality in the Novels of Thomas Hardy.* London: Routledge, 1988.

Morris, Virginia. *Double Jeopardy: Women Who Kill in Victorian Fiction.* Lexington: University Press of Kentucky, 1990.

Mossman, Mary Jane. *The First Women Lawyers: A Comparative Study of Gender, Law and the Legal Professions.* Oxford: Hart, 2006.

"Mrs. Weldon." *Life* 28 Aug. 1884: 163.

Mullen, Richard, and James Munson. *Victoria: Portrait of a Queen.* London: BBC, 1987.

Munich, Adrienne Auslander. "Queen Victoria, Empire, and Excess." *Tulsa Studies in Women's Literature* 6 (1987): 265–81.

Murray, Janet Horowitz, ed. *Strong-Minded Women and Other Lost Voices from Nineteenth-Century England.* New York: Pantheon, 1982.

Neville-Sington, Pamela. *Fanny Trollope: The Life and Adventures of a Clever Woman.* London: Penguin, 1997.

"The New Fictions by Boz and Mrs. Trollope." Rev. of *The Adventures of Martin Chuzzlewit,* by Charles Dickens, and *Jessie Phillips: A Tale of the New Poor-Law,* by Frances Trollope. *Spectator* 7 Jan. 1843: 17–18.

Nightingale, Florence. *Cassandra. Cassandra and Other Selections from* Suggestions for Thought. Ed. Mary Poovey. Washington Square: New York University Press, 1993. 205–32.

Norton, Caroline. *English Laws for Women in the Nineteenth Century.* 1854. 1–175. *Selected Writings of Caroline Norton.* Ed. James O. Hoge and Jane Marcus. Delmar, NY: Scholars' Facsimiles, 1978. N. pag.

———. *A Letter to the Queen on Lord Chancellor Cranworth's Marriage and Divorce Bill.* 1855. 1–155. *Selected Writings of Caroline Norton.* Ed. James O. Hoge and Jane Marcus. Delmar, NY: Scholars' Facsimiles, 1978. N. pag.

Oliver, Caroline. *Western Women in Colonial Africa.* Westport: Greenwood, 1982.

Parliamentary Debates. Ser. 3. Vol. 287. London: Buck (Hansard), 1884.

Parsons, Neil. *King Khama, Emperor Joe, and the Great White Queen: Victorian Britain through African Eyes.* Chicago: University of Chicago Press, 1998.

Paston, George [Emily Morse Symonds]. *A Writer of Books.* 1899. Chicago: Academy, 1999.

Perkin, Joan. *Victorian Women.* Washington Square: New York University Press, 1993.

———. *Women and Marriage in Nineteenth-Century England.* London: Routledge, 1989.

Peters, Julie Stone. "Law, Literature, and the Vanishing Real: On the Future of an Interdisciplinary Illusion." *PMLA* 120 (2005): 442–53.

Petrie, Glen. *A Singular Iniquity: The Campaigns of Josephine Butler.* New York: Viking, 1971.

Pickering, Danby, ed. *Statutes at Large.* Cambridge: Bentham, 1763.

"Police." *London Times* 7 Oct. 1878: 12.

———. *London Times* 14 Oct. 1878: 12.

———. *London Times* 20 Aug. 1879: 12.

Poole, Joan E. *"The Broad Arrow*—A Re-appraisal." *Southerly* 2 (1966): 117–24.

Poovey, Mary. "Mary Wollstonecraft: The Gender of Genres in Late Eighteenth-Century England." *Novel: A Forum on Fiction* 15 (1982): 111–26.

————. *Uneven Developments: The Ideological Work of Gender in Mid-Victorian England*. Chicago: University of Chicago Press, 1988.

Porter, Roy, and Lesley Hall. *The Facts of Life: The Creation of Sexual Knowledge in Britain, 1650–1950*. New Haven: Yale University Press, 1995.

"Portia Arrives." *The Daily Mirror* 30 Dec. 1919: 2.

Posner, Richard A. *Law and Literature*. Cambridge: Harvard University Press, 1998.

————. *Law and Literature*. 3rd ed. Cambridge: Harvard University Press, 2009.

————. *Law and Literature: A Misunderstood Relation*. Cambridge: Harvard University Press, 1988.

"Precedent." *The Oxford English Dictionary*. 2nd ed. 1989.

Queen v. Jackson. 1 Q.B. 671. 1891.

Rajan, Tilottama. "Wollstonecraft and Godwin: Reading the Secrets of the Political Novel." *Studies in Romanticism* 27 (1988): 221–51.

Ransom, Teresa. *Fanny Trollope: A Remarkable Life*. New York: St. Martin's, 1995.

"Remarkable Abduction Case." *London Times* 10 Mar. 1891: 8.

Report From His Majesty's Commissioners for Inquiring Into the Administration and Practical Operation of the Poor Laws. London: Fellowes, 1834.

Resnik, Judith. "Changing the Topic." *Cardozo Studies in Law and Literature* 8 (1996): 339–62.

Rodensky, Lisa. *The Crime in Mind: Criminal Responsibility and the Victorian Novel*. Oxford: Oxford University Press, 2003.

Rose, June. *Marie Stopes and the Sexual Revolution*. Stroud, Gloucester: Tempus, 2007.

Roxburgh, Sir Ronald, ed. *The Black Books: The Records of the Honourable Society of Lincoln's Inn*. Vol. 5. London: Lincoln's Inn, 1968.

Sachs, Albie, and Joan Hoff Wilson. *Sexism and the Law: A Study of Male Beliefs and Legal Bias in Britain and the United States*. New York: Free Press, 1978.

Sadleir, Michael. *Trollope: A Commentary*. London: Constable, 1927.

Said, Edward. *Culture and Imperialism*. New York: Vintage, 1993.

Sarat, Austin, and Jonathan Simon. "Beyond Legal Realism? Cultural Analysis, Cultural Studies, and the Situation of Legal Scholarship." *Yale Journal of Law and Humanities* 13 (2001): 3–31.

Sargent, Lyman Tower. *British and American Utopian Literature, 1516–1985: An Annotated, Chronological Bibliography*. New York: Garland, 1988.

Scales, Ann C. "The Emergence of Feminist Jurisprudence: An Essay." *Yale Law Journal* 95 (1986): 1373–1403.

Scheckter, John. "*The Broad Arrow:* Conventions, Convictions, and Convicts." *Antipodes* 1 (1987): 89–91.

Schneider, Elizabeth M. "The Dialectic of Rights and Politics: Perspectives from the Women's Movement." *New York University Law Review* 61 (1986): 589–652.

Schramm, Jan-Melissa. *Testimony and Advocacy in Victorian Law, Literature, and Theology*. Cambridge: Cambridge University Press, 2000.

Rev. of *Scientific Meliorism. Westminster Review*. Apr. 1886: 250–52.

Scott, Walter. *The Heart of Midlothian*. 1818. New York: Holt, 1969.

Sedgwick, Eve K. *The Coherence of Gothic Conventions*. New York: Metheun, 1986.

Shakespeare, William. *The Merchant of Venice*. Ed. Kenneth Myrick. New York: Signet, 1987.

Shanley, Mary Lyndon. *Feminism, Marriage, and the Law in Victorian England 1850–1895.* Princeton: Princeton University Press, 1989.

Showalter, Elaine. *Sexual Anarchy: Gender and Culture at the Fin de Siècle.* New York: Viking, 1990.

"Sister Buzfuz." *The Evening News* (London), 30 Dec. 1919: 4D.

Smart, Carol. "Disruptive Bodies and Unruly Sex: The Regulation of Reproduction and Sexuality in the Nineteenth Century." *Regulating Womanhood: Historical Essays on Marriage, Motherhood and Sexuality.* Ed. Carol Smart. London: Routledge, 1992. 7–32.

———. *Feminism and the Power of the Law.* London: Routledge, 1989.

———. "Law's Truth/women's experience." *Dissenting Opinions: Feminist Explorations in Law and Society.* Ed. Regina Graycar. Sydney: Allen, 1990. 1–20.

Smith, Patricia, ed. *Feminist Jurisprudence.* New York: Oxford University Press, 1993.

———. Introduction: Feminist Jurisprudence and the Nature of Law. *Feminist Jurisprudence.* Ed. Patricia Smith. New York: Oxford University Press, 1993. 3–15.

Soloway, Richard Allen. *Birth Control and the Population Question in England, 1877–1930.* Chapel Hill: University of North Carolina Press, 1982.

Stallybrass, Peter. "Patriarchal Territories: The Body Enclosed." *Rewriting the Renaissance: The Discourses of Sexual Difference in Early Modern Europe.* Chicago: University of Chicago Press, 1986. 123–42.

Staves, Susan. *Married Women's Separate Property in England, 1660–1833.* Cambridge: Harvard University Press, 1990.

Stetson, Dorothy M. *A Woman's Issue: The Politics of Family Law Reform in England.* Westport: Greenwood, 1982.

St. John-Stevas, Norman. "Women in Public Law." *A Century of Family Law.* Ed. R. H. Graveson and F. R. Crane. London: Sweet, 1957. 256–88.

Stone, Lawrence. *The Family, Sex and Marriage in England 1500–1800.* New York: Harper, 1977.

Sunstein, Emily W. *A Different Face: The Life of Mary Wollstonecraft.* New York: Harper, 1975.

Surridge, Lisa. *Bleak Houses: Marital Violence in Victorian Fiction.* Athens: Ohio University Press, 2005.

Taylor, Anne. *Annie Besant: A Biography.* Oxford: Oxford University Press, 1992.

Taylor, Barbara. *Eve and the New Jerusalem: Socialism and Feminism in the Nineteenth Century.* New York: Pantheon, 1983.

Taylor, Betty, Sharon Rush, and Robert J. Munro. *Feminist Jurisprudence, Women and the Law: Critical Essays, Research Agenda, and Bibliography.* Littleton: Rothman, 1999.

Thomas, Brook. *Cross-Examinations of Law and Literature.* Cambridge: Cambridge University Press, 1987.

Thompson, Brian. *A Monkey Among Crocodiles: The Life, Loves and Lawsuits of Mrs. Georgina Weldon.* Hammersmith: HarperCollins, 2000.

Thompson, Dorothy. *Queen Victoria: Gender and Power.* London: Virago, 1990.

Thompson. E. P. *The Making of the English Working Class.* New York: Vintage, 1966.

Tomalin, Claire. *The Life and Death of Mary Wollstonecraft.* New York: Harcourt, 1974.

Treherne, Philip. *A Plaintiff in Person: Life of Mrs. Weldon*. London: Heinemann, 1923.

"Trial." *The Oxford English Dictionary*. 2nd ed. 1989.

Trollope, Frances. *Jessie Phillips: A Tale of the Present Day*. 3 vols. London: Colburn, 1843.

———. *Jessie Phillips: A Tale of the Present Day*. London: Colburn, 1844.

Tromp, Marlene. *The Private Rod: Marital Violence, Sensation, and the Law in Victorian Britain*. Charlottesville: University of Virginia Press, 2000.

Tuttiet, Mary Gleed. *The Last Sentence*. New York: Tait, 1893.

Wade, John. *History of the Middle and Working Classes*. 1833. New York: Kelley, 1966.

Waits, Kathleen. "The Criminal Justice System's Response to Battering: Understanding the Problem, Forging the Solutions." *Feminist Jurisprudence*. Ed. Patricia Smith. New York: Oxford University Press, 1993. 188–209.

Walker, Shirley. "'Wild and Wilful' Women: Caroline Leakey and *The Broad Arrow*." *A Bright and Fiery Troop: Australian Women Writers of the Nineteenth Century*. Ed. Debra Adelaide. Ringwood: Penguin, 1988.

Walkowitz, Judith R. *City of Dreadful Delight: Narratives of Sexual Danger in Late-Victorian London*. Chicago: University of Chicago Press, 1992.

———. *Prostitution and Victorian Society: Women, Class, and the State*. Cambridge: Cambridge University Press, 1980.

Ward, Ian. *Law and Literature: Possibilities and Perspectives*. Cambridge: Cambridge University Press, 1995.

Ward, Lester Frank. *Dynamic Sociology*. 1883. 2 vols. New York: Johnson, 1968.

Waters, Chris. "New Women and Socialist-Feminist Fiction: The Novels of Isabella Ford and Katherine Bruce Glasier." *Rediscovering Forgotten Radicals: British Women Writers 1889–1939*. Ed. Angela Ingram and Daphne Patai. Chapel Hill: University of North Carolina Press, 1993. 25–42.

Watt, Ian. *The Rise of the Novel: Studies in Defoe, Richardson and Fielding*. Berkeley: University of California Press, 1957.

Weisberg, D. Kelly. *Feminist Legal Theory: Foundations*. Philadelphia: Temple University Press, 1993.

Weisberg, Richard. *Poethics and Other Strategies of Law and Literature*. New York: Columbia University Press, 1992.

Weldon, Georgina. *How I Escaped the Mad Doctors*. London: Weldon, 1879.

———. Letter to William Gladstone. 15 April 1878. William Gladstone Papers. Add. 44456, Fol. 239–40. British Library, London.

———. "Mrs. Weldon on Conjugal Rights." *Social Salvation* Jan. 1884: 2–3.

———. "Mrs. Weldon on Conjugal Rights." *Social Salvation* Feb. 1884: 2–3.

"Weldon v. Semple." *London Times* 12 July 1884: 5–6.

———. *London Times* 29 July 1884: 3–5.

———. *London Times* 29 July 1884: 9.

"Weldon v. Winslow." *London Times* 3 Mar. 1884: 4.

———. *London Times* 14 Mar. 1884: 3.

———. *London Times* 15 Mar. 1884: 4.

———. *London Times* 19 Mar. 1884: 3–4.

———. *London Times* 9 Apr. 1884: 4.

Welsh, Alexander. *Strong Representations: Narrative and Circumstantial Evidence in England*. Baltimore: Johns Hopkins University Press, 1992.

West, Robin. "Economic Man and Literary Woman: One Contrast." *Mercer Law Review* 39 (1988): 867–78.

———. "Jurisprudence and Gender." *University of Chicago Law Review* 55 (1988): 1–72.

———. *Narrative, Authority, and Law.* Ann Arbor: University of Michigan Press, 1993.

White, James Boyd. *Acts of Hope: Creating Authority in Literature, Law, and Politics.* Chicago: University of Chicago Press, 1994.

———. *Heracles' Bow: Essays on the Rhetoric and Poetics of the Law.* Madison: University of Wisconsin Press, 1985.

———. *The Legal Imagination: Studies in the Nature of Legal Thought and Expression.* Boston: Little, 1973.

Wing, Adrian K., ed. *Critical Race Feminism: A Reader.* 2nd ed. New York: New York University Press, 1997.

Wollstonecraft, Mary. Preface. *The Wrongs of Woman; or, Maria. A Fragment.* Ed. Gary Kelly. Oxford: Oxford University Press, 1976. 71–72.

———. *A Vindication of the Rights of Woman.* Ed. Carol H. Poston. 2nd ed. New York: Norton, 1988.

———. *The Wrongs of Woman: or, Maria: A Fragment.* 1798. Ed. Gary Kelly. Oxford: Oxford University Press, 1976.

Women Suffragists and the Lash. London: Humanitarian League, 1899.

Wordsworth, William. "The Thorn." *Wordsworth and Coleridge Lyrical Ballads 1798.* Ed. W. J. B. Owen. 2nd ed. Oxford: Oxford University Press, 1969. 66–76.

Zedner, Lucia. *Women, Crime, and Custody in Victorian England.* Oxford: Clarendon, 1991.

INDEX